Netherwood and Dovecote   *N. Turner*

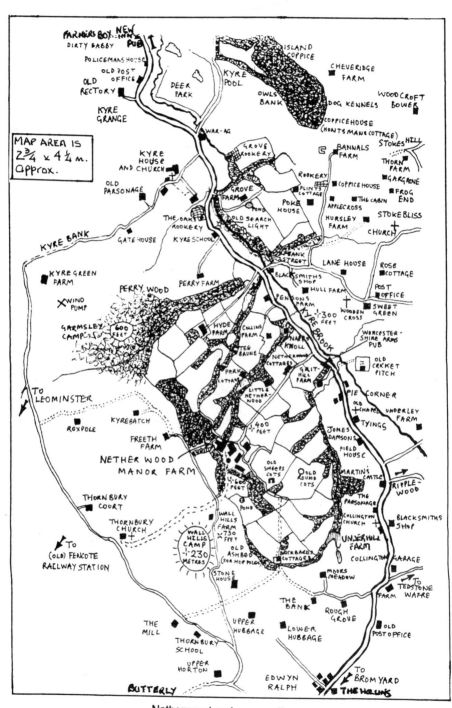

Netherwood and surrounding area

RIDING

ON A

PLOUGH

Ivan Turner

Ivan Turner

A Square One Publication

First published in 1994 by
Square One Publications, Saga House
Sansome Place, Worcester WR1 1UA

British Library Cataloguing in Publication Data

Turner, Ivan
 Riding on a Plough
 I. Title

ISBN 1-872017-80-0

Typeset by Avon Dataset Ltd, Waterloo Road, Bidford-on-Avon, B50 4JH
Printed by Antony Rowe Ltd, Chippenham, Wiltshire

Foreword

by

The Rt. Hon. Earl of Darnley

Ivan Turner has worked at Netherwood all his life. This is his story. As you read it you will realise how completely involved he is with this farm, with its fields and its woods, with the streams that cross it, and with all the creatures that live on it. You also will come to respect his powers of observation and his ability to record the smallest detail that might be of interest. You will become fascinated by his passionate interest in history, which he follows through his discoveries of axe heads and pottery, and all the many other treasures left behind by previous generations.

We came to Netherwood a mere ten years ago, and were instantly captivated by the place. We are delighted that Ivan has decided to publish his diaries, as they will be a permanent record of a very special piece of country, which will help us and those who follow to appreciate it as he does.

Netherwood Manor
26th March 1994

Acknowledgements

I am very pleased to acknowledge here the illustrations by my son
Nigel which greatly enhance this book.
My thanks also to Mr Fendall of Worcester City Museum; Jan Wills
and Derek Hurst – H & W Archeology Department; Hilary White for
her report on the floor tiles found at Netherwood; Anne Sandford of
Hereford Museum; Roger Pye – Lyonshall; my sister Clare whose skill
and patience translated my scribbles into a readable manuscript, also
my sister-in-law Heather, Sandie, and Jill for their efforts on my
behalf.

Introduction by Vesper Hunter

My first meeting with Ivan Turner was on a mild, quiet January day in 1992. I had been shown his diaries which he kept on and off for ten years, sometimes briefly recording some small note of seasonal change, sometimes writing more fully of his day and of the folk around him, and often recording thoughts that had come to him in the fields and furrows as he worked. He missed nothing from the first primrose and the migrating birds to the discovery of the delights of the lift of a girl's skirt or the hilarity of the predicament of a fellow worker's careless mistakes.

I had been asked to read these diaries to help Ivan to order them so that they might reveal to others the insight and vitality that had grown to wisdom almost entirely in the fields and farmlands of the estate where he had lived and worked.

I had not realised when I set out on that January day just what depth of interpretation and meaning this man had wrung from the earth under his feet and from the farming community in which he has grown.

"But it is not my diary that I want to share," he said, "it is the flints." As for all of us, we are so familiar with our day-to-day experiences of life that we hardly notice their significance. It is through these daily discoveries and insights and understandings that our own values are formed and it was of these that Ivan wrote.

When he showed me, first his cabinets where labelled and mounted he had piled sheet after sheet of flint, shard and arrowhead, and then, when we went to the stable where he had displayed pieces of Roman pottery, of medieval tile and more modern fragments of china and bottle, horseshoe, coin or nail, I realised how much these all meant to him, and that his findings had revealed as much to him as did any book or manuscript to a university scholar.

Later we drove the eleven miles from his home to his place of work on the 800 acre estate where he had worked all his life. It was in the heart of rural Herefordshire in still, unspoilt country. We drove past the great Manor House, a listed building mentioned in Domesday Book and going back to the 12th century. We passed barns and farm buildings and crossed fields to the furthest corner of the estate. Turning, we saw the whole of the Netherwood acres lying spread out below in a wide, shallow saucer of gently rumpled land, broken into fields of newly ploughed red marl or green with oilseed rape, and sprouting winter wheat. The skyline all around was edged by low hills and coppices, while to the north was Clee Hill and to the south the dim, undulating outline of the Malverns. In the hollow below us was the Manor House, still and silent, well-kept, with lawn and tennis court, medieval circular dovecot and a long, silver lake beyond. Ivan pointed out the spire of a distant church behind us,

"On a ley-line," he said. "I remember watching from this spot one year the sun rise just behind that spire for it was near to the shortest day." And I felt his close link with ancient lore and belief.

He turned north again. "I was born in that house you can just see in the distance," he said and we went down to visit it. The eldest of his five sons was living there, for they were anxious to keep the family house that had been theirs for three generations. When Ivan married at 26 he had left the family home and moved to the house eleven miles away where I first met him. He did not, however, change his job. At fifteen he began to work on the farm and now, over forty years later, he still works on the same land.

The days at school had had no special appeal, though there he had learnt in schoolboy pranks how to relate to his contemporaries and the society of his world. School for him was the life of Herefordshire where his learning had never ceased. He had learnt the needs of barley and corn, of root crop and potato, of animals and apples and their inter-relatedness. He learnt to coppice and pollard, to hedge and ditch and drain. He learnt to use every tool and the value of every new machine that came on the land. Above all he knew the tractor which replaced the horse and was forerunner of the power and complexity of the machine age which invaded the farmland.

From 1953–1993 Ivan Turner learned from the land and its people, but most of all he learned from the earth itself, as he turned over the furrows from autumn through the short winter days and often after darkness fell, tilling the earth to produce grain and root, fruit and leaf, hay and pastureland.

It was the day on which he turned up his first flint that he found a treasure beyond price. A key that was to unlock for him truths undreamed of about the world in which he lived and which had lain buried for centuries in the earth at his feet.

He tells the story like this:–

"When did I find my first flint, you ask? It was on Saturday, 23rd of October 1971 at 1.15 pm, at The Grove farmed from Netherwood, in the Kyre Valley, on the Herefordshire-Worcestershire border. I was sitting with my back against the crawler tractor facing south towards the main farm having my lunch break, gazing absent-mindedly at the field of clods I was working down, ready for planting. One particular clod a few yards away had a different bit of stone or something in it that did not seem quite natural. We don't get much stone in our red Hereford marl. It kept drawing my eye back to that one spot and, curiosity eventually getting the better of me, I reluctantly moved myself from the comfortable position I was in and prised the small, smooth-looking piece of stone from the soil. Sitting down again, I cleaned the odd bits of earth from this something, thinking, 'This seems unusual', but I did not know what it was or why I should have bothered to pick it up. I put it in my pocket to show Maureen, my wife, that night when I got back to see if she knew what it might be. I thought no more about it and, spreading the sack I had been sitting on over the ground I lay flat on my back for a short nap for the rest of the meal break, listening to whatever sounds were about at that time of the day.

When I arrived home we had a look in the Children's Encyclopaedia and decided it must be a piece of flint which early men had used for their tools. I am a farm worker who did not learn as much at school as perhaps I should have done, and I did not have a clue till then about what flint was, where it came from, or its connection with the history of earlier peoples. I had no hobbies or interests outside work but then, at the age of 33, I suddenly had an unaccustomed interest in something quite different found on land that I had been turning over, planting, harvesting and where I spent most of my daylight hours. Over the next ten years, through that first flint, I was to discover a lot about myself, about Netherwood and nature, and things one can never really understand about life, past and present, and I was to understand also the shortness of man's time on earth, and how temporary is his bodily life."

So, for Ivan Turner, on that October day in 1971, one of the greatest secrets of the world began to be revealed, a secret that in its sheer simplicity might so easily have escaped his grasp.

Little by little, he trained his eye to recognise by a glint here, a gleam or shape there, the flints and shards and fragments in the fields over which, day after day, year after year, he drove his tractor. He realised himself as a small speck on the earth's surface; he cast his mind back to the beginnings of time and then he returned to himself. Where were the bodies of the men and women of earlier generations and centuries? There was no trace of them but only of their work and worth and way of life. So there would be left no bodily trace of him and he saw himself as part of the stream of humanity, and yet at the same time of infinitely greater worth than a mere physical body, because of his capacity to reach so far beyond it, and yet learn, day by day, through natural physical growth, from birth to death. His life was surely not unlike the pattern lived by every man who had worked on that same land before him.

Beyond the wheat and harvest
of fruit upon the bough,
I recognize old Autumn
riding on a plough.

The year has passed its zenith
and now it must decline;
Earth's had her share of summer
As I have had of mine.

PART ONE

Early Days

With my father – already out on the farm

Stoke Bliss & Kyre School 1948/49

2

Born at The Knowle, Kyre on 8th May 1938, my very first recollections would have been when I was about a year and a half old. I had apparently walked down to the brook by the spring where the animals used to drink. The water level was a foot or so below ground level, and I knelt and started to play in the water. I must have fallen forward with my hands outstretched and slipped into the mud. I remember being like that for what seemed like a long time, with a feeling of softness and warmth slowly creeping over me. Whether I started to drown I don't know, but suddenly I was yanked up out of the mud, presumably by my mother, and so started life as I remember it.

The next thing I remember was winter time, with snow on the ground. I was taken outside into the yard, and my bare feet rubbed in the snow, then twiddled about in the contents of the pee pot. This apparently was to stop me having chilblains, which happened a lot in those days. Fifty years later I can say that I have never had chilblains on my feet, only my ears, so it was well worth mother's effort. I've often wondered whether the same treatment on my ears would have done any good!

Then there came school, at Kyre, a mile away. It seemed a rather frightening thing, to be told what to do by a stranger, and a very long day. As far as I know everyone walked there and back. Boys had a separate playground to girls. Nothing comes to mind until I was old enough to move up into the big room, at a guess about 7 or 8 years old. When someone had the cane, it was shared in a way by most of the rest of the class. The teacher would wait until playtime, and with most of the class lined up against the playground wall, would then cross the road and wander up and down the hedge, looking for a suitable whipping stick. The boy to be caned was something of a hero to his mates, but generally a very scared one, as he had to wait till class went back into school and he was hauled out in front to have his punishment.

One autumn, half the class were given the cane as one by one they came into the classroom after an event which most annoyed the teacher. The pupils from Tenbury side arrived on time, but those from Bromyard side were nowhere in sight when time came to start lessons. One of the games we played was to see who could find the strongest snail shell. These were found by scratching in the bottom of hedgerows and pressing them point to point until one broke, the winner then going on the next person, and so on. This particular morning the hedges had been trimmed with a hedgebill and the trimmings raked into tumps, so as well as having the hedgerow bottom there were also lots of snails underneath these tumps. The pleasure of finding these shiny, several-coloured shells is still with me now. The most scarce was a pink one and to find one of those was quite a treat. They were also one of the strongest. The softest was a brownish colour, and in between were the pretty yellow ones, and the yellow and brown striped ones. Even children not normally interested got caught up

3

in what was going on and, time forgotten, the whole of the left hand hedgerow was being sifted through, tumps, the lot. The smell of the half-rotting leaves being moved about was to stay with me through my adult years.

By the time the game had exhausted itself and we were running out of suitable hedgerow, the first lesson was almost over and our last minute dash was of no use. The teacher by then had worked up into a fury, and having armed himself with a suitable stick, he gave us all what for as we entered the classroom. A painful end to a happy episode . . .

The boys' toilets at Kyre School had an open-topped high wall on one side. One of the good things to do was to compete to see who could pee over this high wall. Several of us would line up and have a go. The boys with foreskins were best at it as they could gather a quantity under the loose skin and, holding the end almost closed, squeeze a good squirt out with finger and thumb. The boys who had been circumcised had a greater challenge; they would stand back and run up, willie held tight, and at the last minute loose hold and sort of try to throw their pee up over the wall.

The Knowle is a black and white half timbered house, originally thatched, set in a two-acre orchard, and is now a listed building. There was one large bedroom, a landing room, two rooms downstairs, a cow shed and a room with

The Knowle *N. Turner*

4

Ernie Knight – this is the kind of grate
I remember from my childhood

a copper tub with a fire underneath for washing clothes or heating large quantities of water. The shed round the back which had a hatch out of one side was used at one time to make ladders. The shed around the baking oven and chimney was used for storing wood and coal, and another small high shed for storing hay. There was a pigsty with a toilet built on the side at the top of the garden. The toilet was a two-hole seat, one large and one small, low one for the children.

Toilet rolls were not much in evidence then, and at Knowle we used the Radio Times, each page cut into four, and the pieces threaded near one corner on to a piece of string. Whether the Radio Times was bought especially for this purpose I'm not sure!

Water for drinking was carried in buckets from a spring just over the brook that runs down from Netherwood. The brook formed a boundary along one side of the orchard. Water for bathing and washing was used from a soft water butt at the corner of the house. Occasionally father would put a spot of paraffin on the surface of the water to kill off the wriggly things in it.

Cooking was done on an open fire with an oven by the side. Potatoes and vegetables were boiled in a saucepan balanced on a poker stuck across the fire. On many occasions the whole lot would slip into the fire, the water putting out the fire, and bits of soot getting mixed up with what was being cooked. The kettle for boiling water was usually hanging over the fireplace. Mr. Ernie Knight

5

from Pie Corner is the only person I know locally to still be using this method.

The hedge along one side of the garden has never been laid in the 50 odd years we have been at The Knowle. It's been kept trimmed about three times a year and is still no more than chest high. In 50 years it only grew in height about twice, this was from the bottom, and the whole hedge grew up, unusual seasons must have been the cause.

Four of us children slept in one room until I got too old, and usually it was a bit noisy until things got settled down. One of the nicest things was being tucked up by mother, who usually had to do this before we would all quieten down and slip off to sleep. During the war years we also found room for an evacuee, called Ginny, who is still 'part of the family'.

A pee pot was used upstairs most nights by one or another. The bedroom floor was oak planks on open joists with lots of small gaps between the boards. Over the years there were several mishaps when one of us children put a foot down in the potty getting in or out of bed – for those sitting downstairs the first sign would be a steady drip as the contents seeped through the boards, sometimes on to the dinner table below. Then there would be a mad rush to move things and get newspapers to soak up the wet and stick under the bedroom mat.

Middle School Years – Kyre School

There were several squares of gardens which we kept weeded and planted under supervision of the teacher, Miss Irons. While she was standing over us seeing if we were doing it properly, a couple of us boys would sometimes have a peek at what the teacher wore under her skirt. This once was very little, with a lot of hairs on view. She once took the whole class out along the roadside hedgerows collecting rosehips for the war effort. She later committed suicide at Kyre House lake.

I enjoyed Christmas times at school, especially making decorations such as glueing paper strips together to make paper chains, also making raffia mats. The midday playtime and lunch were an extra long break and it seemed that we must have had a fair amount of freedom, or we took liberties and mostly got away with wandering away from the school playground. The farthest a couple of us got was halfway up Kyrebank, which was about a mile. The school dinners came from the Bockleton direction in a van driven by Mr. Brotheridge, nicknamed 'Snooky'. We had a playtime before we had school dinner. During one of our wanderings, Snooky gave us a lift back in his van amongst the dinner containers and let us out before he backed the van up to the School House. This was enjoyed and so it became the thing to see how far we could get from school and have a lift back. As I said, the farthest we got was about a mile. Whether Snooky was getting fed up, or the teacher had twigged as to what was happening, I don't know, but this time he did not let us out before backing up to the house. Without either of us saying anything we seemed to know this was to be the last ride with Snooky, and crouching down amongst the containers the inevitable happened. The back doors opened and there was the teacher, no way of escape, we were hauled out and left in no doubt that this was not to happen again. Snooky was in the background, looking rather apologetic that it should have come to this.

Another time during our wanderings we came across a place where the brook had been dammed, up near Laundry Cottages. This was just what we were looking for as it was summer time and playing in or around ponds and brooks was what took up a lot of our time, so for several days a quick dash during dinner playtime and clothes off, we splashed and played at swimming, although none of us could swim. Trunks or towels were not thought of, anyway lots of questions would have been asked by parents or teachers if they had been seen.

No one had a watch in those days, so it was a question of intuition as to when to put clothes on to wet bodies and dash back to enjoy the school meal, which, with few exceptions, was much appreciated throughout my school days.

Once when the weather was bad and Snooky could not get through with the dinners, Miss Irons cooked a meal of cabbage and potatoes for the whole school herself.

My mates and I were vaguely becoming aware of sex. Several of us one day were talking to a group of girls through a hole in the fence between the playgrounds. We asked the girls if any of them had been had. One girl said she had, and in a quite unconcerned way, as if saying what she'd had for breakfast, told us who with and where it happened. We were duly impressed for a moment or two, then promptly forgot about what had been said, as did the girls. It's a pity in a way that this attitude does not stay with one later in life as it would have saved me a lot of mental anguish.

A lot of my spare time in school days seemed to be around some farm or another wherever something was going on, whatever was in season. Sometimes I'd get collared and given some job or other to do. The nicest drink I had was when watching sheep dipping at Mr. Dorrell's at the Hall; the people doing the job had stopped for a breather and were given a glass of perry (at least that's what I thought it was), me only being an onlooker in the background almost dribbling at the thought of having some but knowing I wasn't really entitled to any. The farmer must have known, for when everybody had had some, be beckoned me over and gave me a glass, boy it was nice!

The yew trees at the Pensons were then open to the road and amongst the woodpile and nettles and odds and ends, the hens would often lay their eggs. A few of us came across a nest and having overheard some older lads talking about the things they had done – one of which was swallowing raw the contents of a hen's egg whole – we decided to have a go. It's a good job there were plenty of eggs because we found it hard to break enough shell off the egg and still keep the insides intact and tip it in one go down one's throat. After several attempts and a lot of mess, some giving up altogether, a couple of us managed it and kept it down without being sick. The farmer hearing the noise was on his way down the path so we made ourselves scarce.

Always an exciting time was when Jones the Grove washed their sheep in the brook down where Jack Plant's caravan was. Just before the Bank Street brook joined the Kyre brook, the banks were very high. The brook was dammed by old railway sleepers, giving a good depth of water. The sheep I think were thrown in and then left to swim out. As a lad this was good exciting entertainment with the noise of the sheep, barking of dogs and the splashing and shouting that accompanied the job.

When several of us were playing somewhere in the woods, girls as well, one boy a bit older than the rest of us said he was going to have a go at his sister. We had a vague idea what he was going to attempt. His sister, younger than him, seemed quite willing. She was half sitting, showing large blue bloomer type knickers. Whether the boy had any idea what to do we never found out, for as we started to gather round eager to learn something new, their mother's voice came up from the valley calling it was dinner time. Food was then top priority, so the job in hand was forgotten and everyone went off to their respective homes. It was to be many years before I was to find out much more about this sex thing.

Wild strawberries were much sought after in those days, the main places for finding them were the high banks on the corners of the Tenbury/Bromyard road between home and school, but I must admit that the local strawberries were not the most sought after. The largest, reddest, juiciest, sweetest ones were at Rowden on the left hand side going down towards the brook in the direction of the mill. A special journey was made to feast on these.

Part of growing up seemed to be playing at things that grown ups did. One thing I liked doing was sitting on an empty fowlhouse and making butter from the clayey soil from mole tumps, tapping it into shape with bits of board. Girls seem to have had similar habits for they would play at babies and prams for a while, nature's way of preparing them for adulthood.

One thing that fascinated me was at Mr. & Mrs. Francis', the Blacksmith's Shop, Bank Street. There was what we called the bogey hole, the space under the stairs that went up to the bedroom. The Blacksmith's Shop bogey hole was full of what seemed dozens and dozens of pairs of all shapes and sizes of shoes and boots. Children nowadays are not afraid of things as we were. When I misbehaved I was threatened that the Bogeyman would come and get me, it seemed that he came out from this dark recess under the stairs.

One day at school, Mr. Bunn the policeman came. He was looking for the culprit who had broken some windows in Park Cottage, must have been after my grandparents had left. One by one the boys in class were led out into the porch and questioned. When my turn came I was not particularly worried, as I had not done it. It was OK until after saying I knew nothing, Mr. Bunn said, "Right get your coat and we'll go down to the station at Tenbury". That scared me stiff, the thought of going down there was unthinkable, so I said that I'd done it. In desperation, when asked if anyone else had been there as well, I told him all the boys' names in the school I could think of. Whether this satisfied him, goodness knows, nothing more came of it but some time later one of my mates said he had done it, but had kept quiet.

Sunday school was at Stoke Bliss, in the church, taken by Miss Dallow from just up the road.

Father Christmas was a nice thing to believe in and I was sad when it turned out he wasn't real. For several years I'd worked out that no one could get round all the children in the world in one night, but the pleasure of waking early on Christmas morning and finding the thing that you really wanted and hoped for in the pillowcase at the bottom of the bed, made me loath to spoil it all. No one actually told me he wasn't real and, having younger sisters, the pretence went on for many years.

I was about 14 when I was confirmed at Lindridge Church, and because of my lack of mixing with people, it was a rather frightening experience. I had to sneak round the back of the church for a pee before going in. It was Kyre Church, where I was in the choir. Mr. Thomas was the vicar. The hospital adjoining Kyre Church housed children with tuberculosis and one of the girls there would wait out on one of the balconies until church was over, and a relationship was struck up. It got as far as writing letters to each other, which father would deliver as he worked there as engineer. I liked the harvest festivals with all the fruit and vegetables placed about the church.

John and Peter McCall, and I, were playing climbing trees. One of us had a pocket knife which got dropped with the blade open, down onto Peter's head. He, according to his mother, ran crying up to the house with the knife sticking out from the top of his head. No real damage was done as far as I could gather.

When I was 11 a school bus was brought in to take the over 11's to Tenbury to finish schooling. I think till then, children stopped at Kyre school until they were 15, when they left school altogether.

About this time we had a tiddler lamb at The Knowle which my sisters spoilt a great deal. The lamb did not have any fear of man, dogs or fences, and being so attached to the girls did not see why it should not go to school with them. Unable to keep it fenced in, it would get on the bus, jumping up the steps

9

before the door could be closed; the bus driver would then have to wait while it was yanked back out and the door slammed shut, the bus then roaring off with the lamb coming hell for leather behind. At least the tiddler did not chase the bus past Meredith Lane, about 100 yards up the road, thank goodness.

One of my passions was building huts in trees, bracken, anywhere it took my fancy, or was a challenge. Once I made one in the orchard near the house, out of sticks, with dead grass and things woven in, and this particular day had a fire in the entrance. My sister was sitting in the hut enjoying the small fire and I was busy getting dead grass and twigs to keep it going. For some reason or other, the walls of the hut caught alight. It seemed that I just stood there watching, not unduly worried, when out came mother, seeing the danger. In her hurry to rescue my sister, mother sprawled full length just before reaching the burning hut. She quickly got up, pulling her daughter to safety; the hut did not last long. I was justly told off.

The coldest job I had was when father, who had a lorry then, had a load of apples from a farmer to take to Bulmers of Hereford. There were so many rotten ones that, rather than risk being turned away from the cider firm, we took the bags of apples down to where the brook had been dammed and tipped them in. The rotten ones sank, leaving the good ones to be raked out and rebagged – a difficult, cold, wet, miserable operation. I expect all the thanks he got for this was that the farmer would say, "I thought you'd had more on than that" when told the weight.

Winter was very exciting, waiting for the first snow so that we could go sledging. The Knowle was a nice place to grow up in because most things were at hand: the orchard to play in, the brook and the steep hills for sledging, no need to go far unless I wanted to. Sledges varied from a tin tray, staves from a broken water butt, sheet iron, a posh job father made, to ones I made myself – some reasonable, some not much good. A nice steep bit at the back of the house was ideal. A good swift run and not too far to pull the sledge back up. The only problem was the brook at the bottom. The art was to stop or roll off before getting that far. One of my sisters had a go. Not having much idea, she just sat on, not in control at all, so inevitably she ended up in the brook. The sledge had leapt over the brook, ramming a stub the other side. When we got down there my rather bruised sister was still sat on it, slowly sinking through the ice and snow. Credit to her, she was determined not to cry and when asked if alright, just nodded, teeth clenched.

On one of my more ambitious sledges, I put a steering brake either side. This worked well for a while, as I could just sit there and go in whatever direction required, but this one time the mole tumps had frozen under the snow and when going down, the steering brake caught the edge of the hard tump and did not give at all, so my hand got badly pinched against the side of the sledge.

That finished that idea, it was not tried again. Sometimes some of the local girls had a ride, usually sat between my legs, as they would not go by themselves. Once I thought it wasn't going very fast: the girl had got her one leg bent under the seat and was being pulled under. The next go she sat with legs up in the air and my cold wet hand between a warm pair of legs, stopping her from slipping off. There was more to sledging than just sledging! Once Jim Edwards came down from Pie Corner and the two of us went over to Dorrells by the side of Kyre Brook and had a long session sledging, joined by Barbara Dorrell. The bank we were using was covered with ant hills, so there were lots of spills.

We made our own catapults, as the large part of the enjoyment of things in schooldays was the actual making and trying out of one's efforts, be it boats, carts, sledges or what-have-you. Martin Hatton and I had great fun for a while shooting at each other up in the gravel pit on the Low Hill with catapults, an excellent place, as there was an unlimited supply of stones for ammunition. We never saw any danger in this until afterwards, as we always seemed to duck in time. A shot from what we were using would stun a rabbit, so if one of us had been hit on the side of the face with a stone it could have been nasty.

It was with Martin that I learnt to swim. There were no swimming baths handy and we weren't taught at school in those days. After some half-hearted attempts in the brook and at Netherwood lake, we found that a lot of people went up to Kyre pool, mostly at weekends. The popular place was a nook of land the opposite end to the lane that runs across the dam. It was quite a journey to get to this part of the pool: a couple of miles bike ride from home, then along a winding awkward path up the side of the pool, then picking your way through a boggy patch, before reaching the place where it was shallow and hard-bottomed. This then became the place we'd head for most of one summer when we were free from jobs. Weekdays after school or evenings in the school holidays were the best, as usually there was no-one else there, so we could do as we pleased. No-one had told us how to set about learning to swim so we'd just play around trying to stay above water when our feet left the bottom. After a few weeks, I experienced the delicious pleasure of being able to move a couple of feet forward with my feet off the bottom. It was a sort of dog-paddle – that was the first swimming action. Once we'd got a bit of confidence some of the other swimming strokes were soon mastered. We got talking to our mates and sometimes quite a gang of us would be up at the pond swimming. There were sometimes girls there as well and this rather got to one boy who became more interested in one of them than in swimming. In the end the urges that nature instils in boys took over and he ended up chasing her out and around the trees at the side of the lake. This in itself was alright, but his willie was sticking out of his half-off trunks. I think the sight of this spurred the girl on to greater speed, for he never did catch her and it was some time

11

The lake – *N. Turner*

before she ventured out with us again.

At weekends it was rather crowded as carloads of people came, sometimes with a rubber dinghy which to me was quite something to see with people diving and playing around in this in the middle of the lake. Someone up Broadheath way made a small tin boat out of sheet iron. The ridges had been hammered out and two floats brazed on each side. This was left down at the pool, and on week nights when I was there on my own I would use it to explore the parts of the pool which were otherwise inaccessible. There were no paddles or seat, so you just kneeled and paddled with your hands.

There was a picture house in Tenbury and a bus service from Bank Street which was our nearest place to get on and off. They put up posters at the Blacksmith's Shop, Bank Street, advertising what was on at the Regal each week. Eventually Martin persuaded our parents to let us go one Saturday night. Neither of us had ever been before, let alone by ourselves. We caught the bus OK and found our way into the picture house. On Saturdays there were 2 or 3 showings, but the bus times did not coincide with the film times. The Saturday bus left about 10 o'clock from the Crow pub yard. This time was usually before the film had finished, so you had to see the end of the second showing and nip out when the last showing got to where you'd already seen it. Of course we wandered out when the film ended, not really knowing where to go to catch the bus (which had already gone anyhow), each thinking the other

12

knew more than himself. We ended up at the fish and chip shop, had chips and then wandered up and down the street, neither of us saying anything about where the bus was, just somehow hoping it would turn up. By this time about 1½ hours must have gone by and Tenbury was getting awfully quiet. Martins's sister Jean had a boyfriend with a van, and realising something had gone wrong, he came down to Tenbury and found us standing opposite the chip shop, very glad to be found and taken home. So much for our first sample of the complications of the wide world on our own!

In the last term at Kyre School, after we found that we'd be going to Tenbury School for the last years of our education, stories began to filter through from older boys and from friends who already went to what was called the top school, mainly about the headmaster Tom Long, and the things he had done. He was to me the most feared man in Tenbury, even more than a policeman. Of course, I believed all that was said, and the stories about the bullies there; that you would be shoved down the toilets if they did not like you. I had visions of being at the bottom of deep earth closets, so instead of looking forward to the change of schools, it was with dread and fear that filled my mind through most of the holidays. But, unbeknown to me, a new school was being built and we were to be some of the first pupils there. When I found out we weren't going to old Tenbury School a great weight was lifted from me.

Short trousers were worn by most boys my age, until the last couple of terms at school when we had our first pair of longs. School was mostly enjoyed. I once shared top of the class with Cherry Prosser. My greatest fear at school was that I'd be called out to the front of the class and have to read something aloud. Caning, lines and other punishments paled into insignificance compared to this, perhaps because I used to stutter and usually liked to stay in the background of things. It seemed that at times classes were only something to fill in the time between playtimes, when I could go out and do what was uppermost in my mind at the time, one of which was playing marbles. This was done on the partly-made playing fields. It seemed to consist of tossing one marble at another in some form or other. A lot of ground was covered in playtime, and often the rest of the day consisted of carrying a pocketful of won, different-sized, multi-coloured objects around.

Up by the headmaster's office I planted several conker trees in the autumn one year. There was a pear tree in the corner of the school grounds which kept me occupied for several weeks, pelting the pears off – it must have been out of sight of the teachers. Once I had a letter from a girl called Jean in the class below, it simply said "I love you". I wasn't much up on girls then, so did not do anything about it – such things as this do not happen many times in one's life and I failed to appreciate it as much as I should have done!

Pop Evans, the garden master, sold bunches of dahlias which I occasionally bought and took home to mother. These grew up the side of the school drive and I would wander along behind him as he cut a mixed bunch. The different colours and shapes fascinated me as heart in mouth I watched to see if he cut one I especially liked, or go straight past it. He gave us a piece of advice in the last weeks at school, which was to go to the toilet before going to work so it was finished with and off your mind for the rest of the day. This was very sensible as it turned out.

The teachers at Tenbury School must have been quite tolerant people, as among other things I broke a big window with an extra hard snowball and nothing much happened about it. Mr. Holbrook the woodwork teacher, was startled stiff to say the least when I let off a fair bang in woodwork class. This was done by putting match heads in between 2 bolts and a nut. The nut was put a couple of threads on the one bolt filled with match heads, then the other bolt screwed in fairly tight. You then dropped this thing from as high as you could onto the floor, only this time the thing went off better than ever anyone had seen one go before. As it hit the floor it went off with a great crack, then shot off hitting the roof and ricocheting amongst the other boys at different work benches. The hair on the back of my neck seemed to stand up, it frightened me rigid. I'd never seen anything go off like it before, nor ever wanted to again. There was a stunned silence and Mr. Holbrook stood rigid by the blackboard for a few seconds, then to my amazement and relief he carried on as if nothing had happened.

Sport I never got involved with much, as it was required that you went to other schools and places on Saturdays. I liked weekends to do what I liked, too much, so kept out of cricket and football.

Mrs. Davis had the worst job as far as boys were concerned, for she took music and I think history, which most of the boys in my class weren't too interested in, me especially, but later in life I wished I'd taken more notice of what she was trying to teach us.

Mr. McEwan was the teacher I thought the most of. One thing he told us when we left school was to always believe in God. "There will always be people who will try to say otherwise", he said. This turned out sensible advice, for when you go through life and there comes a time when all seems lost and life is not much joy, it is God that you finally turn to for help.

Having four younger sisters, there was always a supply of old pram bodies on wheels, so carts were a passion for a few years. Some were useless as the steering was never much good. Frank Caldicot, myself and one or two others used Meredith Lane most of the time for running trucks down. Looking back, it was a bit dangerous for the lane ran onto the main road by a couple of bends. We'd get to the top of the slope and go as fast as we could. There couldn't have been much traffic as no-one stood where the lane joined the road in case a car

14

came. We'd tear down the lane and mostly managed to get round onto the main road and down the slope to the corner. This one day, Frank got down in a drain manhole through a broken concrete top. When getting back out he gashed his head open and had to be led home, blood running all over his face.

It was where Bannals Lane went over the brook that I learnt to respect wasps. It was when I used to play with Geoff Powell, whose dad worked at the Grove Farm. Having soft fruit at Mr. Selby's The Grove, wasps could be a nuisance later in the year. We'd seen a wasp's nest in the bank at the side of the brook near the bridge so we were given some wasp killer to stick down the hole. This was done with a spoon on the end of a stick. None of us had done this job before, so I had a go. The only way to get at the wasp's nest was to get down into the brook and walk under the bridge. This I managed alright. The wasps were starting to twig that things weren't as they should be. I managed to get a spoonful somewhere near the entrance and it was then that the trouble started for me. As the wasps started buzzing around the hole to their nest, I scrabbled up the bank and out of the brook with wasps buzzing around me. I looked around for the others, who had been watching my efforts from the bridge. They'd gone tearing off up the lane and as I shouted "Wait for me!", the first wasp dug his sting in the back of my neck. I dropped the spoon and can to swat it off and then it was joined by some more that got in my hair and started stinging. I went off up the lane towards home, crying and screaming, trying to get them out of my hair. Nothing had hurt so much as that before, nor had I run as fast as I did then. It seemed to take ages to scratch them off my head and before they stopped stinging. We then had the job later to tell Mr. Powell that I'd lost his spoon and poison, as none of us felt brave enough to go looking for them.

When I went to play with Geoff Powell at his home, the Flint House, his father was doing some mowing or binding. This was before myxomatosis was about and rabbits were very often a meal, so we were always looking out for them. One's parents never said this, it was something one grew up with. So getting up to the house, we decided we'd spend the day down on the field where his father was working, to see if we could get a rabbit or two. They had a sheep dog tied up at the house and we thought it would be a good idea if we had a dog along to help our endeavours, so with a stick apiece, and dog at our heels, we set off. So far so good. Mr. Powell was riding the mower or binder, someone else was driving and the dog, as soon as it saw its master, went tearing across the crop towards the reaper. Whether it had seen a rabbit and was chasing it, or was just keen to be near its master, goodness knows, but it went straight in front of the cutting knife. Too late to see the danger, it got its back legs just about cut off. They stopped the tack by then, but too late, the dog was yelping with pain, trying to drag itself along by its front legs. Mr.

15

Powell took one look, and screaming with rage, ran off towards his house and came back with the twelve-bore and put the dog out of its misery. He then started to turn his rage on us, rooted to the spot a fair way across the field. We heard him say "I'll kill the both of 'em". Something told us to get out fast. Me, I went for home as fast as possible. Geoff really didn't know where to go because he'd have to face his father some time. I don't think I went up near Flint Cottage again as long as Mr. Powell lived there.

I can recall going to watch Rook shoots at the Oaks, Kyre and the Ashbed Grove Farm. There seemed to be more trees at the Oaks Kyre than there are now. The trees are Scots pine, I think, very tall with a few branches at the top. The shoots were so successful that there haven't been any rooks in either of the rookeries for about 25 years. The only surviving rookery is the one up by Bannals Farm, because it could only be shot at by request and so has been able to survive.

Bird nesting was one of my passions. This spanned many years, possibly until the law prohibited the collecting of birds' eggs. I had quite a reasonable collection. Many years of wandering the hedgerows and brooks looking for nests was very fulfilling. Usually, only one egg was taken from each species and blown on the spot. This was done with a pinhole either end of the egg and the contents being blown out through one end, if not too near to hatching. Eggs from birds that nested high in trees were carried down to the ground in one's mouth so as to leave two hands free for climbing. The orchard at the Hall Farm just over the road from The Knowle was where most of the jackdaws nested, as most of the apple trees were hollow, but the eggs were nearly always too far down from the entrance to reach, so bent spoons on bits of wire were used to get the eggs. Many a fright was had while searching for jackdaws' nests, as usually the nest entrance was several feet above eye height, so either you shinned up the tree trunk, or propped a stick against the tree to stand on. Just as you started to peer down the dark hole, the sitting bird would fly up out and startle you. It always amazed me how they managed to get out as quickly as they did. A nice nest to find was a long-tailed tit's. For years one built in a patch of rose briars by the footpath bridge over the Kyre Brook, just along the road Bromyard way. We would usually go back the next day and see if the bird was on the nest. If it was that was good and we went away content, but if no bird was sitting and the eggs were cold a bit of sadness crept into the proceedings. The nest which I liked finding the most was a moorhen's. To see this balanced on a few boughs in the middle of the brook, with several eggs in was most pleasing. If in the mood, and the eggs were not too far gone, I would take two or three, light a fire, boil the eggs in a cocoa tin and eat them.

Finding the first primrose of spring was something my sisters and I liked doing. Jean usually claimed this honour rather to my annoyance, as I was older than she was. This went on into adulthood until her favourite spot for early primroses turned out to be a snake's spring-time place for basking. This put my sister right off, and her visits to the wood at the back of the letter box fizzled out. For me, two of the nicest things in nature are the first showing of yellow in amongst the tightly curled new leaves in the centre of a primrose plant, and a brown hazelnut just ready to fall out of its husk in the centre of the hedgerow.

Nutting was widely done in my schooldays. Many a happy hour was spent clambering up nut bushes and filling pockets with clusters of nuts to be shelled out as I walked towards home or the next tree. Then sorting them out to be put into large Kilner jars with salt to keep them moist. The different shapes, sizes and shell thickness and flavours were numerous. I cracked the nuts in my teeth until my twenties, when I had my first filling and didn't fancy doing it that way any more, so went over to cutting them open with a pen knife. One of the last people I saw doing that was a few years ago (1985) when visiting Mr. John Lyon who used to farm the Hyde Farm next to Netherwood. He was sitting in a big kitchen, a small T.V. at the far end of the room which I could hardly see, a tractor just outside the window grinding corn and a handful of hazelnuts on the table which he was opening with the point of a knife. To me, something

Rookery – *N. Turner*

17

was lost when I stopped cracking nuts with my teeth and went over to a pen knife, it's like losing the flavour of fish and chips when eating with a knife and fork as opposed to eating them with fingers in the open air.

Scrumping was not much of a problem as the orchard at The Knowle had a good selection of apple, plum and damson trees. The one apple we did not have was Worcester Permain, so forays were necessary to the two local orchards where they did grow, up the Collins and over at Dorrells opposite Netherwood Drive.

In conker time the largest and best tree was just by the side of Hall Farm.

Frogspawn was plentiful in schooldays as there were several small ponds dotted about locally, and it was somewhat taken for granted.

Toby Amos and father made up and sprayed two bikes the same colour. I had one, the other Audrey Amos had. Why this stays in my mind is that one sports day, down in Powell's the Perry Field, opposite the milestone, there was a slow bicycle race. Several of us lined up Audrey was one. When the whistle went, Audrey set off at normal cycling speed and was over the finishing line before the rest of us had wobbled and swayed our way many yards. "Look at her" we said to each other and came off, until only two of us were left. About three quarters of the way, it was just me. Instead of then making for the finish at a sensible speed, I tried to be clever and see how slow I could still go. Of course I overdid it and fell off before the finishing line, so Audrey was the winner after all!

One thing about The Knowle was that having a brook on the doorstep I did not have to go far to entertain myself or be entertained. Just by looking out through the window, in winter I could see if it would ice over, or when lots of heavy rain came, I could see if it would change into a muddy brown thing, waiting excitedly to see if it would flood over the bridge that went to the spring. I had a passion for trying to make boats. They had to be short and narrow as the brook was very bendy and not very wide where it went between the trees that lined the banks. By damming up the brook to bank height, there was a fair stretch of water to play on. When building a dam, it was usually with sticks and mud, not lasting many days. The art was to leave a small gap in the dam until nearly finished and then plug it all at once. This meant that the brook below the dam would run dry for a few hours. It was then that the bullheads could be seen and the occasional eel. With the leaves and the trees it was like being in a world of my own, trying to manage a boat that I had made myself, on a stretch of water that I had made available for my own pleasure. Meals were calling distance away, and not having a watch of my own, time wasn't measured in any way. By doing something I liked doing, in a place that I wanted to, on my own, a minute could seem like an hour, or an hour like a minute.

18

The most pleasurable boats were the metal ones made out of army lorry mudguards, flat-bottomed, oblong 4'6" x 2'6", with 4" high sides. These had to have wooden supports tied on to stop them tipping over all the time, and were quite stable. My sisters and their friends liked these. My first attempts were with the tin bath used for washing clothes and people in, but not successful. My last attempt, which lasted for several years, was a sheet of tin iron tacked round a chair seat, making the back of the boat, with the front end folded together to make a point at the front. A couple of tins tied either side for stability, and this was good enough even when the brook was in flood.

The one girl that sometimes had a go in the boats was rather nice, as she would let me take longer than necessary helping her in and out. The close contact we had on these occasions gave me a good feeling.

There is a cave up in Perry Dingle that fascinated Martin and me, so eventually we plucked up courage to have a look in. The planning seemed to take weeks. It had to be done properly, not with flashlights, but with twigs tied on the end of a longish stick, like the explorers in the movies. This worked better than expected, but did not last very long, so there was a quick rush out of the cave as they started to die down. Quite a large cave by our standards, it is still there to the present day.

Father was always good at sharpening tools: saws, axes, clippers or what-have-you. One farmer from a few miles away would make a special journey to have his tools properly seen to. While playing with Geoff Amos one time, we were rummaging around the garage of The Knowle and came across a hatchet. This had been recently sharpened by father and had an edge on it like a razor. Pretending to be cowboys and 'injuns' we were playing with this lethal chopper and I pretended to scalp Geoff. I caught a bunch of his hair in one hand and held it up from his head. I then swung the chopper like I was going to chop a stick. As it swung round, I let go of the handful of hair, just missing Geoff's head and my own hand. An inch either way and I would have caught my hand or Geoff's head. Most things did not seem to worry me, but this time even I saw how daft I'd been. Putting the hatchet back where we'd found it, we crept out rather ashen faced.

For a long time I'd wanted an airgun and finally persuaded mother to let me have one on the pretence of shooting the rats which were a bit of a pest.

They were a problem at The Knowle, especially in winter time when they would set up residence under the fowl houses, also in the sheds around the house, which was worse, as they dug big tumps of soil out from under the house. But when you're young, it's mostly the sport that was had from catching the rats that was of interest. The ones under the henhouses, when the hut was carefully lifted, would crouch still where they were until they saw a stick coming their way, then they would head off down the orchard towards the brook and safety. Unless I hit it with the first swipe, it usually made the brook. The times I've chased one, hitting at it many times as it made its escape. The rats had a sort of bounding run that made it hard to catch. Whether it was good enough to dodge the blows rained at it, or my aim was useless, I was never sure.

We had a terrier type dog for a while, called Jip. She was quite keen, ready to have a go at most things. Father didn't like it much as several dogs would come around courting, often howling outside the house at night. Getting rather fed up with this, he put an electric fence around her kennel; that night there was a yelp and then the sound of a dog howling its way back towards home. Jip was keen after rats, so when cleaning out the old garage this once, she was in keen attendance. We could see the rat in the corner, so I got hold of the stick I had handy, and let someone else move the last bits of rubbish. The dog and I went for the rat at the same time. In the confusion I hit the dog instead of the rat. The poor dog went out with its tail between its legs, and, sorry for what I'd done, I went after it to console it the best I could; the rat quietly slinking off to safety, no doubt thinking how daft humans are.

Until about halfway through school days we had paraffin lamps for light, then father rigged up some batteries and generator so we then had light at the flick of a switch in the downstairs rooms.

I went to Mr. & Mrs. Yarnold, Grit Hill Farm for a fair bit until I left school, doing odd jobs around the farm. I did a small milk-round for them for a while, carrying a pail of milk with a lid on and measure inside, on the handlebars of my bike. This was only to a few houses handy before going to school. This once, pedalling up round the corner of Budd's Bank (Pie Corner), the pail caught in the spokes of the front wheel and threw me off. This was alright, but what hurt the most was the fact that I had to go back to the farm for more milk as the lid had come off and I'd lost the lot. It was during this milk-round that, when calling at Mrs. Knight's, Pie Corner, I was given a message to take to my father. It was that Grandad Turner had passed away that night. Grandad had been looked after by Mrs. Knight, his sister; for several years he'd lived there.

When haymaking fell on holidays or weekends I was able to get involved. This once, Grit Hill was haymaking up past Pie Corner, Collington, and going up to see what was happening, I was sent back to Grit Hill to fetch the horse and rake up the bits of hay that were left around the field after it had been put into a rick. I'd done a bit of work with the horse at odd times around the farm, but it was always hitched up ready to use, so getting back to the farm I had to catch the carthorse. Not having done it before, this was rather daunting. I found it in the orchard by the buildings, but was then unable to coax it to the buildings to put the collar and harness on. I was not tall enough to reach its mane to grab a handful of hair to pull it towards the gate. After several goes at jumping up and trying, we stood looking at one another, me getting desperate. It was then that instinct took over and I found myself getting a bowl with some cattle-feed in and going back to the horse, finding, much to my relief, that after sampling the food, it followed me into the stable-cum-cowshed. Getting hold of the collar, I was able to reach to put it over his head as I could stand on the manger, this was O.K. I then found I could not get it over its head. Quite possibly it was a small collar and a large horse. A panic started to set in again, I found that it went on upside down and I could turn it right way round just behind its head; the rest went on alright. Getting up to the field, I was just in time for tea. This was still done traditionally: everyone stayed and sat round; tea was then dished out by the farmer's wife. If pay was not much, the meals made up for it quite a bit. As a growing lad, food was something to look forward to. After tea, which seemed an unhurried affair, I got hitched up to the horse rake and after a few unscheduled tumps around the field, managed to get the hay into reasonable rows. I think the horse knew as much about what to do as did I!

A job one summer was picking up stones near Grit Hill House. This was when I had what was to be my first of many nosebleeds, which I would get for the next ten years or so. The farmer's wife was most concerned when she found me like this. The nosebleeds got so that they would start just by bending my head down into a bowl of water in the sink when washing my hair.

Feeding the sheep was one of the winter jobs. Mangolds were put in a wheelbarrow and taken out to the field and spread out along in a row. I was usually given breakfast when the farmer had his. This was after milking, so a good appetite had been worked up.

The summer school holidays were something to look forward to very much. The six weeks or so did not seem to have an end. At the start of these holidays when I was working out what to do with all this free time, I could not seem to be able to fill the time in my mind. Those holidays seemed a length of time that I now, thirty-odd years later, look on as a year.

Binding (cutting of corn with tractor and binder) time was filled with anticipation, and listening for the sound of tractors that came from the direction of the corn field near about was enough to send me off in search of sheaves of corn. In those days some of the farmers would cut, by hand, five or six foot around the field of corn that was to be harvested. Sometimes this was done a week or so beforehand, the sheaves tied up with lengths of straw and slung up in the hedge out of the way. The reason for this was so as not to run much corn down the first time round with tractor and binder. After finding a field like this, I made a daily visit until it was cut. The big job, before going off rabbitting for the day, when binding was on, was to cut a suitable stick, usually a springy

21

hazelnut. Much effort was put into this so as to have a heavier lump on the end. It had to be cut right close against the butt of the tree. This was usually done with a pocket-knife that did not cut much. The tree was most often on the edge of the brook, so was a bit awkward. It was from these days that I got involved with Netherwood. The tractor often used on the binder was the John Deere. This had two cylinders and made a distinctive sound which carried a long way, so was the centre of my wanderings during harvest-time.

Jim Tonks rode the binder most the time, and as I stood at one of the corners watching for rabbits to come out, Jim would sometimes put up his hand with two fingers stuck up like rabbit's ears and point to the other end of the field. This would send me off round there, helping to keep my interest going.

Some of the fields were not finished in a day, so it was not much good as the rabbits would get out before the next day's cutting. The best were the smallish fields which were done well within the day. Usually there would be a few rabbits the first few times round the field, then hardly any until the last half hour or so, when it got hectic for a while. Sometimes the tractor driver and binder man would join in as rabbits started running, so everybody could end up with a meal or two. It was possible to outrun the rabbits as they headed towards the hedge, often bumping into sheaves on the way, while looking back to see what was chasing it. It seems there was a bit of the stoat-rabbit relationship when humans chased rabbits, for normally their speed is far ahead of man's.

Fishing was mostly done in Netherwood lake, whether I was allowed to go I don't know, but for several years it was somewhere to go when there was not much on. I liked fishing but did not have the patience to keep trying if they weren't biting. The fishing rod was a stick cut out of the hedge, the float was a cork with a piece of a feather stuck through, the line was whatever thin string I could lay hands on, the bait was worms, usually gathered on the way from under a cowpat or some damp place. Bent pins were tried for a while but were no good so proper hooks were purchased. The fish caught were perch and roach. These I would sometimes bake on the end of a stick over a fire built somewhere quiet. Rather a lot of fine bones to be careful about, but tasty all the same, almost as good as taking them home to fry. Only once did I catch a trout. This was rather a surprise as I wasn't aware there were any in the lake. It was a pictures night, and there was not time to cook it before going out so I asked mother to cook it and I'd have it when I came home. Not having had trout before I was looking forward to getting home and tasting it. However, later when I went eagerly to the kitchen and took the plate down, I was to find that I was second, the cat had already helped itself. I could not bring myself to eat what was left so threw it away. So much for my one and only trout!

The orchard at The Knowle had a mixture of fruit trees: damsons – 14 trees plus a few suckers; plums – 1 Victoria, 1 Early Prolific, 2 Greengage, 1 Jack

Plum; cooking apples – 3 Cheswicks, 7 others, 2 Bramleys; cider apples – 12 unknown sorts, some early, one which was a good baking apple which Bulmers never found out the sort, one which stopped as hard as bullets, 3 Tom Putts, each a slightly different colour and flavour – 20 or so in all cider trees; eaters – 1 summer Quining, 1 winter Quining, 1 Cox's Orange, 2 Rustic Pippins, two or three others that we never found out what they were; 3 cherry trees (2 White hearts, 1 black red when ripe).

I must have learnt to scythe about the time I left school, there were plenty of clumps of nettles to practise on. The first time I tried was in the garden. There was a rough patch with large tussocks about, father gave me his second best to try with. There was no particular instruction, the scythe was put in my hands and I was then left to it (this seemed to be the pattern through most of my farm-working days. You either did a job through instinct or from watching someone doing it sometime or other. You then had to learn the job while actually doing it. It seemed that in farming time wasn't allowed for anything other than very basic instruction). My first attempt was to use it like a hedge-bill and sort of hack it off. This was no good, it did not feel right, so I swung it round in more of an arc nearer the ground. This was better, but I was unable to cut much, the scythe just sort of ran over and around what I was trying to cut. Eventually, by

My collection of birds'eggs

23

having the point rubbing along the ground I made a bit of headway. With these better results, some effort started to be put into it, then the trouble started. At the first bit of tuft or uneven ground, the point went into the ground and started to twist the blade, eventually bending right in half. Father straightened it the first time, but after that I'd stick my foot on it and wrench it back to shape. After several days of getting better, though still chopping at it rather than cutting it in a smooth curving motion, father said to pretend the heel of the scythe was on a wheel and always to keep it just on the ground during both forward and backward strokes. That made all the difference, and in time I could cut the short grass on the lawn. After cutting most of the orchard at various times, it was possible to enjoy the rhythmic motion, feet never leaving the ground, shuffling along with the swinging of the scythe, leaving what looked like two wheel marks where my feet had been.

One winter, the alder trees up Kyre Brook were cut down by Ashworths from Tenbury Wells. Mostly the wood was used for making clogs. They had a yard just as you went into Tenbury. The engine they used to saw the timber up with had a pleasant sound to it. I would dally if possible just to look and listen whenever going by their place.

In my school days, some children each year were allowed time off school to go 'spudding' or for other essential farm work.

School Leaving

The last day of school brought mixed feelings, a little sad at what was past, but mostly a feeling of being glad to go to work, not so much for the money side, but for the chance to do things that up till now I'd only watched others do. Three of the girls about my age (15) on the school bus the last ride gave me a parting kiss. This was O.K., but I'd never kissed anyone, or been kissed on the lips before, so I just sat there grinning with a mixture of pleasure and embarrassment. As the girls came up one by one and kissed me full on the mouth I was unable to stop smiling enough to keep my lips together to return this nice happening until the last girl, when I'd started to pull myself together, so the first girls were very disappointed. I've always been a little ashamed that it should have been that way after their nice gestures. Over the years I often thought how nice it would be to have the chance to put things right!

The previous autumn I had helped to haul mangolds and sugarbeet off the fields at Netherwood, for Mr. Abel Smith, with Jim Tonks and a Massey Harris Pacemaker tractor. One day Jim let me drive the load out to the tump. The tractor, when it had a heavy load on behind, was very light on the steering, so turning was started long before you normally would. I left it too late so went into the ditch, which, thank goodness, was not too deep. By the time I'd put the clutch in the wheels were starting to dig themselves big holes. Jim then had the job of shunting backwards and forwards trying to get back into the field, while I stood back looking at the results of my first attempts at tractor driving.

It was from this holiday work that I was asked if I'd like to go and work at Netherwood when I left school. I had a couple of other offers later from other places. When I started work for Mr. Abel Smith it was a 48-hour week: 7.15 a.m. to 5 p.m., Monday to Friday and 7.15 a.m. to 1 p.m. on Saturday. From the first time I went to work at Netherwood, I was expected to do a man's work. There were 4 or 5 tractors and a couple of horses at Netherwood when I started, 7 or 8 workers, including foreman and stockmen. No-one had a car there then, only push-bikes.

On leaving school I had quite a shock, I was suddenly responsible for myself. I had to make decisions concerning what I said and did. Up till then my mind was free, any money I earned was given to mother and she put it in the bank. I was sent to school, I was fed, I chopped wood because I liked to, the countryside fulfilled my ambitions. I seldom went anywhere much so never got involved with money. There was always something to do and things to look forward to. As far as I can remember the only ambition I had on leaving school was one day to drive the John Deere tractor at Netherwood.

As opposed to father, who when he started work after leaving school went and lived in, only going home occasionally, I was able to stay at home and go to work daily. Vacuum flasks were not in much use then. For several years Jim Tonks brought his tea in a quart cider bottle wrapped in a newspaper to keep it a bit warm until middle day. Most of my early years at work was with one or several people as most jobs were done by hand in some form or other. Generally it was Jim Tonks who had my company and his outlook on life, and attitude to other people influenced me quite a lot later in life when feelings and conflict between people became apparent. He never ran anybody down or criticised them, and if he did, it was in a nice way. When gaffers and foremen or life in general got him down he would suddenly stop in the middle of a job and say, "Fuck 'um all", roll a fag and with a grin say "That's better, now what was we supposed to be doing?"

The jobs then were done with a mixture of horses and tractors. When it was very wet, mangolds and kale were hauled about with a horse and cart. The hoeing of weeds between root crops was done by Jim with a horse hoe. Jim used a smallish chestnut mare which would work far too hard if allowed to. It had one nerve-racking vice and that was that it would start off before it was given a command to. Whether it had been beaten some time or other to get it to move I don't know. Instead of starting off steady when in the shafts (pronounced shaaves), the mare would lunge forward with all her might, almost galloping

25

Workers at Netherwood Manor
when I started in 1954
Wain House in the background is now a Tennis Court

for the first few yards until settling down to a proper walk.

Opening gates was a bit of a nightmare. The stock had jigged up most of the gateways, so it was very muddy. The problem was that as soon as the gate was half open, the mare would charge through, even with Jim hanging on the reins shouting "whoa". The thing to watch was that the ends of the shafts did not get hooked in the end of the gate so I would, as soon as the latch was off, lift the gate out of the mud and run with it to open it as far as possible, then leap out of the way before getting run down by horse and cart. Things nearly came to a head this once when feeding stock in the big tin barn. Sugarbeet was grown at Netherwood then and the tops, after being left for a few days, were fed to the cattle that were being fattened up. The beet tops were thrown out of the cart into the mangers or put in tumps nearby to be forked in when required. This time we were chucking direct into the mangers. I was in the cart throwing out, and Jim was ahead making sure they were clean. In the middle of the operation, with the horse and cart stationary, the mare did one of her galloping take-offs, without being told to move on. This caught me unawares and I was jerked off my feet into the bottom of the cart among the rather slimy tops. The mangers-cum-hayracks were set in between the pillars of the barn, part of which stuck out a bit. Jim, a bay ahead, suddenly caught sight of the charging horse. As I was falling I could see Jim deciding what to do, he half started to go for the horse's head and grab the reins, but must have thought better of it for he turned

26

to run instead, but was in danger of being crushed between cartwheel and a pillar, so in the end he did something I did not think was possible, he threw himself through the gap between the manger and hayrack and rolled out into the cattleyard. Jim was a fairly stocky person and had a job to squeeze through this gap at the best of times, the speed and smoothness with which he managed this impressed me greatly. Me, with visions of the cart being smashed to pieces against the pillars sort of half-rolled and half-fell out over the back into the alleyway. The mare, with the the cartwheel glancing off the pillars, managed to stop of its own accord by the end of the barn, horse and cart none the worse, but Jim and me very edgy for a while after.

The following year a big black horse with a bit of white was used, he was what Jim called 'broken winded', very willing, but could not go far without a rest, and was also unable to back a cart for some reason, so had to go up to a tump forward and be turned around as close as possible, then the load thrown off.

When I first started at Netherwood, a lad by the name of Bernard worked there. He lodged in one of the cottages and had a drop-handled racing bike on which he went to and from work. Meal times and knocking off time, he would go as fast as he could down the drive. This one time he failed to get round the middle cattle grid. The rest of us behind saw him go over the handlebars, nose-diving into the ploughing, the lovely light bike bouncing high into the air, going much further than its owner! A rather dazed Bernard then tried to mount his buckled machine as if nothing had happened before we got level, but immediately fell off in a heap, so one of us carried his bike home for him while he walked.

Another time, Jim decided to have a bit of fun. Bernard's bike used to be parked in the entrance to the big barn. Just before lunchtime, he got a long length of baler twine and tied one end under the saddle of the bike and the other end to the barn. There was a nice slope down from where the bike was, so when Bernard tore off to go to lunch he was going a fair pace by the time he came to the end of the string. He escaped serious injury and the bike didn't come off too bad either. This form of entertainment was not tried again as Jim thought somebody might get hurt.

It was when I was working with Bernard loading beet one cold December that I took a tip from him and that was to sew a button on the top of my jacket opposite the button hole in the lapel. When fastened it helped to keep the wind out. That and a piece of string around the waist was a great help towards keeping warm.

My grandfather, Dick Turner, had worked at Netherwood most of his life, living at Park Cottage. This cottage was demolished in the 1960s to make way for a new dam. His wife, my grandmother, came from the Black Country.

Grandfather was a local man. My father, born at Park Cottage, worked for a while at Netherwood, and been involved in different ways at odd times since, married my mother from Little Netherwood and moved about four fields to The Knowle where he still lives (1986). I was born at The Knowle, went to work at Netherwood when I left school (1953) and am still there in 1994.

My grandfather was born locally, possibly Bank Street, four to five fields away, or Pie Corner where Great-grandfather lived some of the time, five or six fields away. My Great-grandfather Turner also lived locally on a small holding at Pie Corner, five or six fields away from Netherwood.

Mother's side of the family have also been local for a long time. Mother's father had ears that looked like the rats had chewed them, having had a lot of chilblains though the years. The scabs had eaten away the outer edges.

When I went to Netherwood, oats, beans, wheat, barley, kale, peas, mangolds, fodderbeet, sugarbeet, sprouts once, blackcurrants had all been tried. Potatoes and cider fruit were produced. The first harvest I worked at Netherwood I received a harvest ration of food, I think cheese, butter and bacon.

A couple of stories from Jim Tonks' life before he came to Netherwood. One was about a horse a farmer bought from market at what seemed a bargain price, nice looking and looked like it could work. Jim had the job of trying it out – had it between a couple of other horses for a while and it seemed alright. When a job came up for one horse he tried it by itself. It pulled well and did as it was told. After a while he noticed the horse seemed to be pulling one way, so he altered the tack a bit, still no good. After trying altering everything that might be causing the problem the horse still pulled sideways. After several days and ready to pack up trying to find what was wrong he got talking about the problem down the pub and someone up and said "do yee know oo bought him to market?". Jim said he did not, and the chap said "the fellow oo brought 'im in had a barge and the horse was used to pull this barge along the canals". The horse having spent all its working life up till then pulling something that was to one side and not behind, was unable to change. It seems once a barge horse, always a barge horse.

Another was about a relative, or someone he worked with. This chap was leading a horse and cart through a gateway, and somehow he got between the shaaves (shafts) and the gatepost, which crushed his chest. This was before the telephone and the motor car on this farm, so they had to fetch the doctor on horseback. The chap, for two hours, just screamed and screamed until he died. No-one was able to help him in any way, the doctor wasn't found until too late.

Jim Smith was working at Netherwood when I started. He lived in the middle cottage. A year or two earlier a crawler was used for ploughing and suchlike. It was a petrol-cum-diesel International. It was started with a starting handle, had a set of plugs, and started up on petrol, ran for a set time, then automatically turned over to diesel. It could be very difficult to start. Jim Smith spent several hours trying to get it to go this one day out across the fields. Finally, in temper, he flung the starting handle as far as he could and marched back towards the farm intending to tell the farmer or foreman, whichever he met first, what they could do with the so and so crawler. Having a fair way to walk he'd cooled down before getting to the farm and decided to go back and have another go at the thing. On getting there he was unable to find the starting handle, for in the heat of the moment had not seen where he'd slung it, so he had to then spend an hour or so fuming around trying to locate it.

The first year or two the corn was still cut with a binder and hauled up into the Big Barn. This had three roof spans and a lean-to of 13 bays (200' x 150' approx). Pigs, cattle, bales, corn, potatoes, milling, corn-drying and storage was under one roof. We had bait and dinner in there most of the time. I helped to build one rick of loose hay outdoors before pick-up balers took over, and from then on the bales of hay were stacked indoors. The field the hay rick was built in was behind Little Netherwood, the hay was swept up to the stack by a fixed sweep mounted on the front of the John Deere, then forked by hand onto an elevator which took the hay up into the rick being built. It was here that Jim said about a beetle that crawled or fell into his ear while forking hay from

Jim Tonks starting tractor
N. Turner

29

under the elevator. He was unable to get it to come out by banging his head with his hand, also failed to prise it out with a matchstick. There were no surplus people about, so he had to continue working. It was most unpleasant, he said. First the scratching in his ear as the beetle moved about, then it settled down to a sound that was like something banging in his head. After a couple of hours or so of working with this, much to his relief, the beetle found its own way out again.

Binding took on a different role now that I was at work to when I came up just for the day's rabbitting in school days. The job I first did was stooking (standing the sheaves of corn on end in small clumps) after the binder. They were usually placed together in fours or sixes, and sometimes if the crop was heavy one placed either end. They were left to dry if possible until fit to go into a rick, but the weather did not always allow this. Towards the end of the season it would sometimes be hauled straight in. The stooks that had had too much rain on or were binded a bit damp would go a bit fusty and would have to be thrown open for a few hours before hauling in. Sometimes the stooks would get green on top where the corn had started to chit. This made hard work as it was difficult to pull the matted sheaves apart.

When stooking, a sheaf was carried, one under each arm, to where they were to be stood together to dry. If in fours and more than one man working, you would grab a handful of straw near the heads. With one sheaf in each hand you'd place the bottoms slightly apart and lean the tops together. The other men doing this the same time so that all four leaned in together. If stooking in sixes, just one man would place his two bottoms apart, but standing on their own, then another two either side propped against it. This carrying one under each arm was something I couldn't do for long with bare arms as the sheaves soon made lots of little red weals, plus the fact that there were often thistles in it also, so it was a matter of working with a jacket on or with your shirt-sleeves rolled down. It was from handling corn and bales of hay with thistles in that I learned that bait times and dinner times weren't only meant for eating! It was then that you took the opportunity to dig the worst of the thistles out of your hands. No-one seemed to wear gloves in those days, it was another 20 or so years before Netherwood workers took to using them. (I remember watching American films and seeing workers wearing gloves and thinking "what sissies".) I took to carrying a knob-pin in my jacket lapel for getting thistles out of my fingers.

One wet Autumn we weren't able to cut the corn on Calves Hill with a wheeled tractor. A crawler with a Power Take Off Shaft had to be borrowed from somewhere to pull the binder over the wet land. The sheaves of corn were built in ricks in the big barn so I missed thatching in farm-work. To build a corn rick, the bottom layer was started by putting a few sheaves together in the

30

middle, then building outwards round and round in a spiral, the heads of corn placed on top of the bottom half of the previous layer of sheaves so that none of the ears of corn come into contact with the ground. The next and all the other layers started from the outside and work into the middle.

I had the pleasure of riding the binder for one field before the combine harvester took over. It was a double pleasure in a way, as to what followed on from that day. I was sat on the binder in the morning and told who did what by Jim, and away we went. It was a decent standing crop of oats so there was not much to bother about, raising or lowering the sails according to crop height, and seeing that the knotter was tying slightly nearer the heads than centre and wasn't missing any. One of the families at Netherwood Cottages sometimes had a girl to stay with them. This binding day, she and another girl were wandering around the cornfield. Concentrating on what I was doing, I did not take much notice of them. When dinner-time came, Jim and me sat up by the gateway in the butt of the hedge, the two girls came by and had a natter to Jim. As they left, the visitor threw a handful of corn in my direction. At the time all I thought she was 'Hadn't she got anywhere else she could have thrown it?'. The fact she might have been interested in me did not occur to me. The next time I saw the girl again was at Tenbury Show, this time with a couple of other girls. During the course of the afternoon something built up between the girl and me, a mixture of feelings that caused me to hang around in the background. Tea-time the girls made their way from the showground to somebody's car that was to take them back home. While waiting for the driver, one of the girls came over and more or less said that Katharine was interested in me so why not come over and say 'Hello'? (This helpfulness of a third party was to repeat itself more than once as I went through life.) At times like this the body seems to take over from the mind and I found myself following along to where the girl was, my mind not seeming to be taking part in what was happening. After saying hello, followed by an awkward silence, I asked if she would like to go to the pictures. She said 'Yes' and I then had to ask the driver of the car if it was alright, as she was responsible for seeing that the girl got back to the family she was stopping with. With a little bit of persuasion all round, and me saying I'd see she got back alright on the picture bus, the woman said alright, seeing that she knew me. So started my first date. I'd never taken a girl out before, I was about 16 or 17. The girl was possibly 15. The kind usherette at the pictures put us in the back row of the 2/10d's. So far so good. It was a comedy film (Norman Wisdom was the actor). Finally, putting my arm around the girl I started to relax a bit and to think how smooth the skin on her forehead was against my cheek. Then the tickle started, causing me to cough. At each bout of coughing I more or less had to take my arm from around the girl. This, and trying not to cough for as long as possible was making me sweat, so I

31

abandoned putting my arm around her and just sat there concentrating on keeping the tickle from the back of my throat.

Having got the times of the buses sorted out by now, we went out and caught the bus parked in the Crow yard. Must have been cutting it fine as most of the seats were already occupied, so we could not sit together. This was awkward as I felt that I should pay both our bus fares, but was too shy to give the conductor Katharine's fare as well and point out who she was. On looking to where she was sitting as the man collecting the fares went up the bus, Katharine more or less said with her eyes, 'I'll pay my own'.

Getting off the bus amongst several others, we started to walk home. This was O.K., but there was someone behind us. The others had gone on ahead. Wanting to be with Katharine was uppermost in my mind, so with arm around the girl (coughing stopped) we started to walk as fast as possible to put a bit of distance between us and the person behind, but the faster we walked the faster the person behind walked. As we got up by Pensons Farm things came to a head, for the person following put his all into his walk and overtook us. It was Reg Jenkins, cowman at Netherwood. As he breathlessly went past he said goodnight like he was aware of the situation, so for the next half mile the night was ours. Slowing down to a sensible place I started to enjoy what was happening. I don't think we'd spoken hardly at all since walking down to the pictures from the car, other than when I asked if she'd like an ice cream, which thank goodness she said 'no' to. After finding my hand had found it's way up from Katharine's waist to fondle her breast, I discovered what was meant in songs and things when it was said "the stars were shining bright". I found myself looking up at the stars as we neared the house where she was stopping. Whether this was an unconscious act to say thank you to someone, somewhere, for what was happening or what, but I'd never seen stars as bright as they were that night before. Just then I saw someone coming towards us. It was the girl who Katharine was staying with, so, hand hurriedly removed, goodnight was said and sort of "See you again" muttered.

Next morning, as I was pedalling to work at Netherwood, thinking more about what I'd be doing that day than what had happened the previous evening, I was just going past the cottages when a voice shouted 'hello!' On locating the voice, I found it was Katharine leaning out of the bedroom window of the house where she was staying. This was quite unexpected and I was somewhat taken aback. Half slowing down, I managed to wave I think, feeling rather embarrassed because I was wearing a beret. I normally did not wear anything on my head, other than when it was raining. I was to look up at that window for several years, visualising the freckled face under the dark hair.

The first winter's threshing I helped with at Netherwood was done with a

32

proper threshing box which was brought in from outside as Netherwood did not possess one as far as I know. This was parked up one of the alley ways in the big barn. What was done with the straw that year I can't remember. The rowins was saved and later mixed with mangolds (pronounced locally as mangles) or fodderbeet and fed to the cattle in the barn. It was rather dark in the barn with all the dust, machinery and thistle-down floating around. My job was to fork the sheaves of corn to the person throwing up onto the box. After finding out you had to take the sheaves of the stack exactly opposite to the way they were put in, like undoing a jumper or something otherwise you mauled yourself to death, it did not go so bad. As we got down the stack a way I became aware of something warm and soft down my leg. My first thought was "crikey, I've messed myself, what a stupid thing to do". While still working in a chain of people doing something, it is difficult to stop just when you want, then the warm patch moved. It was then I started to sweat, for instead of moving down my leg as it should have done if it was what I thought it was, it moved uphill. As I did not wear pants panic started to set in for I'd come to the conclusion that it was a rat or mouse finding a safe place from the dogs that were having the time of their life darting over and amongst the sheaves on the stack. So, jumping up and down and shaking my leg, I managed to get it to go back down and out the bottom of my trousers. From then on I always wore trouser clips or tied the trouser bottoms with string.

Jim was living down at Kyre Council Houses (now called the Oaks) and cycled to work. What surprised me was that, although he lived farthest away from work, he was usually the first there in the mornings, other than the stockman. The coldest part of his journey to work in the mornings he said was when he came down round the bend from Meredith Lane, and by the bottom of The Knowle drive. Some mornings in winter it was like going into a brick wall as you hit this cold patch of air. Jim would get up to a good speed down the bank and get through it as quickly as possible. Living there, I didn't notice it so much as I was moving out to warmer air when going in in the mornings, but I'll admit it was nice to get to the bottom of Netherwood Drive and be able to walk up between the hedges so as to get a bit of a warm on. In later years, when we had a thermometer, we found that the frosts at The Knowle always seemed that much harder than elsewhere around. This one winter after we had had a fall of snow Jim, being first up Netherwood Drive, must have been in a good mood, for as I followed him about ten minutes later, I became aware that his bike marks had disappeared, then it looked as if he was walking backwards, then the rest of the way up the bank there were all the pretty patterns imaginable made with his feet in different positions.

On Netherwood, in Mr. Abel Smith's time, there were several jackdaws with white on, one was almost completely white. Jim, who had budgies and

View towards the farm,
with woods in the background – *N. Turner*

canaries was most keen to get one, so this spring many of my lunch-hours were spent clambering up trees that had jackdaw nests in them to peer down into them and see if there were any young white ones, Jim anxiously waiting at the tree bottom for my findings. Most of the nests were on Calves Hill. We never did find one with white on.

In Mr. Abel Smith's time I used to help with the milking. There was a herd of Jersey cows there then. When I first got involved and Reg Jenkins starting calling them by name, I thought to myself "this is impossible, I would never be able to remember all of these names, let alone fit the right one to the right cow". There was no other easy means of telling which was which, other than getting to know each cow by sight, but time helped and I found out which was which eventually. Mostly my connection with them was to help the relief girl some weekends. Rosalyn Taylor from Edwyn Ralph was there then, for I remember she asked me to give her a shout through the letterbox of one of the cottages, where she was staying, as I went by that weekend. This was before 4 a.m. and it was still dark. The cows that night were in the stable meadow. I found that having got down to the field to bring them up for milking, while Rosalyn got the tack ready, I could only see the dim outlines of the sleeping cows. Having no torch I went round the bottom of the field and shooed them towards the gateway and farm. It's a good job the cows knew where to go for I could not see the ones in front and just hopefully followed behind. When it

34

got light I went back down the meadow to see if I'd left any behind, but I hadn't. While the main milking was being done with the milking machine, I went over by the stable and milked one, sometimes two, cows that were no good on the machine. The one had a bag that almost dragged on the ground as she walked and the teats stuck out the sides rather than underneath, so it was impossible to get the suction cups under. When milking this cow by hand, you had to milk from two sides as it was not possible to reach underneath from one side to the other. The bucket that was being milked into was nearly flat on the floor and you had to keep emptying it into another one.

Before I went to Netherwood, the milking was done down the lane towards the Parks where a milking bail was used. This was a tin shed built on an old car chassis. This shed was used in later years to tow around the potato fields for the pickers to have meals in. The milk was taken each morning in churns down to Mill Lane, Rochford, where there was a collection for Jersey milk, as opposed to the local farmers who just took theirs down to the end of their drives to be collected. It had to be there, I think, before 8 a.m. It was taken in the green Bedford van.

It was later that I did my first gear change on the move in this van. For the tractors about then you had to stop to change gear. The pleasure I got from changing gear from first to second on the move in this old van was very sweet. It felt like I was getting somewhere in the world.

My first years in farm work at Netherwood were a mixture of everything, cattle, pigs, sheep, a little hedge laying and general farm work, ending up as mainly cattle and tractor driving. This went on side by side for a while, then one day I had to break off in the middle of haymaking to go and do the stock. It was then that I came to the conclusion that I could not do both jobs properly, so I said to the foreman that I wasn't happy breaking off in the middle of a tractor job to go up to the farm to do stock. From then on I was on tractors, helping only with cattle when nothing else was going on.

Before Reg Jenkins left and the Jersey herd was sold, I would help out by cleaning the bull pens out, there was one up by where the old hop kilns used to be and another on the left of the archway. I did not like these bulls much, they had great thick necks and appeared very ferocious to me. When cleaning them out they had their heads fastened in the gate where they were fed, but I was never happy when doing this job, always keeping my face towards them, ready to leap out if one looked like getting its head free.

Eileen Sweeny came to work at Netherwood a bit later than me, on the 29th September 1953, from the Manchester area. Eileen lodged at Grit Hill with the Feyes for a while, then with Mrs. Davis, middle house Netherwood cottages, then in a room at the top of Netherwood main house, then, until she left, in the older part (later sold abroad), which was the wing where the Earl of Essex was

35

born. When I asked in later years if there were any sounds or presences in this old part of Netherwood where she slept alone, she said, "No, only the presence and sounds of modern rats".

Eileen did the relief milking for a while, then after the herd was sold, would milk the couple of cows kept just for the house. She then reared calves for beef. This was done down the Pensons and in the building next to the stables at Netherwood. One of her first jobs was to pull a field of mangolds. This was in the Stable Meadow, about 6½ acres and a very heavy crop. She stuck at it until it was finished and the crop shrank at an alarming rate under Eileen's onslaught. She earned the admiration of most of the workers, as I doubt any of us could have done as good a job. We began to wonder what had come into our midst.

Eileen left in 1973 and went to the Poor Clares Convent, Hereford, on July 11th, the feast of St. Benedict. She felt she had a calling so went to speak to the convent and was not happy until giving it a try. Fifteen years later, when asked how things had gone, she said "It grows on one". One thing Eileen liked when at Netherwood was hoeing in the evenings with a group of people. She used to ride a motorbike when at Netherwood and belonged to Tenbury Motor Cycle Club. She also did a lot of good work visiting some of the older people at Tenbury. Once when visiting Eileen at the convent a few years ago she mentioned that she had prayed for rain two years previously and was sure it hadn't stopped properly since. I've always enjoyed the meals at the Poor Clares when visiting Eileen (now Sister Mary Joseph P.C.). Tea, bread and butter, jam, cake; nice of them to go to all the trouble.

I was brought up with the sound of a pig being killed in different places locally, although we never kept a pig at The Knowle. I don't think I ever watched one actually being killed, I just saw the bristles burned off one at Bank Street once. The pig screams were mostly on weekends and one would overhear parents saying "That's so and so's". I don't know when this died out around Kyre (perhaps in the late 1950s), but the last pig killer I remember was Bert Haywood, who went around doing this job on a Royal Enfield motorbike. You got to know the sound of this bike without ever seeing the person riding it. The last piece of home-cured bacon I had was from Mrs. Knight's, Pie Corner in the 1950s. The slices were cut from a piece of bacon hung up on the ceiling in the kitchen.

The mangolds, until a pit was put in the Big Barn, were stored in buries. This was two thick walls of bales on top of the ground, a bit wider than the cart or trailer. The mangolds were heaped up inside about nine foot high, then covered with hedge trimmings. (Very little got wasted in farming, if a use could be found for something, it got used.) What I used to like was the pretty multi-coloured mangold tops that grew again towards the finish of the bury, when being used up. Hedge trimming was one of the things that Mr. Abel Smith seemed to think that I did alright. This one day, it was a smashing autumn morning, a bit of a frost and the promise of a nice sunny day. I was sent to trim the hedge at the side of Stoneyfield. Looking forward to this very much, I got my jacket off and started swinging the hedge bill (name for a curved hook on a long handle). After doing about ten yards and getting warmed up nicely, I came to a salley stake that had grown. This was extra tough and, taking a good swipe, instead of the hedge giving the handle broke instead, so that put an end to what was going to be a lovely day. This sort of thing seems to happen in different ways quite often, going through life . . .

The other thing the gaffer seemed pleased about was when I turned and baled the bank above the house for hay. Perhaps I'd entertained him for a while as he sat looking out of the bay window facing the green.

For a year or two, bait and dinner used to be had in the tin shed at the top of the wainhouse (now the site of a tennis court), where there was a forge in which the fire was blown by a pair of large bellows. Usually four of us had meals there, as the rest of the workers went home to dinner. The four were: me, who sat by the bellows, seemed to spend most of the meal break pumping the fire in the raised brick fireplace, Jim Tonks, who usually had a snooze, Peggy Francis, who helped mostly with the pigs and Brian Evans, the foreman. This once I must have kept the fire going well for Jim was well down in his seat, gone to the world, his little 'tache quivering in relaxed contentment. When 2 o'clock came, Jim was still asleep, which was unusual, so we made the best of it. We three got up quietly, putting a finger to our lips as Dick Clifford came back from dinner. We then went off to work. Dick, who was a fitter and had his workshop where Jim was asleep said he'd find something quiet to do for a while and keep his eyes open in case the gaffer came out. What time Jim surfaced that afternoon I can't remember, but he was most indignant that we had not woken him up. "What if I'd got caught?" he said. (Under another gaffer I was to find out how he might have felt, for I once dozed off for longer that I should, only that was a combination of courting and sun.)

Once while having his lunch-hour snooze, Jim was lying in the butt of a hedge in the field where he was working, feet out in the field and his head up against the hedge bottom. After a while he felt something sliding over his neck – it was a grass snake. Jim lay there frozen until the snake had passed. That put paid to his snooze for that day.

Ever since hearing that story, I can't relax when sat up against a hedge in summertime, especially amongst bracken. If I have a nap, I move further away into the field.

37

The muck tumps over by the archway, in Abel Smith's time, would nearly always have snakes' eggs in when we came to move them to spread in the fields. One of the worst places for grass snakes used to be around Little Netherwood Lake, and the wood above the Parks. Father, walking round the lake, said the snakes were still in the same spots as when he lived in Park Cottage, fifty-odd years ago.

When we were loading the stock box with muck by hand, at the top of the Parks one year, I was in the lorry throwing up to the front while Jim forked it up into the back. This was alright until I saw the half-grown snakes that were coming up in the forkfuls of muck. It was rather dark in the lorry and it wasn't long before I chickened out and said to Jim "How about a swap?" Jim, being kind and a braver man than me obliged, first getting some string to tie his trouser bottoms. I then rather sheepishly chucked up to Jim.

The tractor paraffin was stored in the round tanks on the garden wall at the bottom of the wainhouse by the bog garden. This was situated just above the two small ponds. The tractors were brought here to fill and grease up. Some were parked overnight in the bottom of the low wainhouse. The standard Fordson tractors were a bit slow stopping when cold, you had to get your foot down on the clutch/brake a fair while before getting near where to stop. I found this out when going to fill up the first time, trying to stop as normal, I suddenly became aware that things weren't right, but it was too late. I couldn't steer away in time, so rammed the garden wall head on. That stopped it. I then had to get Dick to come and straighten the starting handle that was permanently in the front of a Fordson. I was lucky in a way for some time previously someone else had had the same problem, only he was facing the pond at the time, too close to steer away from the edge and he went over the 5-6 foot bank into the water. I suppose that by instinct, as the water came up over his feet, he automatically lifted them up out of the way, enabling the tractor to go on across the fairly hard bottom and up out the other side. I don't know whether this might have been the same one that came over backwards going up the bank above the house. It had strakes on it at the time and only one or two had been put out either side and it so happened that one each side dug in the ground at the same time and the tractor found it easier to come back over itself than go on up the hill. The driver felt this start to happen and jumped off in time. Father said all that happened was a mangled exhaust which he was soon able to put right.

While lugging bales from off the top fields down by the grandstand patch, which is rather steep, I had the John Deere and a trailer with no thriples (skeleton wooden frames put back and front of trailers to stack loads of sheaves, hay and bales against) on the front. I had a fairly big load on, so Dick Clifford said he'd hitch the Massey on behind in case it ran away with me. So off we went, but as we started to go down the steepest part it looked like the load was going to fall off onto where I was sitting, so I applied the foot brakes and went as slow as the tractor would go, but Dick behind had the big higher-geared Massey Harris and only a hand-brake, so eventually he, unable to go slow enough, ended up against the back of the trailer, the starting handle taking the brunt of the contact. From then until we reached level ground I could hear this strange noise from behind, it was the handle being forced back against the engine.

One of the other ways from the top Fields was Calves Hill. This was not so steep, but more of a sideways slope. If possible, the loads would be put on one-sided, so when going down the bank they would be less likely to fall off. There were several loads of bales lost here over the years and what a job it was to pick them up again. The worst part of going down Calves Hill with big loads was changing direction at the top corner to start down towards the bottom, I was usually poised ready to jump if it started to go.

One of the nicest things about the early years at Netherwood was when I'd loaded a load of bales on one of the big green trailers from one of the farthest fields of the farm and was able to stay on top of the load as it was taken up to the farm. There were no good roads, so it was a steady journey all the way back. Just being alone on top of the gently swaying load, flat on my back seeing nothing but the sky and with the occasional whiff of tractor vapourising oil fumes, was very nostalgic.

Cider had stopped being made at Netherwood when I went to work there, but some must have been made the previous year, because for a while after I started it was my job to get a few bottles when threshing or doing other dusty jobs. The barrel was a big one and must have been getting near the bottom because there was what Jim called 'mummys' coming out through the tap. These were bits of green slime which Jim did not like because what I filled were green Gordon's Dry Gin bottles and I was unable to see these bits because of the colour of the glass. I had to keep these bits aside with my finger so that they didn't slip inside the bottles.

Harvesting, in about my first three years at Netherwood, changed from being mostly done with the binder the first year, the second mostly combine, some binder and the third year all done with the combine and, with the combine, came the pick-up baler which made bales half the size of the wire tied stationary baler and about a third the weight. The Massey was used the most on the baler. The tractors then only had one clutch so, when baling, if a large wad was coming up you had to slip the tractor out of gear, leaving the baler running. If it was left too late and you put the clutch in, the baler stopped as well and would jam up, so you got to read the crop a fair way ahead so as to have time to act accordingly.

39

A sledge was towed behind the baler on which a man stood and caught the bales as they came out, stacking them two wide and four or five high, then letting them off the hinged platform at the back onto the ground ready for stacking. The straw bales were usually hauled in as soon as possible and just left as they came off the sledge until loaded on tractors' trailers. The hay bales were a different matter. No silage was made under Abel Smith while I was with him, but before I started there silage had been made in a camp by the side of the lane. It had railway lines in the bottom, so was presumably cut and loaded into trailers or carts. With no silage then, a lot of hay was made. Mostly after baling the hay bales were stacked out in the fields to dry out a bit more, similar to stacking sheaves, anything from fours upwards depending on the crop. There was only a hay pitcher elevator at Netherwood then and that was no good for bales, so for a few years all bales were pitched by hand with pikes until a bale elevator was acquired. The bales were stacked on the trailers about eight layers high, as this was about the limit of the pike-handles. If the bales were not too heavy, one person was able to pitch, but often they were too heavy for one so it was two people to a bale. This is where the fun came in, for everybody had a different way of bale pitching. Some just stood by the bale and threw it straight up forward, others sort of picked it up backwards and turned around as it got above their heads and then onto the load, whilst some put the pike in the bale and ran the end of the pike-handle along the ground until it stuck in , then letting the bale rest on the upright pike, got under it and heaved it up onto the trailer. So with all these different methods you seldom got two people pitching one bale that was the same. Until they sorted themselves out you'd get one going under and one over or backwards, the bale often not getting off the ground and when it did, never even reaching the load, landing on one or the other's head. If one was short of patience he'd soon pack it in and say "stuff the bales", leaving the other to do it alone, who, red in the face and legs buckling, would try getting them as high as he could. The ones that he failed to get as far as the load got left for the bottom of the next trailer. Even when two people got as they could pitch together, occasionally one would leave his pike in the bale as they neared the top of the load and the chap loading, as he pulled the bale the last bit over onto the last layer, would get clouted over the head as the pike, still in the bale underneath, flopped over.

The three trailers that were used for bale carting were ex-sugarbeet trailers form up north somewhere. They were green, very heavy, but stable, with fixed sloping fronts and back and a high V over the wheels. It was quite an art to load these, like loading two trailers that eventually ended up as one for the last four layers, but satisfying when I sometimes got it right. The bales were stacked in the highest span of the Big Barn. It was a fair height so, with no elevator, the

40

bales had to be man-handled up to the top. There was a pitchhold up the end of the bay at the height a man could pitch off the bottom of a trailer, then a second at the height that the man in the first pitchhold could get them; that was usually enough, but with the bales a bit too heavy, a third pitchhold would be made up the face of the stack. The barn was built on sloping ground and so the bays of hay bales had a tendency to bulge at the bottom side if not careful. One or two mornings during the bale carting there would be a mad rush to get some props under an extra bad lean. Usually after the hay had settled for a month or so the props could be removed with no problem.

The first or second year of work, I started going on a week's holiday with Martin Hatton. We went together for a couple of years until our holidays failed to fall at the same time, then I went on my own. The Welsh coast was where we went on our first holiday, to Borth in a caravan that was made from part of a glider. I can't recall us going out much together, we each went our own way most of the holiday. This particular year, on the same site was a girl on holiday with an auntie, so the last couple of days were spent not going far from the area. The girl was younger than me and had dark hair. She was not very tall and seemed keen on making my acquaintance. She being on her own (and me also most of the time) there was no third person to work through. The last day but one the girl and aunt were up at the monument on the high bit of coastline at Borth. I was hovering around in the background, hadn't got a clue how to break the ice, when the girl, with a better grasp of things, came over and said she'd lost two shillings somewhere around here and perhaps I could help her look for it. This I willingly did, so we walked around looking for this coin in the short grass. (Looking back, I don't suppose anything had been lost at all.) The aunt was unobtrusive in the background and after a decent time we gave up. At least we had spoken to each other, but not made much progress as to a further meeting as we walked unhurriedly down to the caravan site when the aunt asked me a bit about myself. On the evening of the next day, which was the last as Martin and I had to be off back home next morning, I saw the girl again in the lane by her caravan. She couldn't stop long, she said, as her aunt was going somewhere. I managed to say that I was going next day and after that I think we both knew there wasn't going to be much chance of making a go of it. Anyway, I had a nice surprise next morning for the girl was there to see me off. We had a nice talk until the bus came.

The other thing that was nice about Borth was that about 4 a.m. every morning the sound of a steam train echoed across the estuary. it sounded like it was pulling a very heavy load and the distinctive, even chuffs seemed to go on for ages. One of these holidays nearly ended my connection with Netherwood in later years.

41

Pigs were kept in Abel Smith's time in the old wooden barn under the hill (pulled down in Mr. Payne's time). The barn was nine or so bays long with originally two openings spaced along the length that went right up to the eaves. This enabled high loads to be taken right into the barn for unloading. Carved in one of the timbers was a date of 1700-something. Meal was ground and mixed on the farm and put into round bins to be used when required. Mr. B. Evans the foreman and Peggy Francis looked after them. Occasionally I would help out with the feeding. The light was not very good in this building and, on getting my arm in one of the meal bins one day found that I was second, there was already a rat in there which did not like being disturbed. After getting over the shock, I got a length of wood and tried to kill it, but it went round and round the bin, making a difficult target. The meal was a fair way down, so it was unable to leap out. I gave up in the end and, unable to tip the bin over, left the stick in the bin for the rat to climb out at its leisure. I got some meal from another part of the building for that feed and after that made sure I put the lids on properly between feeds. For a while there was a steam cooker outside the building in which potatoes were cooked and fed to the pigs. Wood or something was used for fueling/firing. When I did it, not knowing much about the boiler, I was always afraid of the thing blowing up, but the smell of the potatoes when they were done and shovelled into the barrow was nice indeed.

My first combine

Netherwood had its first combine about the second year I was there. It was a tractor-pulled Allis Chalmers with its own engine. Being the youngest, had the job of bagging the corn. On this machine, only one sack at a time could be filled. Behind the good grain sack off-shoot was one for the weed seeds. Sprays had not come in much then. Dick Clifford drove the Fordson tractor that pulled the combine. The full sacks of grain were piled down a shoot and let off in rows around the field. I soon learnt to tie sacks properly as people got fed up when one came undone, moving them then was done by hand. Down Castle field combining once, no one came to collect the sacks, so after finishing the field we had to collect them up ourselves. It was getting on towards dark before we even started. The tractors did not have lights on then so it was a good job there was a moon that night. There was never, at the best of times, much conversation between Dick and me. The only talking was in connection with work. This night we worked in almost total silence. I can remember treading along the swathes of straw trying to find the odd bag that had hung on the shoot and gone past the main line of bags. The trailer was well and truly over-laden as Dick wasn't going to bring another trailer down, so I was helping him to get them up as high as possible and, while he held them, I'd scramble back onto the load and pull them up onto the top. A slow exhausted journey was then made up to the farm. Looking at that load the following morning we were surprised we ever made it. What Dick must have said next day, goodness knows, but we never had that problem as bad as that again. Harvesting must have gone late in the year then. I seldom seemed ever to have any tea with me and going the first time round Collington's was able to fill my pockets with ripe hazel nuts which served as food for tea-time. Another time Reg Bethell took pity on me and gave me a couple of his cakes and a drink.

It was while combining that I lost my first pocket watch; it was stuck in the top pocket of my jacket and when I hung it over the rails of the bagging platform it must have fallen out – a big loss in those days. Dick wore a battered old trilby hat. It seemed to me he only put it on his head as somewhere to carry it until he wanted it for some job or other, like using it to roll up barbed wire, take hot tractor exhausts off, unblock the combine when thistles were jammed in the concave, and many other things. When he put it back on there didn't seem to be a front, back or any shape left to it at all, just jammed on any old way. Sometimes the combine would jam up and the engine stall before Dick could get to it to pull the clutch in. The snag was that the combine engine did not like starting when hot, so often it was a bigger job getting the engine going again than unblocking the drum. The times I've seen Dick on a nice warm day, puffing on a fag, with the tack going well. I could see him starting to relax, enjoying the job a bit. He'd slowly sink down onto the seat, leaning on the

43

mudguard, judging the sound of the combine engine, his one hand easing the tractor throttle a notch or two either way as required. The first warnings were that all of a sudden I was having difficulty in keeping up with the sacking off, no sooner had I taken one bag off the next was ready, before I'd time to even tie the tops. Dick was oblivious to this, his first warning was when the combine engine started to roar. I can seen him now. (He had been in Australia so would quite possibly be dreaming about his time out there). A startled glance over his shoulder and the sudden act of jamming his foot on the clutch brake combination, knocking the tractor out of gear and flipping the catch over the brake and starting to get off to get the combine disengaged. Sometimes his feet never got to the ground before the combine ground to a halt. It was then he would stand rigid for a while, hands gripping the mudguards, then he'd sort of roll his hat down over his face and get off in a slow, exaggerated, manner and we'd start on getting things going again. I'll give the little combine engine its due, it would try right down to its last beat. One year, down in the Parks field, where it hung a bit wet, the corn was choked by redshank. This had gone to seed and when it went through the combine it filled the air with a purple dust. Being a nice still day it hung about like a cloud. Being young, I thought this was very pretty. Dust masks were many years away so I enjoyed making pictures with my finger in the purple dust which was over everything, and at one stage in the day was being followed around by a rainbow that had formed in the dust cloud.

In later years, Mrs. Clifford would take over the bagging at dinner times and I'd drive the tractor while Dick went home for lunch.

I had struck up an acquaintance with a girl older than myself about now. It was more of a mutual friendship than a romance. It was nice to be in each other's company. I was going to the Tenbury pictures three times a week now: on Wednesdays by picture bus, which in its heyday was standing room only before even getting as far as Blackpool Cottages; on Saturdays by bus and on Sundays I would bike down. I only got as far as holding hands with Patricia in the pictures. She would always pay for herself to go in to see the film and for her own bus fare. I think there was a bit of parent disapproval about this happening for it came down to me from the girl's mother to lay off. Just before this warning, coming home one night on the picture bus, sitting holding hands and, knowing me, not talking much, Patricia gave my hand an extra squeeze as we parted, and for some inexplicable reason I knew without a word being said that this was the last time that we would sit together and hold hands and, as it turned out, we never did again. I've puzzled for years how this could happen, this unspoken conveyance of meanings all in a moment of time. I could accept this sort of thing if I'd taken a few hours or days to mull over this squeeze of hands and arrived at some conclusion, but this instant understanding is rather mysterious. Later in life I would come to a possible explanation for this.

Push-biking from the pictures on Sunday nights was rather nice, as I smelt rather than saw the changing seasons. At certain parts of the 5½-mile journey you could smell the mown grass making into hay, the smell of honeysuckle in the hedgerows and one or two other scents that won't come to mind. Another noticeable thing was the change of temperature on still nights as you went down into the hollows and came back out again. Sometimes I would cycle back with Jack Plant who lived in a caravan at Bank Street where the two brooks join, next to the Grove Farm land. One night I forgot to put my lights on. Jack had his on. Just before Bank Street we got stopped by Mr. Cranmer, the policeman, who wanted to know where my lights were. I put them on just to show him that they worked and said I'd forgotten about lighting-up time. At this Jack whispered, "Pedal off home and I'll chat him up a bit". This I did, leaving Jack to talk to the policeman . . .

On the way to catch the picture bus one night there was a girl in blue shorts, playing in an old ash tree at the side of the road. She was younger than me but someone I got on well with. I stopped to talk a while, appreciating what was on show, as Wanda was about head height in the tree. For someone quite young she had a good grasp of things and must have seen that I was getting more interested in talking than going to the pictures, for, with a cheeky grin, said, "If you stop here much longer you will miss the bus". I rather got the impression that the young lady would not have minded if I had. Me being too slow to make use of what was happening I carried on as usual, just getting to the bus-stop in time. I looked back once and Wanda still sat in the tree looking my way.

The last year that the binder was used at Netherwood, the couple of stacks of sheaves of corn in the Big Barn was threshed out using the combine instead of a proper threshing box. The sheaves were thrown down on the floor and fed up into the combine with a pike, or thrown straight onto the canvas by hand as the band was cut. The combine knife had been taken out beforehand. Close to the back of the combine the baler had been parked and the straw was piked into it. There being quite a bit of dust and thistledown about, the combine got a bit too hot and the engine started to smoke and a few flames started licking about. This was put out with a handy fire extinguisher and we were soon able to carry on, but it was not one of our better days, for not long after the P.T.O. shaft from the Massey Harris to the baler broke and the part still attached to the tractor kept going round smashing the back off the driving seat before anyone could put it out of gear. A good job this happened when no-one was sat in the seat, or they would have been badly injured. The one bay we started that year was at the end of the barn and, unable to get baler and combine in the alleyway, some sheets of tin were taken off the end and the loose straw out of the combine was forked outside and then baled up.

The sacks of corn were hoisted up into the granary loft at the barn entrance and stacked up there ready for grinding. The sacks were hauled up with a wire rope attached to the front of a tractor, over a pulley and a length of chain was used to wrap around the neck of the bag. As the sack went up through the hole in the loft floor you got a forward gear quick and let the sack down again with someone above pulling it to one side and onto the loft. Some of the sacks in those days were 2cwt and called Gobsel Browns. The first time I tried to carry one of these was across the granary floor. It was as much as I could do, but the big problem was that there was a lot of loose beams about the floor and being round like ball-bearings, I ended up spreading my length across the floor and the sack spread its contents out through the untied neck. Amusing to the onlookers, but not to me as had to clean up the mess I'd made. On wet days a lot of time was spent sticking patches over the holes in sacks chewed by mice.

Cats seemed to adopt Netherwood, rather than cats brought in for the purpose of catching rats and mice. There were usually some kittens of some sort or another about which was nice, as they got quite friendly. After working late, the next morning you would find the cats sat on the still warm tractor. Sometimes they would get run over. If too many got about, the mess they made over the sacks was almost as bad as the mice and rats. We used to have fencing stakes stood in forty gallon drums of creosote. This one kitten liked to play amongst the tops sticking out of these drums, but one day it fell into the creosote and after scrambling out, blinded, covered by this black liquid, it just ran as fast as possible until it hit something. There was the perfect imprint of its head and ears where it had run into a sack of corn. It must have died eventually as none of us could catch it to do anything. There was one large tabby tom that lasted a long time at Netherwood. I got quite attached to him and would save bits of my sandwiches and feed him at nights. Eventually he would come when I whistled. After several years he developed a large growth on his neck, eventually this burst and he was walking around for a long time with this open wound and flap of skin hanging. I thought that he was a goner, but somehow his neck mended and he lived for a fair while longer.

Jim Tonks rolled his own cigarettes (fags) usually, using A.1. tobacco. These were rather slim things. He never threw his dog ends away, just squeezed the lighted end between finger and thumb and put them in his top pocket. Every so often he would spend most on one meal break emptying his top pocket and carefully unwrapping the accumulated cigarette ends and putting the shrivelled bits of tobacco in the corner of the tin. This had to be done in a building, or on a calm day, for the least bit of breeze and all would be gone. He usually mixed these bits with a bit of good tobacco. It was quite difficult to roll this mixture, as being dry and brittle, it would fall out so Jim ended up with a little thin thing, screwed up each end. When he lit up, the first puff was more flame than smoke and went down a quarter the length of the cigarette. After this first puff, he would hold it almost at arm's length in an upright position and gaze for a moment at the thing in his fingers. I've often wondered how many times some of this tobacco was smoked.

Once, Jim had beaten me up to Kyre Pool and was already swimming up to the top end of the lake. When I got there one or two people were swimming from the road that goes over the dam. There was a lad who had just come to work at Netherwood. I did not know his name. Getting off my bike, someone came over and said this lad had just dived in and hadn't come back up. I tore up to the top end of the lake to fetch Jim who, when he came down, started diving to see if he could find the missing lad. After a couple of dives with no luck he sent me to fetch the policeman. This was Mr. Bunn, who was home at the time. On hearing my story he got the grappling hook on a length of rope and set off to Kyre Pool. I think he had a car then. Jim hadn't been able to find the drowned boy, so the grappling hook was thrown out into the lake and pulled back to the side. This was done many times. Eventually I went off home but the body had still not been found. This put a damper on swimming for a few days, but things soon got back to normal, although it was a long time before I fancied swimming from the road end. I was never any good at diving and that incident put me off ever trying again. I always walked into any of the lakes that I swam in.

When I was swimming on my own at Kyre Pool, a woman came with a party of children in their teens. She asked where the best place was so I showed her where you could walk in on a hard bottom. One of the girls was rather nice. She was called Susan and wore a brown swimsuit, about fourteen or fifteen years old. Being in no hurry to go anywhere I stopped with this party of people until time to go home. My clothes were the other side of the neck of the lake, so I swam back across to change. Susan and another girl went behind one of the trees to change. As they were drying themselves, they kept their heads out of sight but on bending over, two white bottoms stuck out from round the tree. This was an unexpected delight and upon watching further was most intrigued by the way they dried their bottoms. I always put the towel behind to dry when I do it, but the girls put the towels through between their thighs from the front and, bending forward a bit, towelled themselves dry. The method of drying was almost as interesting as seeing the girls' bare backsides.

Sometimes I would swim the length of Kyre Pool, but was a bit uneasy when some of the rough-feeling weed got in the way. It inclined one towards panic if not careful and once there was a snake wriggling its way across the

47

lake, in front of where I was going. I suppose the weed and snakes had as much right to be there.

At one stage in Abel Smith's time fishing was very popular in the lake by Park Cottage. I think that everybody who worked on Netherwood went there. We lined up along the dam and one or two up the sides of the lake. It was very pleasurable to be part of this. Having worked with them for a year or two, it was nice to be with them in a situation of pleasure. They became people in their own right, any aggro or niggles were put aside during the evening's fishing. This sort of thing helped to keep a balance in life and create a sense of belonging to something, especially as this was carried out at a place of work.

When Toby Amos worked at Netherwood he used to catch eels with night lines in this lake.

Mr. Abel Smith thought it would be a good idea if I passed my driving test. I failed at my first attempt, which was taken in my aunt's baby Austin. My reversing put the wind up the examiner, it was up the side of a brick wall and must have been a bit close for comfort as he shouted "Stop! this will do". Before I took another test there was a petrol crisis on and learner drivers were allowed to drive about on their own so long as 'L' plates were displayed. This gave me a lot of confidence, as I could go for a drive around Ludlow without having to bother anyone to come along. For this next test I drove father's Austin 10 van and passed alright.

One winter, I fetched some apple pickers from Bromyard to Netherwood in the old green van. Dick did not put a lot of faith in it, for whenever he took a load of women down the steep bit of the drive onto the main road he would put it in the lowest gear with his foot on the brake and the hand-brake on, switch off the engine and go down as slow as possible. During the course of the apple picking up, a blonde girl showed an interest in me. This must have caught the imagination of the rest of the Bromyard women for on the journey back one evening, instead of the two or three mothers and their children in the front with me (the van cab being separate from the body at the back) I had the company of the blonde girl by herself. The women and children that usually sat in the front had squeezed in the back, intent on giving romance a chance. During the journey we had a bit of conversation, but I must have been quite a disappointment to the rest of the women on that journey. Anyway the girl, having more gumption than I had getting off at Bromyard without anything being sorted out, sent one of her friends over before I drove off to ask if I wanted to take her out or not. I was at a loss at what to say and ended up telling the girl's friend that I didn't think I did. So that was the end of something that might have been rather nice if I had had the sense to give it a chance!

In spud picking time, one of the women from Netherwood Cottages would put me a dash of whisky in my cup of tea. This was rather welcome as meals

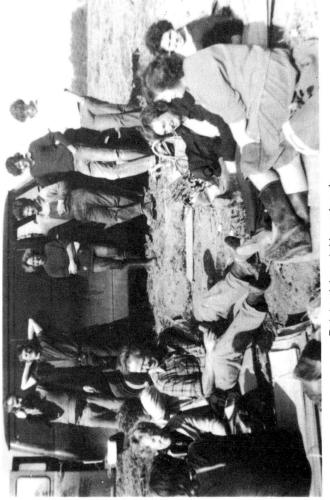

Potato pickers taking a break...
Photo: John Adams

were eaten out in the field where we were working. Some of the time I was on the potato spinner and occasionally got rather bemused by the conflict between the local pickers and the outside gang. Each had their own boss woman or spokeswoman, so when the two gangs had to work together sparks started to fly as to who would be in charge. It seemed to me at the time best idea to keep out of it and let things sort themselves out, as the women in question were rather well built.

The milling of cattle and pig meal was done on the farm by a tractor and hammer mill. The tractors used were the John Deere or Massey Harris as they had pulleys on and were high enough for the belt to go over the wall out of the Big Barn alleyway up to the mixing shed floor. The different sorts of corn to be ground were tipped into hoppers built on the granary floor above. These were about chest height, so any bags that were too low to get on my back had to be humped up. When the tractors were busy in the day-time I would go back up after tea to do some. It always seemed a bit scary as it got on towards dark, being the only one up there and as the mill seemed to vibrate rather a lot I was a bit apprehensive that one of the hammers would fly off, but none ever did. Mind you I'd jump a fair bit when something other than corn went through as a fair old rattle was made. I used to like grinding beans up as the smell of the bean meal was something apart from other smells. This one day, milling during ordinary working hours, I was filling the hopper in the loft with the mill running below, when all of a sudden I found myself falling down the granary floor. One of the castings on top of the upright girders supporting the wooden beams had broken in half, letting half the granary floor down twelve feet or so. There was no warning of this whatsoever. I found myself in the company of sacks of corn, loose grain, shovels, hoppers, empty sacks, sack truck and lots of other bits and pieces that were stored up there, all heading for the floor below as fast as gravity could take them. As the cracking subsided and a great cloud of dust got up I could hear Jim somewhere, calling my name. I was able to scramble out and run around to find Jim and tell him I was alright, much to his relief. The loft was later put back up with the rest of the offending castings removed and a different system adopted.

In my late teens or early 20s, I dug a well at The Knowle. Until then drinking water was carried up from the spring, over the brook, in buckets. After heavy rain, either the spring water got coloured or it was impossible to get across the flooded brook to it. Previously father had someone he knew check for an underground water supply around the house. This the man did with a two-foot steel rule, held under tension between his hands. Whenever he crossed an underground supply the curved (bent) rule would dip. I can remember watching him doing it. He traced this line of water coming under the brook, to the west of the house, from the direction of Collins Farm, through the then cowshed, along the side of the house, across the front yard and back down to the brook, to the north and heading towards Meredith House and Pensons Farm, both of which have wells, in addition to Collins Farm. I think that water was traced first and the houses built on this line of water. To make sure there was water by the house, father made a small hand borer, which I used. This worked well for the first fifteen feet or so, until the marl got hard and a 2cwt anvil had to be mounted on the galvanised water piping that was being used, to get penetration. About 3" to 4" at time was all that I could do, before dismantling the anvil and pulling the borer out to clean the soil from inside. Water was struck at about 23 feet. Up till then it was bone dry. At least we knew that water was down there, so I set about digging a well. I knew nothing about this sort of job. First was to decide what size hole to dig by placing bricks in a circle on the ground, and I found that the smallest diameter hole I was likely to be able to work in – 11 bricks – seemed about right.

In some respects, digging the well was easier than the boring, for towards the 20 foot mark, it was as much as I could to to turn it round at all, with the weight of anvil, length of pipe and hardness of marl. I dug and hauled the soil out myself, being hard marl all the way down, other than the top foot or so. No shoring up was needed which was just as well perhaps, as I can't even remember thinking about such a precaution. Much to my surprise, it was actually dusty until water level. After about the first 7'-8' it got too hard to dig with a shovel, so from then on a hammer and chisel was used to loosen the marl, which was then shovelled into a bucket suspended from a winch and a length of wire rope. Each time the bucket was filled I clambered up a rope ladder I made from bailer twine, with sticks for rungs, to empty it. This was better than a fixed ladder, as a fixed ladder would have got in the way of digging with no one to pull it up and down after each bucketful. With the rope ladder, I just added a rung as required.

All went well until water was reached. This digging was done after work at nights, and at weekends. The water came in properly at about 25ft, so I went another 2ft past this mark and then called it enough. The water never came above about the 20ft level. I then lined it with bricks and father fitted an electric pressure pump. We were now able to have a flush toilet. In the 35 years or so since it was sunk the well has never let us down, nor as far as I know, ever got discoloured.

The banks above Netherwood, where there was no proper woodland, were left rather rough, especially over by Brick Barns. The cattle were put out to graze there in the summer months. It was part grass and part bracken, briars and trees and the cattle used to make paths through the rough parts. Being young, I used to enjoy getting them out of this wilderness, to take them back to the farm – it could take a long time, chasing them through these paths to get them all together. (I can understand how Cecil and Harold Jones failed to find their cows for milking one day, when they had them running on Netherwood banks.)

Sometimes, when rounding them up I would meet a group of them, head on, charging down one of these narrow cuttings. Cattle still had horns in those days, so more than once I took to the side to let them by. It was quite a maze, because Netherwood bracken grew much taller than a man, you could often only hear the groups of cattle, not see them. One man who came to work at Netherwood from a couple of valleys away said he'd never come across such tall bracken before. After collecting them together, several people would help to take them back to the farm buildings. Everything would go well, until the Barn field was reached. This had a road along the top, which led to the farm, the rest of the field falling away to one side. This was where the fun (or trouble, according to your attitude) started. I usually liked the challenge of getting them across this field. As soon as the cattle got through the gate they had this compulsion to run downhill. This was not what was wanted at all. If they kept up along the top of the field it was a short journey to the farm, if not, several men would be employed chasing groups of cattle about the field for an hour or so. Once they split up it was a hopeless job, as each bunch kept trying to join up with their fellows. On more than one occasion the job was abandoned and just Jim and me would have a go later when things had calmed down a bit. The two of us had better results that four or five people, as we would bring them in a calm fashion, all the way from Brick Barns to the buildings, without any bother at all. It must have been Jim's mental and physical attitude which the cattle could somehow sense. It was nice to be part of this achievement, but I was a little sad at not having the fun of chasing around after them in the Barn field!

Castrating the young bulls was at one time done by Jim Tonks. I can remember helping him; he used two hot irons, wedge-shaped pieces on the ends of metal rods. The purse was cut open with a knife and the testicles pulled down clear; then the cords were burnt through with the hot irons and some green-looking oil was put on the open wound.

When a small electric corn dryer was installed at Netherwood, the corn was dried in sacks laid over grids, through which hot air was blown. The first job on a harvest-time morning would be to change these bags over. The sacks were all shapes and sizes, some hardly big enough to cover the hole, while others were so big and bulky they took an extra day to dry through. Heaving these sacks about first thing in the morning used to cause a fair few farts among the men. Jim, ever cheerful, put names to some of them – silent but deadly; sneaky; rip-arse; watery; unmentionable (that one everybody disappeared for a minute or lit up a fag); and embarrassed (where the chap walked away waving his hand behind his bottom)!

After I got my driving licence I would take loads to Kidderminster beet factory and sometimes bring a load of beet pulp back. (This was soaked and fed to the cattle.) The lorry had high sides and it was difficult to judge how much to load. Usually with the mud the lorry was overladen and bottom gear had to be used to get up the hills on the way to the factory. Most of the time I forked it off by hand, as there was usually a queue at the place where they washed it off for you. Some of the beet we pulled ourselves by hand, but if we could not cope, outside help was brought in. One of these was a Mr. Jones, a son and daughter from Tenbury Wells, who also did some draining by hand for Mr. Payne, down the middle of the Parks (Mr. Payne was the next owner).

Sugar beet machines were tried for lifting the beet, but never worked very well in the heavy soil. Pulling beet one December or January was when my hands got really cold. It was one of those days when the frost never really went all day. Nobody seemed to think about wearing gloves, anyway they would have soon got wet. I was working with Lucky Hands at the time, who lived in father's old home, Park Cottage, down by the lake. He had a wife and I think three children when he left Netherwood. The thing to do was to pull as many of the ice crusted beet as possible, until one's hands got uncomfortably cold, stop, to let them warm up a bit, then have another go, and so on through the day. One thing I remember about that day was what Lucky said about teeth. He read somewhere that teeth should either be tightly packed together so that food can't get in between them, or wide apart, so that food can easily be got out from between them.

When Mr. and Mrs. Payne bought Netherwood, there was still some sugar beet to be pulled in the Pea Fields (then Roadside Meadows), in front of Little Netherwood, where John and his wife, Mrs. Beeston, lived. John and I would do an hour's pulling after work, until it got dark, but first I would be taken into John's house and treated to a cup of tea before we set to work. I enjoyed those times.

Mr. and Mrs. Abel Smith had three sons: Wilfred, Fritz and Timothy. Wilfred I never saw much, Fritz I remember with a brilliant yellow car outside the wainhouse and Timothy I remember for being in a hide, shooting pigeons off some kale, down the bottom of Roundcots. This was one Saturday morning, when I was doing something on a tractor and the poor lad was having to sit in there most of the day in the cold. I felt most concerned about him.

Most of my life I've had difficulty keeping my socks up, either because my feet are a queer shape, or I'm too mean to buy good quality socks, or because I like my boots to have a loose fit. One year I stopped wearing them altogether. I even went through the winter without any and the only time I got cold feet was standing shaking apples in the frosty wet grass. People at work were tolerant of each other's strange ways and habits, but the trouble started when I went out anywhere. It was alright walking, people didn't notice much, the worst bit was going to the pictures on the bus, for sitting down exposed my bare ankles above my shoes. Finally when some of the girls started looking and smiling towards my 'bare bits', I tried to make a point of wearing some thin, old socks when going out anywhere, and most uncomfortable it was too!

This work habit can get to you if you're not careful. After being at work for a few years, I had flu and had to stop at home in bed. It was O.K. until I heard the John Deere working at Netherwood, a few fields away from The Knowle. As soon as I heard it, I was up at the bedroom window, trying to see who was doing my job, and why and where and all the other thoughts that go through one's mind. I felt most annoyed that I could not let myself be ill without moithering about work. For several years I seemed to get flu symptoms each spring and autumn. Usually I was able to work through them without having time off, until one autumn, when riding the drill, planting wheat in the Parks, I got so weak and dizzy I could hardly hang on to the back of the drill without falling off. I thought I might be better after dinner, so just lay on the ground at the back of the drill, while the foreman, Dennis Jones went home for his dinner. Unable to face any food and drink, I just lay there on a bag until he came back. I was much worse, and asked if I could drive the tractor to keep myself going until the field was finished. He agreed most willingly, but I vowed then never to work through a bout of flu again.

In about 1958 Mr. and Mrs. Abel Smith sold Netherwood and Mr. and Mrs. Payne bought it and moved in. When the farm was up for sale, I had a couple of job offers from local farmers, but after a little thought I decided to take my chance with the new owner when he asked me to carry on, as he did everyone else I think, except the foreman who moved to another place. Mr. Payne moved down from near Grantham in Lincolnshire and brought quite a lot of machinery with him, some of which is still in use nearly thirty years later. Sid and Mrs. Batterham also moved down, with their two children, Terry and Sheila. Sid was to be the new foreman under Mr. Payne at Netherwood. When Sid started, I had a bit of a job understanding his dialect, and in the first few months, I had to ask him to repeat what he'd said. The names he used for different tools and parts of implements were a bit confusing for a while. Our muck forks he called four-pronged forks, our pikes two-pronged forks. Thriples (the things put on the front and back of trailers for loading hay or bales against) he called gormers;

what we called flays on a plough, he called skimmers, which I think was the book name in this case; and for years confusion reigned about which was top and bottom of a field, after we'd started the wrong end! The trouble was that on Netherwood nearly all the fields have a slope to them, so to us locals, the bottom of the field was always the lowest side or end and the top the highest part of the field, irrespective of where one stood. Whereas Sid, coming from a part of the country that had mostly level flat fields, approached it from another angle. Whichever side of the field they were standing at, the farthest side away from them was always called the top, so any side could be the bottom or the top, according to where one was standing.

Sid's approach to life was different too, more of a direct manner both in speech and in doing work. This took a bit of getting used to. It was almost hurtful some of the things he said and the directness of his orders was a bit of a shock. The local people were rather gentle in manner and speech, almost slow and a bit vague, leaving room to manoeuvre. The way I had been brought up, when someone said 'in a minute', it meant any time in the next hour or so. I must admit, I got to like Sid's way, at least you knew where you stood.

During the year before Mr. Payne took over, I was doing most of the ploughing, with a grey Fergie diesel tractor and three-furrow plough. We had

Barnfield in mid-plough

55

a set of girdles to fit around the tractor tyres for extra grip when it was wet. It was quite remarkable what this little tractor could do. I had always ploughed cops and reans. When Mr. Payne took over and said he was going to enlarge some of the fields, I had visions of having cops and reans at least a quarter of a mile long. I even worked out in my mind how many and where they would be in these new big fields. There was also talk of new tractors and ploughs. Having never had a new tractor to drive before, it was an attractive prospect.

I think one of the most mauling, hard jobs I ever did was when we put down a strip of concrete road out into the Barn field. It was rather a hot time of the year. The concrete was brought in ready-mixed in a large lorry and the mixture was really sticky. This was the way Mr. Payne wanted it. The mixture just seemed to stop where it was put, no flow or give at all and when trying to tamp it level you just could not get enough moisture to the top to skim it off easily. So the day or so it took to do this stretch of unwieldy stuff was very hard work indeed, but having run a crawler back and forth over this stretch of concrete, going from one part of the farm to another for about fifteen years, proved that the hard work was well worthwhile and that the mixture was as near perfect as possible. I've seen some very wet mixtures, much easier and quicker to put down, but which seem to start to crumble very quickly.

By bringing most of his tractors and implements with him, Mr. Payne did not need any of the existing tractors and things at Netherwood, so most things were sold at the sale when Mr. Abel Smith left.

Terry, the foreman's son, and I had a new Fordson Super Major each and Ranson's ploughs to match. The one had wide tyres on and the other normal width (I think this was the only difference between them), but for two identical engines, they were totally different. The one I used, when working hard, smoked like the devil, whereas Terry's hardly smoked at all. They were like this from new and were the same when sold several years later.

I was starting to learn a lesson in life with the coming of the new tractors, and new ways of doing things. The first disappointment was that the new tractor I'd been looking forward to driving was diesel, not T.V.O. I'd somehow always had it in my mind that it would be a T.V.O., and that it might be a diesel had never crossed my mind.

The next thing was a bigger blow. I went to start to plough my first field under Mr. Payne, with his new tractor and plough. It was the small patch, at the side of the roadway through the Parks. I was, to my amazement, told to start ploughing around the outside. I thought, well, perhaps they're just seeing how the plough goes before starting the first cop. But no, I had to keep going round and round the field, until I got to the middle, then do the same in the next field, and so on and so on. That was the way the ploughing was going to be done from then on. I can still feel the sinking feeling I had, as I struggled to get the plough round the bends in the field boundary. I'd always tried to plough as straight as possible with the cops and rean method of ploughing. To sit there, day after day, having only an occasional straight side to a field to follow just about finished me with Netherwood. I think that was the nearest I ever was to packing in, all over that change of ploughing method. I suppose, up in Lincolnshire the fields are mainly flat and straight sided, so drainage was not helped much whichever way of ploughing was used, and perhaps the field being fairly even in shape it was easy to work back out from the middle. Whereas Netherwood fields were mostly on a slope, and being heavy soil, benefited from ploughing straight up and down a slope, so the water could drain off more easily. Most of the fields bordered on a dingle, so often there were some very difficult curves to follow round. Over the years, we had lots of trouble with strained front furrows on the ploughs, and when the man from Ransons came and tried putting things to right, he said, "If you will try to plough round corners, you must put up with bent ploughs, it's your own fault, ploughs are meant to go in straight lines, not the way you use them." But I must admit, I learned how to put lengths of wire and washers behind certain parts, to help straighten things up a bit.

It seems that change brings as many disappointments as pleasures. One only thinks about the apparent advantages, not enough about the side effects. Changes that happen in one's own life and in the world in general never seem to be wholly good. As time goes by, the bad effects of change come out into the open, as if there is only so much good and so much bad, as if everything has an opposite in the world. When a farm goes over to making silage out of grass instead of making hay for feeding livestock the effluent often gets into streams and ponds, killing fish and other things that are dependent on clean water, whereas generally speaking, the only thing that suffered from the effects of hay was man himself, from breathing mouldy dust out of bad hay.

I heard of a farmer who found what was happening to his trout lake and dug a large drain through part of the farm, diverting this effluent into a nearby stream. Stories of similar instances make me rather sad, as I am in some way connected with all of this. The side effects of change almost outweigh the advantages unless the side effects can be dealt with in a way that is acceptable to the world and the people and creatures that live in it.

All these pollutants spread on the land, mostly end up in the streams and springs. Two instances come to mind during my years in farm work. One was when I was ploughing and in the adjoining field a man spread a load of liquid slurry from a tanker. About an hour later, as I was going up the side of the field, I noticed that one of the drains coming into the open ditch was a strange colour. Not taking much notice, I carried on ploughing. A bit later, I had to do something to the plough near this drain head, so I took a look to satisfy my curiosity, and on bending down near this funny coloured water I could smell what it was. In an hour the slurry had drained through the soil, into the nearest length of drain, and was running merrily on down into the nearest brook. The speed of this quite shook me. I might have expected that in a couple of days or so it might seep through when some rain came along.

The second incident was when I was ploughing with the crawler. There was a place where a drain came out of a field and joined a small stream that went through a culvert, under the lane. The crawler and plough used to get filled with fuel and greased up at this point and usually getting my hands covered in grease and mud, I would go down to this drain head to wash my hands. The fine silt in the bottom of the ditch made quite a good soap, cutting through the grime and gunge, and the water running out of the drain was fine to swill off with afterwards. This day, a chap with a sprayer was working nearby and before he went off the farm I saw him tootling about with his tractor and sprayer in the corner of the stubble field, near where I filled up the crawler. He just seemed to be driving idly about, doing nothing in particular. I thought I saw something coming out of the bottom of his sprayer tank; "Ah well", I said to myself, "he has to get rid of it somewhere", and promptly forgot about it. When the crawler worked hard, the fuel tank did not hold enough fuel to work until 9 or 10 o'clock at night, so I had to fill up at tea time. Having done so this day, I jumped down into the ditch to wash the diesel off my hands, saying to myself at the same time 'What in heaven's name is that?' for the water I washed my hands in was a pretty yellow colour. The spray that had been let out had worked its way down into the drains and was showing up in the water coming off the field. That stopped me washing my hands there for a few days, but I was more worried about the frog who lived in this bit of ditch, for I used to see him most mornings when going to wash. So it seems that things do go through soil, in some cases quite quickly.

Having to wait a while once when I was at the barbers in Tenbury, in my teens, I picked up a booklet to read, and a bit in there was about Kyre, where I lived and worked. It said the old name for Kyre, which I think was spelt Cear, meant 'Valley of the Springs'. I thought how fitting, as Netherwood was part of the Kyre Valley where I worked, and having ploughed or done some operation with a tractor in most of the fields and accessible hilly bits, had either got bogged down, backed off, gone round, or left the tractor stuck till next morning, to be pulled off by another one because of wet places. (Even in later years the same thing still happened with the crawler, but that comes later.) I once worked out that there was not one single field on Netherwood that I couldn't get stuck in. Ancient man had got the name just about right.

Before Mr. Payne bought Netherwood, Abel Smith had sugar beet on the Parks, and it had to be hauled up to through the top of the field. In an effort to make sure we would be able to haul it off in the winter, the foreman and I spent several days hauling stone with the lorry from Bromyard tile works quarry, and making a road down the side of the hedge, by the side of the Parks meadow. I must say I enjoyed what bit of lorry driving I did in those days, as there weren't the restrictions and amount of traffic as there is now. The lorry was, I think, a Bedford 3 tonner, with a sectional stock box to fit on as required. When Mr. Payne took over, I half expected to carry on doing some of the lorry work, but Sid had other ideas, he said he wanted me on tractor driving and that the two would clash, so Dick Clifford took over the lorry for a while.

During the first year or so after Mr. Payne took over Netherwood, it must have changed more than at any other time since it was a Deer Park, for he bulldozed (pushed) out several hedgerows, and made bigger fields, in some cases as many as four fields were made into one. This suited his style of farming and the bigger machinery that was becoming available, as well as tending to level any humps and hollows. This happened before I got interested in amateur archeology, so I didn't take much notice of what was going on around me – it was all rather exciting and stimulating. What did strike me after the first couple of years was how cold and small the farm had become. This was because until then, there was double the number of fields, and each one had a hedge round, usually overgrown and with mature trees along it. This made you feel, as soon as you had gone into the first field away from the buildings, that you were in a world of your own, in as much as you could not see the farm house or buildings, and in some cases not much of the neighbouring farm either. To go across to Collington's or Brickbarns along rutted dirt roads, and through several high-hedged gateways made it seem a long way indeed. Also it was very sheltered from the winds, whatever direction they were from. Wherever you were working, it was never far to go to have a pee or find shelter from a storm.

As soon as many of the high hedges were pushed out and things generally tidied up, one found one could suddenly see the farm from most of the fields and, what was worse, Clee Hill came very much into view, this being north of Netherwood, and any cold winds seemed to come straight off this hill and hit Netherwood duff.

I'm not criticising Mr. Payne, as he turned out to be a good farmer and kept a balanced farm, and in good heart. By running stock alongside grain, he managed to have plenty of farmyard manure to plough back into the land. This is more than can be said of some of the big farming companies about today.

Having seen the results of when someone new comes into the area to take over a farm or something, what they do often is upsetting to the local people. It would be nice if there was a body of people who knew the area that the newcomer was taking over, to explain if there was anything of interest that would benefit from being left as it is. I must admit things are getting better in this respect, as the public in general is becoming more aware of its environment.

About this time the footpaths on Netherwood were closed which was sad as my parents and grandparents and generations before them had used these paths in their daily work and activities. After making a few inquiries, I found that they were indeed closed. Apparently a small notice had been put up in Ludlow or somewhere, presumably stating what was proposed and any objections or anything had to be in by a certain date. If you don't know about a certain thing, how can you object; by telepathy or something? It seems the Law then was loaded a bit one way. How the Law stands now on such matters I don't know, but it seems logical that a notice should be put at each path or bridleway to be closed, where people are able to see it and so do something about it if they feel inclined. My personal view is that generally so few people use them, unless it is a place of outstanding beauty or a national monument or something, things are best left as they are. Poachers or other such people wouldn't bother either way I expect. Take the paths and rights of way on Netherwood over the years before they were closed for instance. I saw less than a dozen people use them in as many years, and nearly all were local people anyway. One was a man from Thornbury direction, who used to take his horse to be shod at Charlie Bethell's, the blacksmith at Collington. He used to come down across from Brickbarns through Collington meadows and over the bridge into Underhill Farm. Of about three serious walkers I saw, one was a fellow with a dog tagging along behind him. This was rather a nice sight, I wouldn't have minded joining him for the rest of his day's walk. Cecil and Harold Jones also used them occasionally. Nowadays, however, the motor car and other such forms of fast transport make them less important, but still of interest to many of us.

Back to wet fields! Mr. Payne set about draining the worst wet holes. This was firstly done by a local contractor with a digger on the back of a tractor. One was Adams of Underley, who have now moved abroad. The trenches were dug out by him and us workers at Netherwood put the pipes in the bottom and then threw waste floor tiles hauled from Bromyard tile works on top about a foot thick. This solved the immediate problem, but an even bigger one was looming up. By pushing out hedges and upsetting a few of the drains and ditches accompanying them, associated with circular ploughing, water was starting to pool where it normally didn't before, and as ploughing was done with one tractor wheel in the furrow, when it got wet this produced furrow smear. After a few years it got to the state where the water would not drain away because of the furrow smear. It got to the point that the crops were starting to fail where it remained wet. It came to a head in the Roundcots field. One year the autumn-planted wheat crop had completely failed in the wettest areas in this 30 acre field. Only about 15 acres were any good as it was patchy all over the field. It was not possible to plough up the worst bits and replant, so it was decided to plough in what was left of the crop and plant up the whole of the 30 acre field again with spring corn. This was some of the strangest ploughing I'd ever done, for usually the wheel in the furrow was where you got your main traction from, but in this case the furrow bottom was slimy from the previous ploughing, the land not having had time to settle properly, so much of the time I was shooting across the furrows as the land wheel was doing all the gripping. It seems my instinct was right about this circular ploughing on Netherwood.

It was at this point (Mr. Payne had been at Netherwood about eleven years by now), presumably, that Mr. Payne had to change his way of farming or go out of business. He then took the rather big step of buying a crawler and plough so as to stop the furrow smear and get his land back in good shape. It so happened we ended up with a reversible plough, so I was able to plough in straight lines again, but still not as interesting as cops and reans from my point of view. The continued use of the crawler, combined with what seemed like miles of draining, done by T J Read of Hereford over several years on Netherwood seems to have kept the farm in good condition as far as the arable side is concerned.

Things seem to go round in circles. Mr. Morris, one time owner of Netherwood, had a very early crawler, Mr. Abel Smith had a crawler and now there is a crawler back again.

Back now to when Mr. Payne took over Netherwood. As I said, everyone of the workers carried on, except the previous foreman, so in fact there was one extra with Terry, Sid's son, who was a bit younger than me. He never liked the hilly roads in the district. Back up at Grantham it was pretty flat, ideal for cycling, but down here no good at all he said. I got on well with him, especially at work. He and I had two different meanings for the phrase 'Old boy'. My interpretation was the local one meaning tramp or old man. His was when he referred to one of his mates in their teens, when he called them 'Old boy'. Other than this there was not much difference in our different regional outlooks.

Jim Tonks and Dick Clifford left after about twelve months or so. Jim went to work for the council. I was sad to see him go, as I think he shaped my outlook and attitude to life more than anyone. It gave me great pleasure to wave and have a chat with him whenever I saw him working at the side of the roads in the area. George Allen came to be lorry driver then after Dick Clifford.

During my visits to Tenbury I became interested in a dark haired girl who worked in a cafe. She had a beauty spot on one cheekbone, whether this was real or not I don't know. After a while she returned the interest which was nice. She lived in Tenbury and I used to think she had the smoothest, nicest legs in town as she walked up through Tenbury after the pictures. One thing I couldn't come to terms with was that she liked dancing, which was perfectly natural, but to me then the thought of going into a dance hall was more than I could face as I couldn't even dance. The thought of going in with this girl was then more than I could cope with. I had once seen her dancing through the open door in the hall that used to be on the corner of Berrington Road, and had an awful sinking feeling of getting out of my depth if I were ever to get as far as taking this young lady out. Things progressed nicely for a while with her helping things along as best she could. It got to the stage when going to the pictures that I used to sit below the balcony in the 2/4s and when the girl and her friends saw me, they would come in and sit behind in the 2/10s. I was bombarded by their ticket stubs and such like, a form of attention I didn't mind at all. I think in the end she gave me up as a useless case after one Sunday night visit to the pictures. She used to walk back home the same way as I cycled and as I went slowly past where she was walking she wished me goodnight nicely, trying to break the ice that I seemed to be encased in. Typically, I was too slow to cotton on to what was happening. For a start I could hardly believe that it was me she had spoken to and by the time I did, I was many more yards up the street and getting too far away to reply, even if I could have formed the words. She took my silence as lack of interest and I heard her say as I cycled on up the road "Oh don't speak then", which more or less signalled the end. After that evening I had a few miserable nights' sleep, as all the dreams and hopes had suddenly been shattered. My own fault of course.

It surprises me just how much feelings, thoughts and emotions can be experienced from just looking at a girl, never even speaking directly to her, or touching her, just a meeting of the eyes.

About this time I went on holiday by myself to Dyffryn near Barmouth in Wales, but at the time we were in the middle of beet hoeing. This was done on piece-work outside working hours. As it happened, my holiday fell in the middle of the first time through, which was when the plants were singled into even spacings. The next time through was to hoe the weeds that had grown off. If I'd gone on holiday and left half the crop I'd been allotted, it would have been a right mess to come back to, so I decided to try and finish it before I went. The only time available was before 7 in the morning and after 5 in the afternoon. So for a week or so I would get up at about 3 a.m. and have a bite of food and cup of tea, then go up and sit and wait for it to get light enough to start hoeing, which was fairly soon as it was very close to the longest day. I'd work till about 6.30, go back home and have a proper breakfast, then do the normal day's work, then back to the hoeing until it got too dark, sometime around 10 p.m. As this took place near the cottages, it was nice to observe the houses coming to life and to notice which people were first about. Terry Batterham was the first. He had some pigs of his own, down the dingle from where I was working. It was nice to see him walking, bleary-eyed, with a bucket of food down to his stock. This early morning work has never appealed to me a great deal, as my natural body clock thinks 9 o'clock is the proper time to get up in the morning. It was good to get the hoeing done and I really enjoyed the long sleep in the caravan on the first day of my holiday.

While on about Terry and his pigs, it was then that we learned how much pride, or whatever you might call it, the gaffer had in his corn crops. Terry had taken a tractor and trailer with some stuff down to his pigs. He had to go through a patch of partly grown corn, which he did by going round the headland and in doing this he ran down some of the corn with the tractor and trailer wheels. When the gaffer found out he went up the wall, tearing down to the field in the land-rover to have a look at the damage. He rammed a gate post in his temper and that completely put the tin hat on it. He threatened to stop money out of Terry's wages for the damage done to his crop. This got a bit awkward, as Terry's father was foreman, and said he would pay for the damage there and then. Things cooled down a bit then and as far as I know no money actually changed hands, but we all learned to be careful from then on – until I had the misfortune to make a similar balls-up the following year. I was rolling winter corn in the springtime and, having several fields to do, was trying to get on as fast as possible. When it came to change from one field to another, instead of going a long way round the road to the next field to be done, I cut across the nearest field. This happened to be one that I would have to roll later in the week, so I thought it would not matter, but the gaffer saw what I'd done and there was nearly a repeat of the Terry episode. He let it be known, in no uncertain terms, that he was displeased. I must admit I felt rather sick about the whole thing for the next few days.

I'm not sure how I got to Dyffryn, whether it was part way by bus and the last part by train or not. A large part of that week's holiday was spent at Barmouth and, not having a lot to do, I fancied having a go in a rowing boat. Having spent a couple of half hours learning to row at Ludlow on the river below the castle, I thought I was good enough to go on the sea in one. So I hired one from a fisherman, down below the railway bridge that runs into Barmouth across the estuary. He let me have it for about an hour at a reasonable rate. As he pushed me off into the water he said something which I could not understand as he was very Welsh, so I just nodded my head and set off. The tide must have just turned, for there was a good rush of water coming through the railway arches and forming a fast current out to sea. I enjoyed this, as I could get into it and go out to sea at an exhilarating speed, then row back up against the harbour wall and have another go. Getting quite engrossed in this, I was suddenly brought down to earth by some irate voices above me, along the top of the sea wall. These were fishermen and I hadn't seen their lines and was trying to row back up through them, causing much havoc. Shipping the oars and shouting I was sorry, I gently extracted myself, sorting their lines out as best I could and then shamefacedly got as far away from them as I could. I did this by heading up to the railway bridge and starting to row through one of the archways, but after a while it dawned on me that I wasn't getting anywhere. The water coming through under the bridge was going so fast that I had got half way under and wasn't moving. Lining myself up with a bit of rock, I saw that the situation would stay the same unless I managed to find a bit more energy. After what seemed like a long time, the sea must have relented a bit, I was actually moving, be it only half an inch on each stroke. What a relief when I finally made it and had a large expanse of water to row about in, with no one else in view. After guessing that an hour had passed I went back under the bridge. Coming out the other side was rather like a cork coming out of a bottle owing to the fair speed of water. Having got back, the fisherman was there to give me a hand out of his boat, saying as he did so, in hardly understandable English, "Well young sir, you did very well indeed". Wondering what he was on about, I was enlightened when he said "Did you not hear what I told you when you got into the boat?" I said "No, I had not understood what was said". "I told you not to go near the bridge as the build up of water was coming out too fast from the other side to be safe." I suppose he'd sat there wondering if he'd ever see his boat again in one piece, after seeing me heading up to the bridge. I've always cherished this compliment, even if I was in the wrong!

There were a couple of Amusement Arcades near Barmouth beach, with juke boxes in, which I spent a fair amount of time hanging round, as did lots of girls. I hardly ever put any money in them as I felt too shy to walk in amongst the girls to do this. The record that week that was played over and over again was Brenda Lee's 'Weep no More my Baby'. After a couple of days I grew to like one fair-haired girl with a rather nice figure who would come and stand around with her friend. She and several others decided they would see if they could make me smile. One or the other would come and stand in front of me with a mocking smile on their face and stop there, just looking. After a while I could feel my lips starting to tremble and, quite unable to stop myself, broke out in a big grin. The girl would then march off triumphantly to her friends, looking back at me as if to say "Beat you!" I never actually spoke to any of the girls over the several days that this was happening. It was a bit embarrassing at first, but I quite got to like the attention. On the last full day of the holiday I found out where the girl I'd taken a liking to worked. She was a waitress in a fish and chip shop, on the land side of the main road that runs through Barmouth. It was up a long flight of steps. Having spent a couple of hours wandering about plucking up courage, I finally went in. The girl and her friend were there, but apart from them the place was empty. On entering, the girls' first words were "Found it at last then". Getting my fish and chips, I sat down at one of the tables, but was not going to be left in peace to eat them. The two girls came and sat with me, asking where I came from and such like. When I said I came from Worcester there was a bit of a silence, so I added, in Worcestershire, thinking that they did not perhaps know where Worcester was. At this the two girls burst into laughter, repeating several times Worcester in Worcestershire. In my embarrassment I went to put my foot on one of the rungs of a stool nearby and my foot crashed to the floor. At the same time the young lady I fancied said, smiling yet more, "There's no rungs on our stools here you know". After that the other girl went and busied herself on the other side of the room and I then had a nice conversation with the girl for the rest of my meal. The owner then appeared from out the back somewhere, saying, "Come on you two, I don't pay you to chat up customers". Whether I paid for the fish and chips I was never sure. Having to go back home next day, I could not pursue the relationship any further.

A year or so later, when waiting at a level crossing or station near Dyffryn, a train came slowly by. As it did so, I was hit on the side of the head by something chucked out of the train window. Looking to see where it came from, I saw this same girl looking at me with a big smile on her face, eating from a packet of chips. Sitting beside her was a young man and from some instinct or other I was sure they were married. As she went past out of view, I could have sworn she said or mouthed the word Worcestershire. My hand picked something off my collar – it was the chip she had tossed out to attract my attention.

Going to Barmouth over several years for holidays I came to recognise some of the faces, especially those in one of the cafes, and it was nice to be greeted by one or the other as I went in each year. Having got quite attracted to the place and the girls, one winter I made a couple of journeys up for the day on a Saturday, after finishing work at 12 o'clock, I'd have dinner, then push-bike down to Tenbury and pick up a hire car from G E T H Maund Garage. This was a reddish, column gear-change Hillman car that would do the ninety-odd miles in good time. Barmouth, like most seaside places I suppose, seemed to withdraw into itself in winters. Instead of walking about the sea front one had a tendency to keep to the town, where it's more sheltered. As it got dark early, I would end up in the dance hall. This was a bit out of character, as I would not go within a mile of one back home. It was also a strange feeling going into this dance hall and seeing the girls' faces known from my week's summer holiday and their looks as if to say "He's familiar, but it's the wrong time of year". Having satisfied myself as to what the seaside in winter was like and worked out that if I got serious about a girl it would be rather a long way to keep popping back and forth, I stopped going any more. The one good result of these winter visits was that I could now go into a dance hall without my legs turning to jelly, thinking that everyone was staring at me. This made me a little less timid on my home ground.

The big barn at Netherwood had been altered. One alleyway was done away with and incorporated into the cattle pens. John Beeston had moved and was now living in one of the cottages. He was the cattle and pig stockman. The cattle in the barn were fed with silage in the mornings and hay in the evenings. There were no milking cattle at Netherwood during Mr. Payne's time, apart from during the first few years when one was kept for the house. There are two things that have stood out during my connection with Netherwood. One was the first time I saw milk delivered to Netherwood House in milk bottles. I thought to myself, "What on earth is farming coming to when a farm can't produce milk for itself?". The other noticeable thing was when a big bakery bought up all our local bakeries and everybody had to have the same bread from this centralised thing. We had contractors at Netherwood at the time and I happened to go by where they had their lunch and, to my disgust, saw half-eaten rounds of bread thrown on the ground. We, at Kyre, were still having locally made bread at the time and you never wasted anything anyway. If you couldn't eat something it was saved for the next day or given to the cats or dogs or fed to the fowls or pig. It was never wasted, everything was used to feed something. Jim used to have a bit of paper between his thumb and finger when he ate with dirty hands, so as not to waste any of his crusts. Even now, nearly thirty years later, I don't like chucking things about the farm, I either take them back home, or put them out of sight somewhere. A month or so later, when we had to have this newfangled bread baked somewhere miles and miles away, I understood the disgust these contractors felt and could in some way forgive this symbolic throwing away of something that had the texture of soap. I've never taken to it; in my opinion all it's good for is toast, which it makes quite well.

The silage John fed to the cattle in the barn was forked out of a clump by hand. This was hard work as, in those days, the silage was put in as it was cut at its full length. It was put in the clump with a buckrake and more less left as it came off, apart from a bit of levelling. So, when forking it out in the winter, it had to be taken out as it was put in, otherwise it was almost impossible to get any out at all. One day in winter, four of us were loading up a trailer to be taken out to be fed to the sheep. They were fed in hayracks out in one of the fields. This particular morning we were having a lot of fun throwing forkfuls of silage over each other, but things got a bit wild and resulted in me sticking

66

one of the tines of my fork through George's hand. It was more or less in the middle of his palm with the tine sticking out the other side. Instinctively he pulled it out again and seemed all right, but was persuaded to go and have a tetanus injection later.

John Beeston was one of only two men I ever saw steaming when working. Having cattle and pigs to look after, I suppose he liked to get as many fed before bait time as possible. The silage he fed to the cattle was hauled around the barn on a hand-pulled four-wheeled trolley. I happened to go in one morning after he'd just about finished. I stopped to say something to him as he was standing with the light behind and I saw a gentle cloud of steam coming off his whole body through his clothes. He must have put a lot of effort into that morning's work. The other person was Arnold Olive, who at the time was heaving heavy concrete blocks about and as he stood for a moment in the cool darkness of the part-built piggery, I saw little spirals of steam coming off the top of his head.

The pigs then, or should I say the sows, were kept out in the orchards. Several covered railway huts were dotted about the various patches for them to live in. The sows were generally brought into the building just prior to farrowing. Occasionally one would slip the net and farrow outside. To see a sow carrying mouthfuls of grass and stuff to make a sort of nest to have her young was a pleasurable sight. One young litter of pigs of several weeks, had the free run of the farm and buildings, which sometimes happened when they found they could squeeze under gates and get out where they shouldn't. It is one of the most entertaining things I've ever seen. It's almost impossible to catch them as they all charged at once at a furious speed, stopping for nothing. They just seemed to bounce off things till they got where they were going.

Terry Batterham used to take great delight in sneaking up on the pigs when they lay in a tump in the middle of an empty cattle yard, amongst the dry humps of dung. Getting as close as possible, he would shout "Boo!", and they would immediately scatter in all directions at top speed. Terry would jump and shout, egging them on to greater confusion and speed. This was great fun for us, but when the pigman came to do anything with them he had a hopeless task because they were so wild. I bet he cussed us on the quiet!

John Beeston then had, I think, three daughters and a son. Janet, Lesley, Wendy and Terry. Terry came to work at Netherwood for a while to help his father with the pigs and to do general farm work. One day, when he was taking pig nuts out round the orchards, he tried to climb one of the apple trees with the tractor. He misjudged it whilst trying to avoid a pig. Later, when he had a car and was working away from the farm, he was noted for his impressive hand-brake turns in front of the cottages, and as the one who was able to get his car, with a cold engine, up to the highest speed between the cottages and the main road.

At about this time, when the pigs were out and about and were sometimes to be found in one of the orchards, a chap who worked for one of the contractors is reputed to have taken one home occasionally under his coat.

Over the years the Saturday morning hours came down as the hours of work were reduced, until we just had to work four hours on one Saturday in four. This was in order to fill up the pig bins around the farm and feed the ducks and pheasants, but after a while some of the workers found that they could do this on a Friday night or come in early on a Saturday morning and often finish before the usual starting time. Things came to a head when the gaffer came out one Saturday and asked if the duty worker would do something. He was told that he'd already been and done his hours and gone back home. This soured things a bit between the gaffer and the workers for quite a while, but I suppose this was about the only time he had met any resistance about anything connected with work from us.

Saturday morning working then more or less fizzled out and we were down to a five-day week. The abolishment of compulsory Saturday working was one of the best things that happened in farming for me. I still always went in when asked, but I now had the freedom of choice. It was as if a weight had been lifted from my shoulders and I felt a new zest for life. I suppose as a working person, I am, more or less for most of my life, being told by someone or other what to do. As a child, by parents; at school, by teachers; at work, by gaffers and foremen; when married, not quite so much, but there are still things one's wife asks one to do and then there still seems an obligation, or sense of common decency to help one's parents in things they require. So until a working person retires, he is restricted as to what he can do to a certain extent.

We used to have a student who would come for a year or so to learn about farming. I liked this, as it was nice to get to know a person I would not otherwise have met, particularly if he came from abroad, as I have never been out of Britain. One of the first was John Duggan, from Birmingham, who stayed in the foreman's house. When I had my shirt off in summer, he would stroke the hairs on my chest and say it was just like stroking his hamster. He once tried to tell us a joke about a rarey bird whilst weighing potatoes. It took him ages to get through it as he kept getting the giggles. He became totally useless and could not even lift a half hundredweight of spuds off the ground without falling in a heap. The afternoon was almost over before he got himself right again. He went to live in Australia I think and got married out there.

Jim Lightfoot from Evesham and Roger Banister from the Kidderminster area were another two. I think Jim was more interested in cars than farming. He was very pleasant to get on with. Some twenty years later, my son Richard

68

met him in Australia where he was playing in a band in his spare time and working on a cattle ranch, riding a horse. Roger was a stocky fellow with a farm to go to on the other side of Clee Hill. On one of his first days he was humping spud bags about and put so much effort into it he split the seams of his trousers. He was most embarrassed and had to wear something tied around his middle for the rest of the day.

Patrick, from Bridgenorth way, was the first of many of us to knock the end off the wall where the pig muck was kept. He had a Triumph Vitesse and let me have some spares for my Vitesse and would not take any payment.

Howard from Shrewsbury way was very neat and conscientious. He lodged with Tom and Edna West and their two daughters, Cheryl and Shirley most of the time he was at Netherwood. At another place where he lodged he had the distinction of being fed on roast lambs tails for a while. He went on to be foreman/manager at Mr. Bulmers, Puddleston. Howard once failed to negotiate a sharp left-hand turn through a gateway and tipped a trailer full of silage over on its side, on top of the gate and post, holding up silage making for a while until things were back on four wheels. He also used to hang his socks out of his bedroom window at night.

Jack, from up north, came for a few months. He smoked a pipe and nearly always had a drip hanging from the end of his nose. He was the only person who could take the filler cap off the fuel tank on the crawler without unlocking it.

Bill Butler, from Africa, used abbreviated words, such as bro for brother. He got on the wrong side of the people he lodged with after a late-night party. One of the things he said he'd like to do when he got back home was to farm wild animals in their natural environment for meat, rather than fencing patches off and rearing cattle. He always worried about the way we ploughed up and down slopes, as where he came from they always ploughed across, in an effort to stop soil erosion. Bill was the one that went the farthest distance along the top of a hedge with a tractor and trailer when he failed to negotiate a bend by Kyre School, as he was going up to the Grove Farm one day.

Nick Kerr, from another part of Africa, walked around in his bare feet in summer and brought his balaclava hat with him, as where he came from it was very cold in the mornings until the sun came up. He was the wettest, muddiest person I've ever seen on Netherwood. We were trying to finish drilling a field of corn and it had just started to rain. He was riding the drill and ended up wearing a fertilizer sack with holes cut out for arm and neck. With the mud flying off the wheels, as I was going rather fast, he looked terrible. I later got told off by the people he lodged with for getting him in such a state. He came and visited us again a few years later, with his wife or wife-to-be, before he went into the Ministry. It was nice that he had taken the time to come and see us again, I much appreciated it.

69

Stewart, from near Craven Arms, was very tall. He had been in the army and was used to giving orders, so he found it a bit difficult being told what to do by the likes of us. He's the only person I've come across to pronounce the word 'bastard' with such force and feeling, and in such an appropriate way, particularly on one occasion when he had to reverse a tractor and trailer up the alleyway in the barn, ready to be loaded with silage. It was quite a way and a bit narrow and the tractor was rather hard on the steering. This was his first job in the morning and we chaps would line up on the manger wall waiting for him so we could load up. He did not get on very well the first few times and would completely lose patience after about ten minutes. He would stand bolt upright, one foot on the clutch, the other on the brake pedals, two hands gripping the steering wheel which, surprisingly, he never pulled off. His head would go back and as he drew a deep breath he let out, in as loud a voice as possible, a long drawn out "y..o..u bastard!" I suppose us lot sitting on the wall grinning did not help matters much. He was the first person I saw to eat all of an apple, core, top, bottom, the lot. He sat next to me in the bait room and would read his post. He must have had a letter sometimes from a young lady, as I was greatly entertained by his murmurings and shifting about in his seat while he was reading these. Once when Terry and I were howling like wolves while painting the girders in the barn he came to see what the noise was. He stood for a while, just looking, not smiling – nothing – and then walked away, apparently dismissing from his mind that two people could make such a strange noise for no apparent reason. He was going into farming.

One lad, came from a large estate up north England, When we were silaging he tried to see how far he could drive across the silage clump in his car. He got a fair way onto it, but could not get back off again, so several of us had to part carry it back off. The car made some strange noises and obviously did not take kindly to what was being asked of it. He would talk about the scenery up where he came from and it sounded very nice indeed.

Michael was another one. He came from near Leominster and we used to drive across in his Morris Minor to Collington Lake during our lunch hours to go swimming. He went into building and came back in later years to do some building work at Netherwood.

Stewart, a lad who was connected with horses, spun off the road in his car, up near Collington Garage.

David was fairly local. I gave him a bit of moral support one day in spudding time. I walked up with him to where a young lady, Catherine, who he fancied was sitting with some others having her lunch. He later married the girl. It was during this meal break that I had the pleasure of watching her friend Kathy brushing her lovely long auburn hair. I've been a fan of that colour hair ever since.

Steve, from just up the valley, would have nothing but plums or whatever fruit was going for his lunch during the fruit season – no bread, cake, biscuits, nothing. He once ran over a set of harrows, owing to muddy windows and the sun in his face. I don't think that to this day he knew he had done it. They were right way up so no damage was done. He went to New Zealand to have a go at farming.

Henry worked as a tree surgeon before coming to Netherwood. He went on to buy and sell grain in London.

I hope Edward, another of the students, makes a go of farming, as he was one of the few people who was patient enough to do a job properly and see it through to the end. He liked the Charleston type of music and dancing. He once asked me to help him put a length of fence up where there were a lot of bricks and stuff. It was hard to get the stakes in so took longer than he expected. I was in the middle of sawing a large bolt through on the plough at the time and so, feeling very guilty, refused his plea for help. I also felt that if he was going to have men working under him later, it would be of benefit to him if he knew that some jobs took longer than expected.

That seems to be most of them. There were others, for lesser periods, including some of my own sons.

After having been without any students for several years, a more recent one is Jackie Smith. She comes from somewhere near London and is interested in herbs as medicines. She mainly helps with lambing and is quite at home with animals or machinery. One memory I have of her was watching her driving a tractor harrowing. She, unlike most men, was letting the tractor do the work, just sitting there bobbing up and down over the rough ground. Most men seem to be mentally egging their machines on to greater efforts, which is reflected in the way they sit and look, whereas she reminded me of the gentleness of a group of house martins as they quietly hover, gathering nesting material from a small muddy patch at the side of the road after a rainstorm.

Netherwood started to expand a few years after Mr. Payne arrived. The Pensons Farm adjoining was bought when Mr. & Mrs. Mantle left, then the Hyde when Mr. & Mrs. John Lyon moved. Grove Farm, just up the road from the Hyde, was farmed from Netherwood when Mr. & Mrs. Wrighton moved – to Scotland I think.

When Mr. Payne was first at Netherwood, quite a lot of the old grass fields were ploughed up and planted with corn and the steeper slopes re-seeded. Once a couple of us were ploughing on Calves Hill which was a bit steep and we were only ploughing down hill and coming back up empty. About a quarter of the way along from Brick Barns, as I was backing up under the trees at the top of Calves Hill, I became aware of some buzzing. This didn't bother me too much, but on coming back up empty from the bottom, I saw my mate waving his arms as if a fly were bothering him. Arriving back at the top, I found that the hollow ash tree I was under had a bees' nest in, the entrance was about four feet from the ground. The bees were very annoyed by the disturbance and set about chasing me off. As soon as one stung me that was it, plough lifted up and I was away as fast as possible. This was rather dangerous, for while swatting away the tractor was inclined to go its own way – down hill. This made things a bit dodgy for a bit, but we could not pack in ploughing, so we covered ourselves up the best we could. I put my sou-wester hat on and tied bags around myself and had another go. After a few bouts we were clear and could shed our protective clothing. Once we were far enough away from their nest the bees left us alone.

The bees had several goes at me over the years. I found that if I ran as soon as one started buzzing around, with a handkerchief twirling around my head like a helicopter blade, the bees would leave me alone half way down Calves Hill field (about 150 yards) from their nest.

Later on, we got on better together and those bees gave me great pleasure in observing their comings and goings. The hole in the tree faced almost east so they got the early morning sun through their entrance. Even in the coldest days of winter when I would go and poke my nose in the entrance and take a deep breath, the smell that came out was very satisfying – a mixture of rotten wood and the smell of the bees and their home, with a hint of warmth. On these occasions two guard bees would show themselves, take a bleary-eyed look and disappear back out of sight. Only once did this not happen, but the bees were still there next spring, so all was well. On the 13th May 1974, I sat and had my bait while watching them come in, some with orange sacs on their legs, some with yellow ones and others with nothing on their legs at all. In later years the gaffer cut this nest out with a chain saw and put the bees in a hive.

In my early years at Netherwood there were several wild bees' nests in trees: at the top of Calves hill – ash tree; Big Orchard – oak tree; Bottom of Stable Meadow – oak tree; Barn Meadow – oak tree; Tee Baune lake – oak tree; at the top of Hyde Hill – elm tree. In 1986 only one remains – the one at Tee Baune lake. The trees in Big Orchard, Hyde Hill and Barn Meadow were all bulldozed out in the progress of farming. The nest in the tree in Stable Meadow became sealed up as the tree grew together and the nest at the top of Calves Hill was commercialised.

When the big hopyard was ploughed up, John Beeston was rather sad as it was the last field on Netherwood that he liked to put his cattle on to graze. It was such a good mixture of grasses that the cattle, he said, spent most of their time lying down contentedly, whereas with the modern leys, the cattle seemed to be wandering about, never seeming to settle properly.

As more of Netherwood got ploughed up, so overtime became more of a regular thing. It was during a long bout of ploughing, until about 9.30 at night, that I found out what it was like to be cold. The tractors in those days did not have cabs so there was not much protection from the weather. I took all my meals in the form of sandwiches to work – bait, dinner and tea. These were usually eaten sat up against the tractor wheel wherever I was working. During daylight hours it was not too bad, but as darkness fell, so did the temperature and in frosty weather it was a job to keep warm. I found that several sacks helped a lot, one over my knees for normal daytime, then as it got dark, one over my shoulders and one tied round my middle so as to drape over the back of the tractor seat to keep my back warm. Then if it got too bad I would wrap two more around my legs. In those days I never wore a hat, so I subsequently suffered with chilblains on my ears. As a lot of time ploughing is spent looking behind, the scabs would get rubbed off my ears by the coat collar, causing them to bleed which became a bit painful at times.

With all these sacks draped around me I used to dread having to get off the tractor to unblock the plough or something, as I would get cold and frustrated, having to unwrap and wrap myself up again. When knocking off time came there were often several gates to open and close to get back to the farm and the temptation to nudge them open with the tractor wheel was great indeed. When I was very tired, I felt it would be easier just to go to sleep there and then, sat on the tractor, rather than face opening the gates. After several weeks of this, the cold got into my very bones. I would get home at night and sit in front of the fire with my overcoat still on to have my dinner-cum-supper. My skin would burn, but the heat would not penetrate through to my knees, which seemed to get the coldest. Even in bed I didn't seem to get really warm even with piles of clothes on top of the blankets.

After stretches like these, it would take several weeks of non-tractor driving before my bones felt comfortable again.

The first tractors Mr. Payne bought did not have a ploughing light on the back so you were unable to see what was happening when ploughing at night, so several of us found or scrounged some old lights and fitted them up on the backs of our tractors. This was alright until one tried to out-do the other and started drilling holes in the mudguards and fitting flashy chrome things that caught the gaffer's eye. That was it. The order came via Sid to take them all off as he (the gaffer) was not going to have his tractors looking like someone had machine gunned them when he came to trade them in. So, for the rest of the time I had the tractor, all I had for light was a back light bulb, with the red glass removed, which was not really adequate, as sometimes you never knew that the plough had blocked up until you lifted it up at the corners.

Sid, the foreman did the combining for the first few years, then his son Terry took it on for a further few years until he left. One year, Sid was combining the Collington's and I was bailing the straw about an hour behind the combine. It was a very hot day, ideal for what we were doing, the only snag was that I'd had a few late nights courting and was a bit lacking in sleep. Normally this is OK when you're working on your own, but when you're with others it's not so good, as it seems that the body, in its efforts to compensate for lack of adequate sleep, narrows its field of vision and thought to concentrate on the job being done. This does not leave much room for what someone else might or might not do. On this day the bailing was going fine, until the unexpected happened: Sid, instead of keeping going when he dropped the bed of the combine in to start a fresh cut as he normally did, stopped and started to get off his machine. Me, in a bit of a haze, misjudged how close I was to the back of the combine by about an inch. The bailer just caught the back of Sid's machine, putting a kink in it and Sid was almost thrown off the steps by the impact, as the poor combine flexed. Much to my relief, the combine was still able to work alright and did another couple of seasons, with this bend in its back end. There was no damage to the bailer, other than a small scratch in the paintwork.

This lack of sleep and lack of awareness of people around me caused another mishap. It happened during spudding time. One morning we were greasing up the tack in the tractor shed. I was in the doorway working on my tractor and trailer and John was inside with his. To get a bit more light to see what he was doing, he moved a bit closer up behind me and took the grille off the front of his tractor and was doing something inside it. In a bit of a fog, I started up the tractor I was working on and backed it up a bit to get the steering straight so as to get at the grease nipples better, completely forgetting John was behind until I heard his muffled shouts. I had gently pushed him so that his head was wedged up against the radiator and his shoulder jammed in the opening in the grille which he was working through. On drawing away, I ran around the back to find John freeing himself, with the marks of the radiator impressed on the side of his face. He was a bit shaken, but OK. The marks on his face quietly came out during the course of the day.

A silly thing I used to do, due to high spirits and the build-up of energy from sitting on a tractor all day, was, when knocking off at 5 o'clock after ploughing or whatever, to tear into the tractor shed in top gear and apply the brakes at the last minute, leaving several yards of skid marks in the oil and gunge on the floor. This was silly in itself, but what was worse (looking back) was the fact that the workers often lined up against the tractor shed bench just before knocking off time and were in direct line with the doorway as I came tearing in. I could see them starting to go pale and beginning to lift themselves up onto the bench out of the way, as I stopped within an inch or so of them. Then, after stopping the engine, my ears were assailed with appropriate swear words. Eventually, it got through to me that it was not appreciated, so I started to take a little more care. Anyway this stopped after a while as once we had tractor cabs we could not get in the shed at all because of the low doorway.

Jim Tonks would often say, when I'd done daft things like that, that I would end up behind a big high wall. Years later I still think about his remark, for when I got married, the house I went to live in had a high wall round most of the garden. This was not quite what he had in mind, but it still makes me smile when I think of his comments.

When John started at Netherwood he would sometimes have violent arguments with Sid the foreman, who was also his father-in-law. When asked to do a job that he did not approve of he would ask why. This was a bit awkward for Sid to explain, as usually when he gave an order it was carried out by the rest of us without much to-do. Once I had to walk away, as the argument got so heated and the language so bad that it shook me a bit. I have found that there appears to be several ways of getting through life, your (my) way not necessarily being the best or only way.

Until 1962 I'd never had any transport of my own other than a push-bike and often when cycling along the road into Ludlow I would gaze rather enviously at the lads going by in their nice cars, with pretty girls sitting beside them. Seeing this used to knock the edge off cycling a bit. That autumn, while wandering around Tenbury, up by the station, I saw a car in a showroom. I'd not particularly planned to buy one, but I quite fancied this one. I didn't know much about cars, but went ahead to buy this model through Carmichaels in the Butts, Worcester. They didn't have one in stock, but said they would get one for me by the 1st January next year, in a month or so's time. On looking into what I was buying a bit more, I found to my surprise that it had a bigger engine under the bonnet than I had thought. The car was a Triumph Vitesse (I still drive this car when writing this in 1994). After collecting it, on the first Saturday in January 1963, I had difficulty in getting it up the drive at The Knowle, because of heavy snow. My sisters had to help me dig the drive clear in the dark before I was able to get off the main road. It sat there in the shed for quite a while until the snow went and I was able to use it. A large part of the pleasure of owning the thing is often the anticipation, for once it's yours you're somehow responsible for it. I know I was quite thrilled as the time got near to collecting it, so much so that in my exuberance one day at work I leapt over a forty-gallon drum, just catching my heel on the rim as I went over. This sent me sprawling along the concrete yard and I ended up rather shaken. It served to bring me back down to earth very suddenly. The rigmarole of getting hire purchase was quite off-putting, as I had to get some of my aunts to vouch for me in case I fell behind with the payments. Thank goodness buying a house was much easier.

It seems that I was meant to buy a car to go to Scotland, to meet three girls and to appreciate the beauty in things, especially Netherwood. Up until then I had looked at things from farmer's point of view: everything had to have its use, nothing was a thing of beauty in its own right. Trees I looked upon for what could be made from them – how much timber, how many posts and stakes, how much firewood from the bits that weren't of any other use. Cattle I looked upon in terms of how fat they were or how much milk they gave. Lakes were things to swim in and catch fish in. It seems that I was not aware of the beauty in things. So after I had been on my week's holiday around England, Wales and Scotland in the car, I came back to Netherwood to see it in a different light.

On this holiday I went down to Land's End, then on to London, where I spent the night. I spent a pound on a visit to a strip club and managed to go on the Underground for free since I didn't know that you had to buy a ticket before going down into the Tube! When I got to my destination and was asked for my ticket, I couldn't remember where I'd got on. There were two kind chaps there who said, "Get out of sight, quick", which I did. When I got back to the car in one of the car parks to have a sleep I found most of the cars had gone. I settled down and had just nodded off when I was awoken by the police, asking what I was doing and who I was. Satisfied with my replies, they left. I was just about asleep again when along came another police car. When I told them I'd just been visited by their mates they left me alone and I had a fair night's sleep. It was in one of the cafes in London that I first experienced the sight of a woman picking her teeth, and where a cup of coffee was a shilling a cup as opposed to 4d back home.

Next day, I drove on up towards Scotland, stopping at Worcester to have the car serviced for an hour or so. On my way up north I gave a lift to Edinburgh to a lad who was going to see his girl. He was short of money and asked me for 10/-. I said "No" as I didn't know how much I would have to spare and wasn't in the habit of giving people money. He gave me his coat as a deposit, saying that he'd get the money from his girlfriend and bring it to me the next morning, saying that I should be at the railway station at a certain time the next day. I parked in one of the side streets in Edinburgh and kipped down for the night. I don't know whether I had a visit from the police or not, but in any case I found that if you said you were just passing through they were amiable enough. The next morning I had to find the railway station. I asked a bloke on his way to work and ended up totally confused for I could not understand his directions. He spoke so fast and in such a way that I could only make out one or two of the words he was saying. 'Railway station' came out as one word, which I managed to grasp after his third attempt at explaining. By then he'd lost patience with me completely and walked off to work shaking his head and saying something like 'Bloody foreigners'. I found the station eventually and waited about an hour, but the chap never turned up, resulting in the loss of 10/- and the gaining of a coat – which I wore for the next 5 years or so.

Travelling further up into Scotland I came to a ferry somewhere and whilst on this I caught sight of three girl hitch-hikers. They had just been offered a lift in one of the cars going over and were putting their gear in the boot of the fellow's car. As it took a fair while for the ferry to cross the stretch of water I got out and had a walk round and asked one of the girls where they were going. Apparently they were doing the same as me – touring round Scotland – but by hitching lifts from place to place. On finding out that I was going their way, the girls decided to come along and so, much to the man's amazement, they took their things out of his car and put them in mine. As it had been raining the girls were a bit wet, especially their feet, so when I saw them take their socks off to wring the water out I offered to put the heater on and dry them on the air vents in the car. The next next fifty miles were a bit steamy and warm, which suited the girls, giving them a chance to warm up and relax.

The three girls were Argentinians, staying in London and were seeing as much of the British Isles as possible, before going over to the continent for a while. Their names were Elena Gallino, Irma Etchemendigaray and Margarita Levere. Elena did most of the talking as she spoke the best English. They were most interested in Scotch Whisky and the English teas which they had heard about and these subjects came up in conversation over the next few days. It wasn't long before the phrase 'beauty spot' was used, when a particularly nice view came into sight. Up until then the only 'beauty spot' I'd been interested in was the one on a female's face and so I was quite amused by this other meaning. It was agreed they they would spend the next few days going round Scotland with me, sleeping in Youth Hostels at night, while I slept in the car. I would drop them off near a hostel so that they could walk in and in the mornings pick them up a little way down the road from where they had stayed. The first night was spent in the Trossocks and I passed a nice night just off the road, amongst several different coloured rhododendron bushes. It was there that I saw the clearest water. I washed in a small stream and was astounded at the clarity of it. I could see right to the bottom, just as if there was nothing there at all. It seemed a sin to dip my hands in, so disturbing this beautiful clear water.

The following morning we agreed that the girls would supply the food and me the transport. After several more exclamations of 'beauty spot!' as the day progressed I began to look at the trees and surroundings in a different light. Up until then I was only interested in getting from A to B as quickly as possible, taking very little notice of what was in between, or around me, at any particular time.

At times the girls would start discussing things and break into their own language until Elena would say "Stop, it is wrong to speak amongst ourselves

77

when someone (meaning me) can't understand what's being said". They were very fair amongst themselves, as each day a different girl sat in the front seat. One day when things were nice and relaxed and they were enjoying being where they were, the three girls broke into song. They sang in their own language and so it sounded a bit strange to me. The effect of the singing, the pleasant proximity of the girls, the car going well, the beautiful scenery, caused me to break out laughing, by way of emotional relief. My laughing stopped the girls singing and Elena asked what I was laughing about. They must have thought I was ridiculing their song, which would seem a pretty natural conclusion to draw. Unable to understand and interpret my feelings I was unable to say why I was laughing so it was all left in mid-air. (At times like this I would have liked to have had a better command of the English language.) They never sang again in my presence and I've often felt very guilty about not putting their minds at rest on this score, but as the day passed it was forgotten and we settled down again to enjoy the beauty of Scotland.

Part of my holiday plan was to visit Land's End and John O'Groats. The girls were more interested in the scenery, so when night fell and we parted company till next day I said I was going on up to John O'Groats and would see them on my way back down the next day. Going on up north until about 10 o'clock I decided to find a proper bed to sleep in for one night as the car wasn't very comfortable. I found a bed and breakfast place, had a bite of supper and asked how early breakfast was next morning. I think it was about 8.30 a.m. I wanted to be on my way before 7 a.m. so I said I'd get myself off. This didn't happen, as at 6.30 the next morning I was aware of activity in the house and on getting up found that a bleary-eyed pretty girl was getting breakfast for me. This was a nice surprise and quite strange, having this girl sitting near by as I ate my breakfast, bringing the food and half-swaying in her seat as she started nodding back off to sleep. When I came to pay the bill, which was 17/6, I gave the girl a pound and sat there while she rummaged around for the half-crown change. This was achieved eventually, by her finding odd pennies here and there around the house. After about 50 miles I suddenly experienced a deep feeling of guilt and meanness. What the poor girl must have thought of me, goodness only knows, after getting up at that unearthly hour and me not even giving her the 2/6 change in appreciation of what she had done. She must have gone back to bed thinking all the tight people are not in Scotland it seems. I still feel pangs of guilt about it, even now.

On the last but one day of the holiday, the girls had seen as much of Scotland as they wanted and said they would hitch-hike back down to London over the next couple of days. It seemed wrong to abandon them like this, so I said I'd take them back next day. They thought this was a good idea and so on the last day of the holiday I went and gave them a look at the dams at Rhyader in Wales and on down to London, arriving at the girls' lodgings sometime during Sunday night/Monday morning. I knew there wasn't much time for sleep as I had to go to work that morning after I'd been to the local police station to produce my driving licence after a minor accident at some traffic lights. I seem to remember getting Mr. Cranmer out of bed before I went back to work, so that I could show him my licence.

When I went to work that day I took a fresh look at an old oak tree. Instead of gazing at the tree and wondering how much fencing we could get out of its timber, as Jim and I used to do, I now looked at the shape of the tree, the colour of its leaves and the way it stood out against the skyline. I wondered how old it was and how many people it had seen and the changes at Netherwood it had witnessed, hoping it would still be there for many years to come.

When the holiday photos came back I went down to London one weekend to give some to the girls, but when I found out where they were staying, I was stumped as to how to get into their flat. I'd been used to knocking on a door and someone coming and letting you in. The system there of pressing a bell and someone unlocking the door from some remote room to let you in was quite baffling to me. For a start I didn't know what to do or what happened

Trees – N. Turner

79

when I did start pressing buttons. After hanging around for a bit to see how people got in and out, I lost my nerve and went back home without seeing the three young ladies. I later posted the snaps to them. It was nice to receive an occasional letter or postcard from them as they journeyed around Europe. I am pleased that I bought the car and was able to be part of their lives for a while.

Ploughing, when it is going well, is a pleasant job, but when the ground is hard and dry and difficulty is experienced in keeping the plough at the required depth, it can be a bit of a sod! Once, we were ploughing what is now part of Roundcots field (father called it the long-length). Part of the field was OK, but when we got up on to a bit of a knob, the plough would not stop in the ground at all. We were both getting very frustrated and my mate was the first to crack. He suddenly lifted his plough out, jammed on his one independent brake, went round and round in a circle a couple of times – tractor flat out – then tore off up the farm, completely browned off with the job. Taken aback at what he was doing, I lost concentration and started up across the furrows, making an even worse mess than was already there. I then had the field to myself, so I plodded on as best I could to finish. On looking at my mate's tractor next day I found that, in his temper, he had bent both linkage arms somewhat. The next field to plough was the Big Hopyard, a bit better, but not a lot. So trying all I knew I ended up doing a bit of a compromise job. The gaffer was not pleased with my efforts – he wasn't a very happy man at the time as things were probably not going too well. Most of us dreaded him when he was like this, for no matter what you did, it was wrong. It ended up that whenever he came into a field where you were working, you might just as well stop the tack and wait for his comments.

After a while we got Sid, the foreman, to have a word with him about it. This was alright in theory, but Sid was a very blunt man and did not mince his words. So, in his efforts to sort things out I think he actually made things bad for himself as far as the gaffer-foreman relationship went as they never did seem to get on very well after that. It helped as far as the workers were concerned, as the gaffer did make an effort to be his usual pleasant self.

Another awkward thing to plough was mustard, which was used as green manure after potatoes. This would grow six to seven feet high and it got a bit dry and old and was very hard to bury. Once, when up to four of us would do the ploughing, I was trying to plough some in, in the forty-acre Pensons. I was not getting on very well, so did not do much the first day. After having to stand some derisory remarks next morning, I was told some of the others would come and show me how to do it. Rather downhearted, I carried on the best I could. One of the others came down and had a go in the morning before he went spudding. He went once round the field making as bad a mess as me and said, "That'll do me thank you very much" and left me to do it. One other chap had done some before so knew what a cow of a job it was and kept out of the field altogether. The other chap came down after tea to show me how to do it. As he tore across the top of the field, the plough apparently going beautifully, my heart sank as I watched from the other end of the field, and I said to myself that I'd pack it in when I got round to the gate and leave him to it. I lapped him twice while he was adjusting his plough, feeling that I wasn't a total failure after all. His patience lasted about 1½ hours and then he too went out of the field, leaving me on my own again. Having now time to fiddle without someone breathing down my neck, I was able to get things to go a little better. Eventually, over the years, we found the best way to deal with it was to roll the mustard the same way as it was to be ploughed. This rolling was often done after tea. Once John Adams was doing it in the dark and as the tractor lights were lower than the crop, a lot of concentration was needed to see where you were going. Next morning, the gaffer asked John why he did not stop last night when he'd come down to see how he was getting on. John just hadn't seen him and could easily have run him over with the roller. Thank goodness the gaffer gave up and went back home.

Whilst at the bottom of The Knowle drive, waiting for a lift back to work one tea time, I was squatting down against the telephone pole when around the corner came a girl on a horse. It was warm weather and the girl just had a T-shirt on her top half, covering a delightful pair of breasts. The horse was sort of walking, causing her breasts to jiggle up and down in a rhythmic manner. The amount of movement up and down suggested she had an elastic bra on. She caught sight of me, gazing goggle-eyed and took a quick glance down to see what had caught my attention. She started to smile as if to say "Great, aren't they?" then sat a bit more upright, continuing at the same pace and movement towards me. I could feel myself sliding into an upright position against the telephone pole in appreciation of this beautiful sight, pleased that the girl allowed me this nice moment in time with her apparent blessing. As she went out of sight round the next bend, I slowly sank back onto my haunches, saying 'phew' to myself.

I seem to remember that for my twenty-first birthday I was given about eight ewes. Mr. Powell of the Bank Farm Rochford had thirty to forty ewes and he let me pick the ones I wanted. They were carted to The Knowle in father's A40 van. They did well on the mixed grasses and other plants that grew in the orchard. When they lambed, Mr. John Lyon of the Hyde Farm let us have an orchard opposite the Blacksmith's Shop, Bank Street and some of the time we had them down at Kyre Hospital, where father worked. When the

81

lambs' wool was sold it was a nice bit of pocket money for me. There is also a lot of satisfaction to be had when leaning on a gate or fence, just looking at the animals you're responsible for. I can quite see how people get hooked on farming. Eventually the Hyde was sold and as there wasn't enough land at The Knowle to keep sheep all year round, the sheep were also sold.

When Mr. John Lyon left the Hyde he returned a Grandfather Chair given to him by my father, when he first moved to the Hyde without much furniture. I still have the chair and have always been pleased that Mr. Lyon saw fit to place it back in the family.

Middle Work Years

Once, when baling at the top of Old Roadway, after a late night out and not much sleep, I decided to have dinner sat in the curve of the rear wheel of the tractor, in a sheltered part of the field, by Rabbit Bury Coppice. The sun was warm and lulled me into a heavy nap, dead to the world, so to speak. Eventually I became aware of someone calling me and, rousing myself as best I could from this sun-induced sleep, found the voice was coming from Eileen Sweeny, on her way up Calves Hill. She shouted out asking me if I was going to do any more work that afternoon. Looking at my watch, I found I'd overslept by about three-quarters of an hour. Jumping straight up and onto the tractor, I went back to baling. Within a few seconds I felt completely disorientated because of my panic. Now I knew how Jim must have felt when we left him asleep in the Blacksmith's shop. I vowed it would be the last time I'd jump straight up after a nap. It was tea-time before I felt alright again.

The first time I did any haymaking with Mr. Payne it was not as happy as it might have been. Different people have different ideas and ways of doing things and it was a couple of years before I could get into doing things the way he liked them, rather than the way I was used to doing them. When turning the hay I had gone too fast and lumped it up together somewhat, which he did not like. The whole staff was sent for, including Frank Hatton, the gardener, who had done this sort of thing before and who showed us the way round. For starters, we had to shake all the lumps apart, spreading the green undried grass out so that the sun could get to it. It was hard work, but nice to be doing something altogether for a change, as farming jobs had by now become more split up with one man doing a job that several would have done in previous years. A year or two later, in this same field, the near Sallybed, there was a more pleasant memory of haymaking – the gaffer came along one tea-time and took over the baling for half an hour or so, bringing with him fresh strawberries and ice-cream, along with the children and their nanny. The strawberries went down well indeed.

Suzie, the Payne's second daughter, once asked Terry Batterham, soon after she'd started school, if he liked making love. Presumably, she did not know what she was asking, just something overheard at school. Terry, taken aback a bit, scratched his head and, rather to my surprise, made a pretty good job at answering the question.

Feelings are sometimes like smells: a different combination or a different happening brings forth a feeling not quite the same any others felt before. One of these occasions was when I was having a snowball fight with Joanna and Suzie Payne on the front lawn of the house. I can't remember whether Richard Payne was about then. Anyway, the gaffer came and joined in and snowballs were then flying in all directions. I admit that it did seem rather strange, lobbing one or two in his direction.

Joanna, his eldest daughter, Suzie, and later Richard, spent a lot of their free time helping or watching what was going on at the farm. When they were there I often seemed to be trying tactfully to settle arguments between the two girls, such as who was best at something. Later, when they started having a go at driving tractors, Joanna offered to teach me to ride a horse, which I never did get round to doing.

During silage time she liked to come and play in the fresh cut grass. Once Suzie asked me to go with her to collect some crab apples. Unfortunately I was busy at the time and did not go, and still feel a little peeved that I didn't take the time to enjoy her company for a while – this sort of opportunity doesn't present itself very often.

One cold winter's day, Joanna had been out hunting and I happened to be around as she got back home. I have never seen anybody looking quite so cold before; she looked like she'd been frozen into the shape she was in. How she ever got off the horse and made it into the house, goodness only knows. I used to like waving to Joanna as she went off to school at the beginning of term and when she came back to Netherwood at the end of the school term. I must admit I used to discreetly hang about if I could, so as to get the chance of doing this, as she seemed so much a part of Netherwood.

My wife, Maureen, came to Netherwood to look after Richard Payne soon after he was born. Richard was a bit of a handful at times. As he grew older, he would like to have a go at combining and driving the crawler. He mastered these, but not without the odd mishap. Once, when he was discing, he turned a bit too sharply and the crawler tracks caught in the drawbar of the discs. Being metal to metal, nothing gave and the discs then appeared to be trying to get into the cab with us as the track lifted them up off the ground. A quick stop was made and things put themselves right again. I don't think Richard ever realised what had happened.

The big tin barn at Netherwood largely consisted of three round roofs. In the winter the snow would collect in between these to quite a depth. The rainwater gulleys underneath froze solid, the melting snow could not get carried away, so hundreds of gallons of water would cascade down inside the barn. It was then time for us workers to get up there to shovel and wheelbarrow the snow out onto the ground. When you got near the middle, it was a fair journey to each end to tip the snow off. This was one of the few occasions that the gaffer gave us a bit extra in the way of refreshments. During this snow-clearing operation he brought out flasks of hot, milky, sweet coffee, and much appreciated it was too. One other time, on an extra-cold day's beating he brought out the Cherry Brandy. This appreciation of when something is done above the normal run of work keeps things ticking over much more smoothly.

When Park Lake was part-drained by Old Harry, he slept on a pile of old potato sacks on the hearth in Park Cottage and used to shave in cold water. He once left his Sunday joint of meat on the Saturday picture bus and proceeded to shout abuse after it as it disappeared up Bank Street. The lake, after having been empty for twelve months, had grown thousands of willow trees in the mud. It fell to us workers to wade in to cut them down, prior to the dam being rebuilt by Reads of Hereford. We'd mastered the art of building fires on stumps sticking out in the water and mud, but our foot attire was not up to this, so we put our feet in plastic bags, which helped considerably. Frank Worrell, the shepherd, was involved in the cutting down of these saplings at the dam end, which was chest-deep in water. He proceeded to put us all to shame. For after slashing away for a while and getting wet from the splashes of water, he lost patience and stood for a second, looking, deciding whether to pack in or what. He chose what, and went into the lake in the clothes he stood up in, slashing in a most purposeful way. I wasn't able to help much as it was the day after the Worcester to Tenbury walk and I had blisters on my feet and could hardly walk.

Tishy Winnie was one of the nannies and one whom I had the pleasure of sitting next to at the annual Christmas dinner, given by Mr. and Mrs. Payne at the Royal Oak in Tenbury Wells. All went well, until the soup was served. When I'm talking, I'm inclined to use my hands and arms, gesturing as I speak, and during conversation my hand caught the edge of the soup bowl and neatly flung the contents over myself and Tishy's pretty party dress. She handled this very well, giving her dress a quick sponge down and carrying on as if nothing had happened. When I offered to have the dress cleaned, or buy her another, she would not hear of it.

Margaret was another nanny at Netherwood. If she happened to be anywhere near where I was working when taking the children for a walk she, as others did, would give a lovely wave. This used to brighten the day up no end for me, as it gets a bit lonely going up and down and round and round fields for days on end by oneself.

Annabel (now Mrs. Richard Elliott), came to Netherwood as a secretary. When the interviews were being held, I thought she was one of the most unlikely candidates for the job, as she seemed very young and had a cold at the time. But I was proved wrong, she got the job and over the years got to know about the farm and the running of it so much that at times it appeared that she knew almost as much as the gaffer about its management. She had the distinction of tipping her car over on the same bend at Kyre School that Bill Butler failed to negotiate with a tractor. Annabel kept a dog or two and once when I had a lift with her and the gaffer back to Netherwood from the Grove, the dogs were in the back of the vehicle. As I went to crawl in amongst them, Mr. Payne got out of the front and insisted I had the front seat, while he crouched in the back with the panting, licking dogs. This gesture did a lot to help gaffer-worker relationships as far as I was concerned.

Once, when spudding, I was digging the potatoes with the two-row digger and was stood up on the tractor gazing intently up the field, waiting for the women to pick up their stints (so many yards of potato row, so each woman had an equal amount to pick up), when a small voice came up from by the tractor wheel, saying with a long drawn out "a-n-d what are you looking at?" This caused me to sit down a bit quick, as it was quite obvious what was holding my attention. It was neat lines of a pair of knickers under a thin summer dress of the next woman up the row. The voice belonged to Jean Passey, who quietly worked up her stint, and seeing what I was looking at thought it best to bring me back down to earth. Jean, I seem to remember, was the last person to wear a skirt for potato picking, as over the years most of the pickers went over to wearing jeans or trousers. There was one person who I can't ever recall seeing going to have a wee during her twenty-odd years of spudding at Netherwood. Most women would visit the dingles once or twice a day for this purpose. Sid said, when he was working up in the Fens, where dingles were a long way apart, he would, on cool autumn days, see an occasional patch of steam rising from one of the spud rows. The women would, if wearing skirts, just pause for a few seconds, where they were working, have a pee, then carry on picking, leaving just the tell-tale patch of steaming ground to say what had happened. He also said that in that area, at one time, the farmers would, when spring came, go out into their fields, take their trousers down and sit their bare bottoms on the ground to see if it was warm enough to start planting seeds.

I've been rather grateful for spudding over the years, as it is a way of meeting people. I had virtually no social life, I don't often go to pubs, so any chance of meeting people, other than through the Church or work, is a bit remote. Some of the spud pickers have been coming to Netherwood for many

85

years. Their children, when under twelve months old, were sat in prams in the mothers' stints when picking commenced. I admired these women very much as I watched them change nappies and feed their babies and themselves and cope with the weather, hauling their prams up and down the cloddy field. I would entertain these children a little as I went up and down the field. Each child had things they liked doing best, be it just waving, sticking up a thumb, or the very young ones would shake their heads from side to side, or up and down. Some of the more reserved ones would only go as far as putting their heads to one side or the other as I went by, then sitting back upright when I'd passed. Some of the babies grew up and then came spud-picking themselves when old enough. They would then get married and bring their own babies spudding, so completing this circle. Whether there will still be spudding at Netherwood, enabling this cycle to continue, only time will tell. (Potatoes stopped on Netherwood in 1989.) I always took the sight of prams in the spud field for granted, but when someone came over from Canada he was fascinated by the sight of these many prams with mothers and babies lined up down the field. With the coming of machines this will become a rare sight I suppose.

With some of the people who came year after year it seemed as time had stood still in between the end of the last potato harvest and the beginning of the

No time wasted, even at break time!
Photo: Jean Passey

next, for it was possible to carry on a conversation from many months ago, just as if it had been the day before.

The smiles and enthusiasm of the young people who were about to leave school and who had not long left school were nice to experience, as it filled one with a sense of purpose and encouragement for the future. One young lady often talked about getting on her push-bike, cycling as far as she could for as long as she was able, for the sheer pleasure of seeing things and places. For two pins I would have jacked things in and gone with her.

Early mornings, when fetching the pickers in the van from around and about, I was alone with one girl for a while, until we got a bit farther along the round. It was as if she had just got out of bed and walked straight outside into the vehicle and sat near by the side of me. To look into those wide, not yet fully awake brown eyes, morning after morning, used to knock me for six. I didn't know I could drive so far without looking at the road, and to see her ample breasts jiggling as we went over the rough ground did not help my driving concentration much either.

One of my best conversations was with Sabina, in the middle of a muddy, wet, potato field. I've never really talked much, usually listened when I've been with people. This time it was a two-way thing and we became totally absorbed in what we were talking about; so much so that her mother, another of the women pickers, asked what we were finding to talk about that was so interesting. I couldn't even remember, it's just that for once I was at one with another person for a while.

Sabina once shared a little of her growing up with me, for one year at the start of the spudding season, I was helping one or two to pick up until things got sorted out that morning. When I came to help Sabina to pick some up I found my eyes a few inches from her partly unbuttoned shirt front, showing something that appeared to have grown faster than it should have, and looking rather pleased and proud of the fact, she let me have my visual fill of them. It looked as if her breasts had suddenly put on a spurt of growth almost overnight and suddenly grown too large for her skin to accommodate, which had stretched so smooth and tight that I could see the delicate blue veins through the almost transparent skin. It's nice that she saw fit to let me be part of her coming into womanhood in this way.

Over the years, various types of fun was had between us and the women pickers. Once when they were giving us a bit of stick, hiding our hats and coats and filling bate bags up with indescribable objects, a couple of us decided, when they were busy, about mid-morning, to get their spare clothing and lunch bags from under the hedge at the end of the rows of potatoes. Unobserved, we took them out of sight of the field and tied their bits and pieces high up in the trees, to the side of the dingle. It's a good job a couple of the pickers were young and agile as some of the trees were rather hard to climb. We viewed this from a safe distance, thinking that if they didn't get a move on their lunch hour would be over before they get their things back down.

One year a good-looking girl of about seventeen came for the spudding season. One hot Monday she caused a bit of a stir amongst the male staff. Over the weekend, someone had put a neat line of love bites starting on her neck and disappearing out of sight down between her breasts. She had quite a lot of attention that day, as one or the other of us tried to get a closer look at this unusual work of art.

Some women only came for a few days, as they found the work harder than they could cope with and we never saw them again in the spud field. One girl won the admiration of several of us blokes; she hadn't done any spudding before and was a bit slow on the first day. The second day, even slower, ending the day crawling on her hands and knees at the job, unable to straighten her back. The third day, when no one expected her to come anyway, it was almost pitiful to watch her struggling, spending most of her meal breaks trying to catch up as she was so far behind. Then, with a weekend's rest and some more sensible clothing, she got into the swing of the job and was able to keep up with the others.

Joan, who had several daughters, had permed her hair and when I started digging the spuds out, not having seen who had come that morning, I asked someone if Joan had brought another of her daughters or someone fresh in her place. When I got closer I realised it was Joan with her fresh hair-do. I told her what I'd said to the others and thought to myself that I had never seen a person take a compliment with so much pleasure – Joan literally curled up and purred with delight like a pussy cat.

Once when unloading spuds from the boxes into which the pickers had put them, and tipping them into a trailer I misjudged getting the contents of the last box of the row onto the top of the trailer and almost half the potatoes landed back on the ground. I said 'blast', or suchlike to myself, and was about to get off the tractor to pick them up again, rather to my embarrassment, as it's not the done thing to make such a hash of it, four of the women pickers came straight over and, before I even had a chance to get out of the tractor cab, started picking up the spuds that I'd upset, spuds which they had already picked up once. I looked on in astonishment, which turned into a great love and affection, as they had just finished their stints and were about to sit down for a quick breather. They would have been well within their rights to have sat there while I picked them up, casting deserved comments of an undesirable nature my way instead. I could have hugged them all to say how much I loved them for their kindness.

Digging spuds, week after week, and month after month, gets to be more than just a job, as clashes of wills develop, and feelings arise that are sometimes disturbing and which upset the general pleasantness of of the job. Sometimes, it is between the women themselves, several against several, or one picker against another picker, or pickers against you. Over the years I'd become very sensitive and tuned into these underlying currents of feelings. A woman, who I had got on with for years would become upset by something I had done, such as getting an extra row out just as they think they've finished for the day, by giving one woman an extra box to the others to pick up in or making a hash of measuring their stints out, and one thinking she's got more than her neighbours. When measuring out, some of the pickers count your steps between each stick that divides the stints up. This person can, without saying anything, just by her lack of a smile and general attitude, make the day very uncomfortable. When things have become extra bad on occasions, one will pack up there and then and get herself off home. One woman, after a huff, took herself and her children and walked the five or so miles back home, not waiting for the afternoon's transport. Thank goodness she cooled down overnight and was back at work the next morning as right as rain. This sort of thing can effect some of the people that do the potato lifting to such an extent that I've actually seen a man shaking with the emotion of one of these conflicts. But the dazzling smiles one is treated to in the more pleasant moments of the job by some of the hard-working females far outweigh the down side of potatoing.

There is also the entertainment value of watching people working day after day, season after season. The little things such as a woman who is afraid of mice trying to pick one up in her gloved hand to move it to safety. Her actions and shrieks are a pleasure to behold. There is a great deal of competition between two pickers, not to be outdone by each other as to the speed with which they can pick their stint up. You will see them picking up bucket for bucket, and if one gets a bit behind, she will, as soon as the other's back is turned, break into a little trot between the row and the box, keeping an eye on the other person so as not to be caught appearing to be hurrying. When several of the children get together they can be a handful and often the day is shattered by a full-voiced woman calling her offspring's name. One lad was walking about where some of the men were working, out of sight of his mother. He was not properly out of nappies and had a large turd weighing down his pants and in view. Several of us had looked, shrugged and turned away back to our work. But one chap, who on the face of it wasn't very keen on children, took this innocent toddler to the back of the hedge and emptied his pants of this offending sight. I'll admit I had a bit more respect for this chap after that.

How some of the women cope with the washing amazes me, for I've seen several children of the same family standing in a rut partly filled with water, waist high, and getting plastered from head to toe in mud from larking around in it. It seemed that as soon as their mothers get home they have to start work all over again. There was one lady who came spudding who, even in the most appalling muddy conditions, would go home at night as clean and as impeccable as when she arrived in the morning – most impressive. Once there were two women larking about and I was teasing them a bit. One got hold of me and while she held me, the other scooped up a handful of mud and rubbed it all over my face. This was rather unpleasant for a bit, but turned out alright in the end, as one of the women kindly wiped it all off again!

In later years, when I would walk into the barn late at night, where the potato pickers had been riddling and bagging the potatoes, I would get an overwhelming feeling of their presence. Just as if everyone was still there, but not in a form that I could see. This feeling was so strong that I would virtually run out of the shed in confusion at such an unexplainable emotion. I started to experience this sort of feeling in the bait room, when having tea on my own in the winter. It's as if the people were still there, but not in a physical sense. When in a certain state of mind I would pick up something coming into my mind and becoming known to me in a way that I could not really comprehend. I had to talk myself out of letting these feelings become too strong, or I would be unable to go into places on my own where people I knew had been.

Soon after I bought the car, I said to myself, if I don't find a wife or girlfriend whom I'm likely to marry within the next twelve months, I'd sell the car and leave my job and go and see something of the world for a while. Almost at the end of the twelve months, I became acquainted with Maureen, who as I mentioned earlier, had come to Netherwood to be Nanny to Richard Payne. The following autumn we were married. On the Saturday morning of our wedding day, I offered to go into work as normal, as I thought it would keep me occupied until the service in the afternoon. Sid wouldn't hear of it and said that no one was working under him on their wedding day.

The wedding ceremony was at Stoke Bliss Church and the reception held in a marquee at the New Inn, Sutton. What I thought was nice was the patience of the people at the reception, when Maureen went to change before going off on our honeymoon. It seemed ages. Perhaps I was a little impatient to get going and that made it appear that way, but everybody was still there waiting to see us off. I'd never had a holiday in the autumn before as it was a busy time on the farm. I think the gaffer, if the truth were known, would have preferred me to have picked a better time of year to get married. Anyway, I was able to see Scotland in its autumn glory, which was superb. The frosts had already begun up there and helped to turn the bracken a beautiful brown. This was set against the clear sky, hills and multi-coloured trees. It was a great pleasure to wake up on a clear frosty morning at the Bredlebane Arms, Aberfeldy, to hear the rippling stream alongside the hotel and to go outside and scrape the frost off the windscreen of the car parked in the square. I felt pleased that I was able to be in such a place at that moment in my life.

In the north of Scotland the weather changed completely and it rained non-stop. The wet orange look of the autumn landscape was something the like of which I had never seen before. I had never driven so many miles before along a road and met so few cars. I only saw three cars on the journey that day. Farther on down the western side, we came to a place where the road just disappeared into a loch. We hadn't been looking at the map much, so we did not know quite where we were. A house could be seen on the other side of the water and as we sat there for a while wondering what we should do, a boat started out from the other side. It turned out to be a ferry. It came over empty and picked us up. There were no other cars or people about. I sat in the car while we were ferried over the water and drove off the other end without even talking to the two ferry-boat men, or paying anything for this, to me, most unusual trip.

When we decided to get married, I had a Saturday afternoon off and went house-hunting. First I went to the other side of Ludlow, to look at a bungalow I could afford. I thought it was a bit out of the way, so I went to Giles Smith, Hereford and found a couple of houses to look at. One was just out of Hereford, which did not really appeal. Then, rather late that afternoon, I went to look at one in Bishop's Frome. This house felt right, partly because some of it was brick built and I thought to myself, goodness, fancy living in a house with straight walls. The house I'd been brought up in was black and white, with higgeldy-piggeldy floors, ceiling and walls. This was before timber-framed houses became sought-after. Finding that this house was still for sale, I told the woman owner that I would buy it. On the Monday I rang the agents, telling them of my intentions and they asked me what I was prepared to pay. Not knowing about haggling prices down, I told them the asking price, which seemed to startle the man a bit. Asking him to stay open one evening until I had finished work, I went and discussed whether I could afford a mortgage. My farm worker's wage was not quite enough, even though the gaffer had given me a pay rise when he heard I was going to get married. After a bit of head scratching and me saying I could earn extra by doing piece-work, he said O.K., fine. Buying a house was much, much easier than buying a car, which seemed a bit strange to me.

When the documents and things were sorted out about the house, I found that someone, somewhere, had been on my side, for 12% had been knocked off the price I'd agreed to pay, without me even knowing about it. The house needed a fair bit done to it in the way of alternations. It had a large garden too. Farm workers' wages were not as high as some, which meant that I had to work long hours to earn enough money to do the work on the house, which of course meant that there wasn't much time left to do the actual work required. For the first few years I never sat down in my own home, other than for meals. Even Christmas days were used to catch up on the work. After about ten years of this and other emotional problems, I was getting into a right state of mind.

I still worked at Netherwood after moving to Bishop's Frome, going to work in the first few years on a scooter, the sound of which most people along the route got to recognise. Mr. Howe, the headmaster at Bishop's Frome school, when he lived at Bromyard, used me as his alarm clock as I went to work along the Old Road, by his house. Also, people knew when I knocked off work at night. Some would be most concerned about the hours I worked and would say so whenever I happened to bump into them, telling me to spend more time at home. I found out later that Mr. Dorrell at the Hall Farm, over the road from The Knowle, had talked to my parents about it, saying that I should spend more time with my children. It surprises me somewhat, the extent to which people in a small scattered community are involved with each other, their

Vicarage Cottage *N. Turner*

92

concern, anger, pride, or annoyance or what have you, with the things going on around them.

I did not heed the warnings and concern of these people to any great extent, just thought it was nice of them to worry about me. But one foggy, end-of-autumn morning, something happened that brought home to me what they'd been on about. Going up past Peacock Heath, 1½ miles from Bromyard on the Tenbury Wells road, and only able to see a few yards in front because the fog was so bad, I started to get a feeling of light-headedness, as if I was becoming remote from my surroundings and what I was doing. I was aware of things around me, but was unable to relate my actions to cope with controlling the scooter. The body refused to take any commands from the brain. I could see and was aware of what was going on, but couldn't do anything about it, as if my body had been trussed up and someone had sat me on a moving scooter. I was unable to shut the throttle down, apply the brakes, use the clutch or even steer at all and my balance went as well. I started to veer over towards the white line in the centre of the road, at the same time as a large white lime lorry loomed up out of the fog. I was sure I was going to end up crushed under its wheels, but somehow the lorry seemed to push me away and start me off on a course back to the side of the road. I more or less observed myself going into the ditch, just past the Tack Farm, thinking what on earth am I going to do when I crash, as my body was still not responding to my brain.

After what seemed a graceful exit from the road then travelling along the grass verge for a little way and falling with the scooter into the ditch, I lay there with the engine slowly dying from its unnatural position. I felt half-embarrassed and half-afraid that I would never be able to move again. Then, after a while, anger crept in and in the half-light of the morning my body gradually got its feeling back. In the panic of being afraid of being found in the ditch by someone I knew, I was able to untangle myself from the bike and was much relieved to find I was able, if somewhat shakily, to move and walk again. Hauling the damaged scooter back onto the road, I was able to start it again and proceed to work, saying nothing to anyone and just feeling queer for the rest of the day. It's as if I'd pushed myself too far for too long and my body was telling me to ease off a little.

Not having ever told anyone about this happening, it seemed more than coincidence that not long after, Mr. Payne said he was a bit worried about me travelling home late at night after working long hours and thought it would be better if I had something with four wheels instead of two. So he bought a van for me to use – petrol supplied which was much appreciated. It's as if we each have a part of us on another level, that somehow communicates with someone else without our conscious mind being aware of it, like the squeeze of Patricia's

93

hand on the picture bus and me somehow knowing that that was the last time we'd go out together.

This unspoken communication is perhaps what animals and birds have, such as when a flock of peewits take off into flight from a field, and the unison with which they fly and wheel around the sky. Perhaps man was like this before we developed speech. It's possible we have been nurtured this far by some god or force of nature and are slowly being given the chance to plan our own future, for at the moment I seem more comfortable following my instincts and taking things as they come, rather than trying to manipulate things and the future. Who knows, man may end up on this earth as a single man and woman with the knowledge of all mankind that has been before him and so be given the chance to be creator or keeper of another world somewhere.

The first tractor I had with a cab was a Massey Ferguson 175. This must have been soon after I got married, as the gaffer enquired, when we were going to change the one I'd had for the past three and a half years, whether I intended stopping at Netherwood, or whether I was thinking of changing my job, because if I was, he was not going to buy a new tractor. I said, I wasn't thinking about leaving and made a sort of verbal agreement that I was hoping to stop for the next ten years. So things went ahead. I was really looking forward to having a tractor with a cab fitted, thinking how warm and dry it would be, but again change brings about other changes that one hadn't thought about; in particular the noise. Having not been in a tractor cab before, this came as a shock. There was no padding or anything to deaden all the different sounds, so my first day with a cab was quite a disappointment. But hanging and stuffing a few bags in and around the cab (can't seem to get away from bags (sacks), even with a cab), and stuffing bits of rag in my ears, things became quite acceptable.

Within the first week of having the 175, I came very close to being without a cab again. I'd been so used to parking in the old tin barn, going under a low doorway. One night I came tearing home to the farm and swung into my usual parking place, completely forgetting about the cab. It wasn't until the bonnet of the tractor started to go under the low doorway, that it hit me. Fortunately I was able to stop just as the cab started to become wedged against the barn. For the first few weeks I also still put my arm up to fend off tree branches, even though the cab deflected them.

About this time, Mr. Payne had bought the Pensons Farm, the Hyde Farm and he also farmed the Grove Farm. This made Netherwood spread out a bit so to speak, giving us workers a change of scenery and a new zest for work, especially for me. It was like a second childhood, especially the Grove Farm, not having been over the farm much since schooldays. So, as I worked my way around the farm, ploughing and suchlike, lots of half-remembered places and memories came back which was rather nice, especially as the farm was in

94

between The Knowle and Kyre Pool, which was one of my favourite places to wander off to play during the school holidays.

It was in the first year of the ownership of the Grove that the crawler was bought. Funny how things keep coming around again, Morris had one when they farmed Netherwood, Mr. & Mrs. Abel Smith had one, and now Mr. Payne was sort of forced into having one, due to furrow smear and soil compaction. I quite enjoyed going around and meeting people in connection with buying the crawler and plough. We ended up with a Track Marshall 90 and a Dowdswell five furrow reversible plough. Mr. Dowdswell was one of the few firms about that would take notice of any ideas or suggestions we made in connection with his plough, having had a few teething troubles during the first twelve months of its use. It was nice to be shown around the works by him, and to see his drawings of future ploughs. The plough is still in use twenty years later (1990), although some of its wearing parts have been changed many times.

Crawler driving is somewhat different to driving a wheeled tractor, it took me about three years to settle down to it properly. With the wheeled tractors, up till then, I could, at most jobs, go as fast as the engine would allow. This habit was hard to break, for the gaffer had worked out the top speed he wanted the crawler to be used at. It was quite a mental strain for me to sit there doing a job, when there was enough power to go up a gear or two. The gaffer started to get rather ratty when I sort of forgot myself, and started going faster than he thought fit. Having amicably warned me a couple of times to slow down, the third warning, he started to look white about the lips and it came home to me that if I was to continue working for him in an amicable fashion, I'd better do as he wanted or our relationship would become very strained.

When ploughing with a wheeled tractor you dropped one wheel in the furrow and then more or less forgot about steering, until you got to the other end of the field. Whereas with the crawler, you stopped on top of the land and had to steer a few inches away from the furrow at a set distance, so as to keep all the furrows the same width. This demanded a lot of concentration all day, otherwise I either dropped in the furrow and made a mess of the ploughing or wandered off too wide, so making the plough try to turn over more than it could cope with and eventually straining the front furrow on the plough.

Having never had anything to do with a crawler before, I was alright until the steering brakes needed adjusting. The snag was that the instruction book was for the previous model, as the ones for the machine I was using had not yet been printed and I wasn't sure whether there was any difference between the two models or not. So, not taking any chances, I asked one of the contractors pushing out hedges near where I was working, if he knew how to adjust the brakes. He said he couldn't be sure, so I thought it would be best to leave things alone and ring up the makers. They didn't seem to be sure which model we'd got, so they decided to send a man down from Gainsborough, several hours' journey away. The job took him about a minute and a half to do. I felt so embarrassed at having got him here for such a simple thing that, years after, I would inwardly squirm whenever I thought about it!

The more acreage farmed from Netherwood, the less variety there was in jobs. Towards the end of Mr. Abel Smith's time, I was doing, or helping to do, most things on the farm, but as more land got ploughed up each person took over two or three main jobs, as it was not possible to plough, cultivate and plant when large acreages were involved. So, instead of several of us doing one job together, one person ended up doing one job on its own, which has continued up to the present day. The only jobs we all worked together were bale hauling and beating for pheasants, although these two have now near enough stopped, as small square bales are being replaced by large round ones, which one man can haul himself, and the beating has become a weekend job, so half the blokes don't come anyway as the pay is not very high. My father, when working with Frank Briscoe, rabbitting on Netherwood in the 1920s, used to get a pound for a day's beating locally and I, in the 1970s, would get a normal day's pay plus a few pounds extra and a brace of birds as well. In 1987, it's eight pounds a day and a couple of cans of beer. Some things don't always continue on the up.

So, I've gone from when I started working with several men and women, to working a large part of the year on my own. The crops have changed. During my spell at Netherwood they changed from fairly modest acreages of wheat, oats, barley, beans, peas, potatoes, sugar beet, cider apples, milking cows, beef cattle, sheep, pigs, turkeys, damsons, fodder beet, mangles, kale, swedes and hay through to much larger quantities of only wheat, barley, potatoes, beef cattle, pigs, about the same of sheep and cider apples as before, but less hay. There was also grass silage, which was extra and mustard for green manure. In 1986 they had changed to: wheat; barley; which had changed from mostly winter- and some spring-planted to mainly winter-planted; potatoes, a bit less acreage; less sheep; beef cattle; pigs; and fewer cider apples. New crops to come in were stubble turnips, oil seed rape, maize for stock feed, silage, Christmas trees and beans again. Potatoes went in 1989, beef cattle about 1987 along with maize, as it was grown as their feed. In 1989/90 two men, who had been at Netherwood for a long time, went in exchange for a manager/worker.

In the 1960s there were some concrete sectional grain siloes in the Big Barn and these had small ventilators in the bottom, covered with wire mesh. It was near these that I fed the big tom cat with bits saved from my sandwiches. A mouse had somehow got into one of these small openings, behind the mesh, and as the bin was full of corn it was unable to get out again. It survived for many weeks, presumably just living off the corn. It never had any water. In the end it seemed to get bloated and eventually died. It used to worry me, seeing this mouse week after week, unable to get out.

When I started work in 1953 potato planting was mostly done by hand. Hundredweight (cwt.) sacks of potatoes were distributed down the bouted out ridges and the spuds planted by hand with a bucket. Then we borrowed a two-row planter which went behind a tractor, with two people. This was followed by Mr. Payne with a three-row planter, with three women on, one of whom was often my mother. The planter was quite heavy, so the tractor was light on the front. One day, feeling in high spirits when turning at the end, I kept my foot on the steering brake and went round and round several times on the spot. It was fun to me, but the three women on the back got the wind up a bit and told me off somewhat, so I didn't do it again. After this we went on to a two-row planter with one man, that went many times faster than the previous model and was still in use in 1987.

Again in 1953, when I started, potato lifting was done with a single-row spinner and women picked them up and put them into 1cwt. hessian sacks. The potatoes were tipped and stored, then riddled and sold during winter, or if difficult to get rid of were sold to the Ministry for stock feed. These had to have purple dye poured all over and in the sacks of the carefully sorted potatoes. This is alright when you get used to it, but after several days or weeks of carefully sorting the potatoes, to see someone stabbing holes in the bags and then tipping watering cans full of this dye over them, it is inclined to make a person angry. Particularly the women sorters, who had never seen it done before. They would become most indignant to see this happen after their hard work and care. It would have been better if the Ministry chap had done this work out of sight of the people sorting, as it was rather demoralising.

Then, for a few years, we went over to using wicker hampers which held about 1 cwt., which the women picked up into. A couple of chaps would grab a handle apiece and throw the hamper of spuds up onto the trailer, where a chap tipped them out. By then, we were starting to sell potatoes directly off the field. These were sold for a little while in 1 cwt. hessian sacks, although this only lasted about a season and then half-hundredweight paper sacks came in. There were lots of derisory remarks from the workers about the lightness of the bags, going on about them being twice as much work and handling, and what was farming coming to, having such light small bags that even women can handle with ease? We were then sacking off the grain in 1½ cwt. sacks, so the half-hundredweights were a bit of a joke, but after a season we soon got used to them.

Potatoes were then picked directly into these paper bags, weighed on some scales towed behind a tractor and trailer on the bale sledge, tied and stacked on the trailer ready to be loaded on lorries at the end of the day. The women picking up spuds into these would have the job of sorting them as they went along, as no other sorting was done. A watch had to be kept on one or two pickers who weren't very fussy as to what went into the bags – clods, potato haulm and what have you. Each woman's stint was kept separate and she was paid by the amount she picked up. This was a bit awkward sometimes, as some of the women would try to get you to dig them up faster and some would be telling you to go a bit steadier. By then, we were using a two-row digger elevator. One of the snags with picking up in paper sacks was when we got behind with the weighing and a storm of rain came. This made a lot of extra work and put us further behind. When things were going well, with lots of potatoes picked up that day, we would have to come back after tea to finish off. One evening we were still weighing by moonlight, behind the Pensons. It had been a lovely October day, and the hundreds of unweighed sacks were dotted about the field with their tops open. The spiders had made lots of gossamer webs criss-crossing these openings and when the low sun was reflected off them it was a very pretty sight indeed.

Then we tried a potato harvester, which had seven or eight people on. We sorted, bagged and weighed, all on the machine. Like the early bagger combines, this was not very successful. So then a sorting/bagging/weighing set-up was put in the nearest convenient barn and the potatoes were then hauled in bulk from the harvester to the sorting machine in the barn. This was not too successful as the soil on Netherwood was inclined to be cloddy and in a wet season a lot of unnecessary soil was hauled up with the potatoes. We had been picking up into 5 cwt. boxes by hand just before this, which was rather labour intensive, and for this reason the harvester was tried, but to keep up daily tonnage the harvester had to be used after tea. This brought the boxes back into favour somewhat and for a while the two systems were run side by side. Over a period of years, the harvester was abandoned and we settled into picking up by hand into boxes, which is how it was still being done in 1987.

When there is a thunderstorm, there is one place on Netherwood where it strikes more often than anywhere else. Once, while loading bales of hay onto a lorry and trailers in the big hopyard field, a thunderstorm developed. No rain as yet, just thunder and lightning. All of a sudden, there was a crack as the lightning hit an ash tree in the hedge at the bottom of Calves Hill, causing the hedge to burst into flame. Over the years, observing the number of trees around the farm that had been struck, by far the highest number are along the hedge and nearby trees at the bottom of Calves Hill and Brick Barns bank adjoining, apparently following the line of the old canal or ditch.

With the coming of artificial fertilizers, there seemed to be a decline in the mushroom population. Whether the two things were linked for sure, I don't know, but that's the view we had at Netherwood. In the cold early springs of the year, fertilizer spreading was a bit of a job, as the tractor did not have a cab then. The spreader held about a ton of fertilizer. At one time, this was stored in a big stack, at the bottom end of the sheep pens, out in the open with no sheets or anything on. This was bought in the autumn, so it was outside for several months before it was used. Consequently, if any of the bags in the stack had any holes, the contents would become wet and sticky, or some fertilizers would go like concrete and have to be smashed up with the back of a shovel.

Not having fork-lifts, or any other aids, the hundredweight bags had to be slid down from the top of the stack, then came a few rows of level loading, after which the lower bags had to be humped up by hand into the spreader. Being the low side of the sheep pens meant that the bottom bags were covered in sheep muck and the like that had run through the bottom of the stack. I'd get a sweat on loading, then get perished driving around spreading it – not the best of jobs sometimes. The fertilizers then were very varied. In those days some ran like sand and others hardly ran at all. I developed a bit of a skill in judging, after once or twice around the field, whether I'd got the setting right. The spreader was run off the land wheel, enabling it to be driven at high speed around the fields, if the application rate was not too high. This had its problems, for on several occasions the spreader would come unhitched, pulling the hydraulic pipes out of the back of the tractor and ramming the spreader drawbar well into the ground, and so tipping a fair amount of the contents out into a heap. After scooping it back up the best I could by the double handful, a lot seemed to be left, therefore killing off a patch that would be brown and bare for a long time, causing the gaffer to make some appropriate comments.

In the early Mr. Payne years, we were given a day off, with pay, to go to the Three Counties Show, transport provided if required. This was at the beginning of June so it often clashed with silage making. One year I said I'd like to go on the second day of the three-day show. The foreman said OK, so I arranged to go with my wife and her parents. Came the day and we still had a day's silage to do, so the gaffer said to go on the third day instead. This was OK as far as I was concerned, but made it a bit awkward for the people I was going with, which upset me somewhat, being caught in the middle of things. From then on I never made positive arrangements to go anywhere with people, as work seemed to come first.

Silage time was usually the start of the fine warmer weather, so I used to look forward to this and to taking my shirt off to start getting a tan. The first silage I helped with was built like a rick of hay, all built by hand from an elevator with unchopped grass. Then to building a wedge shape on a piece of sloping ground with the aid of a buck rake, still with unchopped grass. Then a pit was made in the Big Barn as it was built on sloping ground, which enabled the grass to be buck-raked in on two different levels. A direct cut silage harvester was used now, up till this time the silage was got out by hand. A hay knife was used for a while to help with the forking out, then an electric blade was acquired about the time we went over to a double chop silage harvester. The grass was first cut with a finger mowing machine with a crimper behind. This was to cut down on the amount of moisture taken to the silage clamp. The grass was allowed to wilt for a day or two before being brought in. With long grass it was possible to build straight walls on the clamp and get the tractor near to the edge when rolling it. I had to be more careful with the double chop, as it did not bind quite so well, but with care, a straight wall could still be achieved. One year we had a lorry come and seal the clamp with a layer of lime, but mostly straw bales were used. About the time of the double chop, the big tin barn burnt down and a new, larger clamp was built in one of the new barns put up. Plastic sheeting was coming in then, which was used for sealing the silage. Discarded car tyres were used to keep the sheet down, so preventing the air getting to the silage.

For the first time, the silage was got out mechanically. I've often thought this was one of the reasons John Beeston left. This distancing of the stockman from his cattle, having to sit in a cold tractor on a morning, instead of being able to get a good warm on first thing when feeding. The chance of finding a man or woman who likes both tractors and animals is a bit remote. A stockman is quite happy to get his hands covered in the muck of whichever animals he's working with, but loathes getting near oil and grease and vice versa for the tractor driver.

The meter, or precision chop, came in then. The grass was chopped up quite fine so that a straight wall could not be built with this stuff. A slight 'taper in' had to be achieved. In trying to find an appropriate slope, we had a few landslides. Not the best of things to be greeted with first thing in the morning. Having to make the face presentable again was hard extra work. The face is the end of the clamp that has no support to hold it in place (up to 18' high), so as to make it easy to start getting it out again for feeding in the winter.

When the silage pit was about three-quarters full, several of us, including the student who was at Netherwood that year, would see if we could get across the span of the barn by going hand over hand along the girders in the roof. Few of us ever made it, but it was not for the want of trying. Sometimes, when the grass silage was brought in a bit damp, it would stick in the trailers, so when it was tipped it would go past centre, with the weight behind the wheels and lift the back of the tractor off the ground, leaving just the front wheels touching the ground and causing some strange expressions on the drivers' faces. With the tractors which were heavier it was no problem, until the hitch came undone unexpectedly. Either the trailer drawbar knocked the rear window out of the cab, or when the trailer was being jerked the tractor shot forward, ripping the hydraulic pipes off, leaving the trailer pointing skywards.

It would appear that the Hyde Farm had to be tacked onto Netherwood before I was to see my first pair of dippers in adult life. There may have been some at Netherwood, but I'd never seen any. When doing lots of tractor driving, it was nice to get away from it for a bit, so I'd take my bait bag and walk to the nearest wood or lake to have dinner. While ploughing the Quarry Field, Hyde, I'd walked a way up the brook in Perry Wood and was sat down at the side of one of the small waterfalls. This was a very pretty place before some of the mature beech trees were felled, which let the light in, enabling the briars to take hold there. These briars survived well as there were no rabbits to speak of, because of myxomatosis, to nibble the young briar shoots off. The sight of these two birds walking in the brook, at times disappearing under the water, I found very interesting, as I didn't know what they were. Not knowing much about anything, I have found great delight in life discovering about what is in and around where I work. These dippers, 'though quite ordinary birds I discovered, gave me several days of pleasurable thought, even at the present time the picture in my mind is still as fresh as the day it happened.

About 6 acres of blackcurrants were grown for a few years at Netherwood in what was called the Park Orchard, or Broken Orchard. I helped to set the rows and spacings out for the young currant bushes and to take part in the planting. It was satisfying when we'd finished, to look down the rows at any angle, and see the neat lines of young bushes. I would go currant picking after work and at weekends. Generally there was no picking on Saturdays, but Sid the foreman, seeing I was keen, made an exception and let me pick on Saturdays. A bit strange, suddenly having a whole field to myself once a week. Not having picked currants before, I'd see how different people picked and copy what appeared to me to be the best method. The fast ones appeared to pick currants, leaves, the lot, as fast as they could into a bucket, then spend a little time picking the leaves out. I didn't like this way much, as I preferred, when I'd picked a bucket full, not to have to turn round and sort through them again. So I tried grabbing the berries off with both hands, leaving all the leaves and some of the stalks on the bushes. This was OK until Sid commented that my trays were starting to look like they were already jam. So I plumped for picking

101

whole sprays fairly carefully between thumb and finger with no leaves. After a bit of practise, it turned out to be a reasonable job. Park Orchard was then, and now, referred to as the currant patch, the current bushes were grubbed out about six years after planting, as currants clashed with the lifting of early potatoes.

In the days before bulk grain and sufficient siloes, corn was sold in bags and for a few years was also stored in them after being dried. The 2¼-2½ cwt. Gobsel Brown sacks died out a few years after me starting work. We then had 1¼-1½ cwts. Many weeks were spent in the dryer, sacking off corn, mostly in the winter. During the autumn, there were usually three or four of us with one bagging off, which was the dustiest job, but in some ways the easiest until you put on a bag with a hole in or one slipped off. Panic then set in, as before a new bag could be put on, one was slipping and sliding about in the grain from the uncovered spout! This was before dust masks were supplied, or even heard of to any great extent. So, you had an easier job in the dust, or a harder job tying the sacks, from which, after a couple of days, you got very sore fingers. When I was doing this, someone showed me how to tie them properly, which then gave a bit of job satisfaction. This entailed pulling the neck of the sack into a straight line after shaking the contents down, then making neat, even, folds, gathering the neck together, keeping the top level, then tying as close as possible down near the contents. Before I was shown this, I'd just cobbled the tops together as best I could. This is the case for having a go at all the various jobs, because if the first part is done properly, the rest goes much smoother, such as when a badly tied bag drops off the elevator onto your back and the top comes undone, you soon learn to do all things properly.

The tied sacks were either put on a trailer or stacked three high on the dryer floor. The third layer of the 1½ cwt. sacks were stacked by two of us, a stick clasped between us, put at the bottom of the bag, the top pulled back by our free hands and swung up into place. The first time my back gave way was when loading a trailer on my own with these sacks. Up till then, I was able to put my all into what I was doing. I have now learnt when to ease off and to recognise just how much I can or can't attempt.

In the autumn, after combining was finished, room had to be made in the dryer. The sacks were then stacked five or six high under the granary floor, down in the big barn. Not being able to get tractors or trailers right in, the sacks were carried on one's back up the planks, to get the top couple of layers on. After about three days of sacking off, I'd end up with the same symptoms as the flu and weekends were spent getting right again, so a couple of us bought dust masks in later years from the chemist and another used a folded-up handkerchief over his nose and mouth. Still before dust masks, a sealed silo

102

was put up in a bay next to the granary, in the big barn. Undried barley was stored in this, to be fed to the cattle over the winter. This would occasionally go mouldy and stick to the sides. After John Beeston had poked as much down as he could with a hook pole through the small opening at the bottom, someone had to go in and shovel the rest of it out. Terry and myself often as not ended up doing this. It was rather worrying as reports were going about as to the effects of this mouldy dust on farm workers. It was a job I'd rather not have done, but someone had to do it. One year we had the compressor going, so we blew a bit of fresh air onto one another as we worked at shovelling the bin out. I was glad when this job ceased to exist, but not the way it came about, this was by fire in later years.

The Grove farm was the best place to be to watch and hear the Canada Geese flying between the lakes, mainly Kyre Pool and Netherwood lakes. To hear their honking and watch their straggly line flying low over the farm, with the low winter sun on them, was very humbling; this sharing of an area between man, birds and animals. In the misty, foggy weather, they'd only be heard, not seen. Too many are a nuisance, but a couple of families, the local farmers should be able to put up with. They have nested at Netherwood a few times and reared half a dozen or so young. When a group is grazing in a field, there always seems to be one with its neck stretched high in the air, keeping watch, while the rest get their fill. Once, after feeding in the field by The Knowle, father had been watching them on and off for a couple of hours, when they took off and a low circle was made around the house, as if to say "We've been watching you watching us". As the line straightened out and the geese gained height, father, standing in the garden, gave a couple of realistic honks and much to his delight the dozen or so geese all turned their heads as one, at right angles to their necks, in response to his call. During the shooting season, one might be potted. Once, a tiny little dog belonging to the gaffer, about a quarter the size of a Canada Goose managed to grab one and hang on to it until a shooter arrived to deal with it.

Canada geese seemed to take over as the swans disappeared. From earliest childhood, there had always been swans about the area. As a pair would fly over The Knowle, we would all stop work and wait for them to come into sight, as usually the whistling sound of their wings would precede them. Even father would come out of the garage and watch then fly over.

The last swan's nest was possibly on Tee Baune lake. One winter one of the last swans to grace the area apparently died trying to swallow a whole potato that had been put out to feed a duck. Most sad to see this swan with a large bulge halfway down its neck. One year at the Grove farm, during spudding time, a mother and about eight young grey, half-grown, cygnets seemed to be moving to another lake. Quite an arresting sight to see this line walking down

Grove lane, a rather hot looking mother in front, followed by her waddling young. People were trying to help, but there wasn't a lot anyone could do, other than keep a distance away and see no vehicles ran into them. Someone stopped with them when they got to the main road, heading towards Kyre House.

We were once graced by a solitary black swan that visited the various lakes about. People were getting quite attached to this bird, boasting about how they'd seen it that day. Suddenly it was seen no more. It came about later that someone Bromyard way had taken a fancy to it and in an effort to keep it on his own lake had clipped one of its wings to stop it flying. This was bad enough, but he also had a couple of dogs that took a dislike to this swan and one day managed to catch it. As the black swan was unable to fly it couldn't get away and was killed by the two dogs. The desire of one person deprived himself and the community of something common to us all.

Woodcock may have always been at Netherwood, but it wasn't until the woods that Mr. Payne had cleared and planted up again had become established that I noticed them. They increased over about ten years until, when beating on certain parts of Netherwood woods and dingles, as many woodcock as pheasant were flushed out. I've often asked myself about the rights and wrongs of pheasant shooting. I'm inclined to follow my mother's dislike of any form of cruelty, but, the way I see it, the longer a thing has been going, the longer it should be before it is done away with. It's a part of farming that I've grown up with and my not going would not make any difference. It's more sporting than having birds cooped up in small wire cages and it was nice for all of us on the farm to do something together. I very much like walking through the woods and dingles of Netherwood and beating gives me an opportunity to do this. It's also a chance for my children in turn to savour a little of where I work. Pheasant is a taste I grew to like. Perhaps it gives farmers something to look forward to, as it's the time of year when things are not very busy, so stops them breathing down their workers' necks so much. Also, it seems that if one thing is stopped or altered in the way of life, something else just as bad, in a different way, springs up.

If one looks at nature, one thing eats another, often whole and still alive. It seems for the moment there has to be killing in some form or other, be it for the production of food, or for pleasure. Me, I have great difficulty in killing anything, be it only a mouse that's doing mischief. This might not have happened if myxomatosis had not come about, so doing away with a free meal off the farm. Perhaps I'd still be happily bashing rabbits on the head with a stick, but also there would not be any rabbits walking about with bloated heads and blind eyes until they die what must be a miserable death from this despicable disease. Since this disease came about, the venom I've heard come from men's

104

lips about its introduction, whether deliberate or not, was often worse than when they were talking about Hitler. What they would have done with the person, or persons, responsible for doing away with the poor man's meal is nobody's business. So, I'm inclined to carry on beating, with slight reservations, but enjoying the walks through the woods and meeting different people, whom I would not otherwise have met. There was a girl called Catherine from New Zealand who came beating a couple of times. I think she was here in England to learn something about horses. The last time she came beating she was about to go off back home and while waiting for the guns to change positions, we had chance to have a talk, standing in the frost, and cold, at the top of Rabbit Bury Coppice. Once this girl got talking, I just stood back, rather amazed at the way she got going, rather as if she'd been wound up somehow and the words had to come out there and then. A most pleasant ten minutes for me, being able to observe at close range the face and body of this pretty young lady as words poured forth in an unbroken flow. Mrs. Payne stood a little way off, leaning on her beating stick, with a slight smile on her face, taking it all in.

Another time, things were not so good. I was cleaning the leaves from the overflows of the lake, soon after a new gaffer had come to Netherwood. It was raining heavily at the time and I had a sack around my shoulders and a sou'wester hat on. I had the misfortune to arrive at Tee Baune lake just before the new gaffer and The Colonel came up the other way, shooting duck. I'd not been told about what was going on, but I must have presumably frightened off any duck that might have been there, just as they were about to have some sport. I just carried on cleaning the leaves out as if nothing had happened, cursing the foreman for not putting me in the picture, the gaffer for perhaps not telling him, the weather which caused the lakes to overflow and me for being there at the wrong time, the people for shooting duck in such lousy weather anyway and generally wishing I was somewhere else other than in farming (all this hopefully under my breath).

In February 1970 I ended up with my foot in plaster. This happened when I was loading a trailer of bales on my own. I was throwing them down from the top of a stack in the Big Barn. When nearly finished, I stood a bit too close to the edge, trying to get a better view of where I was chucking them. The bale on the edge gave way and I found myself falling, heading straight onto the metal corner-post of the trailer. In the short time of falling, I was aware of thinking "If I land on that I'm a gonner". I seemed to be twisting like a cat as I fell. When I hit the trailer, one leg went outside the tailboard and the other was wedged inside, between the tailboard and a bale, and acted like a big spring. The whole weight of my sideways-moving body was supported by this one leg, which let me nearly onto the floor and sort of pulled me back up again. On freeing myself, I found that I was able to hobble about, which was a relief. On getting to hospital, I found that just one bone had been fractured in my foot, so several weeks were spent in plaster. Many years later this bone still aches occasionally.

The news that the garden wall had fallen against Bowler's lorry shed came when I was baling or hauling bales in the Roundcots. The message came that the wall had partly fallen, but was held up by a 'table'. Not much concerned by the news, as none of the walls were that bad, I thought, I went home when I'd finished what I was doing. It was a bit of a shock when I saw what had happened. Thirty yards or so of the main garden wall had leaned the one yard distance between it and the shed, and still in one piece. The many tons of this wall of stone and brick, fifteen foot high at its tallest, was leaning against the large lorry shed, slowly pushing it out of true. The 'table' turned out to be an electric cable running along part of the wall. This was being stretched across the gap at one end of the wall. The ground level on the garden side was six foot higher than the lorry yard side. There was no way of getting any mechanical aid to the collapsed wall, so all the work was done by hand. In order to take it down to an acceptable level, several relatives lent a hand. There were lots of odds and ends stored between the shed and the wall which made it harder work, trying not to damage these. Nigh on the next three years, spare time and holidays were spent by me taking it down completely, digging the garden back and getting down to the original foundations. Not having done much building, if any, on my own before, I found this an absorbing task. Not having enough money for sand, cement and mixer, I decided to mix the several ten-ton loads of sand, appropriate cement and lime, by hand on a piece of sheet iron. As there were a couple of other bits of stone wall lying around the place, surplus, I decided to build the new wall wholly in stone, with some of the bricks for a weather-proofing top.

When I'd got the foundation trench out and was building my way up to the lower ground level, I found the trench kept filling up with water after a storm of rain. Getting fed up with emptying this out all the time, I decided the next time it rained I would go out and try to see where all the water kept coming from. It turned out to be a blocked drain taking the water off the lorry shed roof. Whether this had been part of the cause of the wall falling down, goodness knows.

When taking the wall down and cleaning the bricks from the garden facing wall, I came across several bricks with hand and finger impressions in them; other than that nothing of interest. But one brick which had the number thirteen cut into it brought back all the old superstitions that I'd been brought up with but had largely abandoned or forgotten. Like not cutting one's fingernails on a Friday or Sunday; crossing knives; breaking mirrors (seven years' bad luck);

106

burning elderberry wood; knives dropped on the kitchen floor meant there'll be a visitor soon; not killing pigs unless the moon's in the right place, nor letting a female salt them down because it won't take; putting a new pair of shoes on the table; walking under ladders; putting part-burned sticks on the house fire a second time; greenery, holly and mistletoe for Christmas decorations indoors before a certain date; unlucky number thirteen. Looking at the brick with thirteen on it, I thought "you sod", thinking partly about the brick and partly about the person who may have put it in the wall. I said to myself, perhaps this is one of the reasons it collapsed – well it's definitely not going back in the wall or anywhere else that I know about. So, carefully wrapping it up, I put it in the dustbin, just hoping that it wouldn't prove unlucky for the refuse tip it was taken to. The bricks I saved from the wall were enough to top another thirty or so yards of garden wall, a length of dividing wall, seven foot high, part of a porch, an inspection pit in the garage and some to cover a patch of yard.

N. Turner

PART TWO

The idea of writing a diary came to Ivan first when, in the war years, the farm-workers had to record daily on a work sheet where they had worked and what had been achieved. Ivan's very brief and occasional entries are reminiscent of these records. As time passed his entries grew longer as he recorded the particular experiences the day had offered or a train of thought sparked off by an observation. Gradually the reader identifies with a man whose life, which might by so many of us be found monotonous, with neither change nor excitement, proves that opportunities lie around each of us if we allow life to reach us, teach and mature us and share its truths with us.

V. H.

N. Turner

The Diaries

1971

February

4th   Ploughing.

March

1st   New Crawler.

9th   Discing. (Working land down prior to planting)

14th   Rolling corn.

17th   Fertilizer spreading.

April

6th   Planting potatoes.

16th   Rolling corn.

26th   Combine tractor course at Stoneleigh. Several tractor drivers from around the country attended. Course lasted several days. We all slept in accommodation on site. On the course were a couple of black Africans who seemed to find the brown boots I was wearing of great interest. Much looking and commenting went on while looking in my direction. Short hours of work between meals and breaks which took a bit of getting used to, not that I minded for it made a change from the long hours in farm work. I over-indulged myself with cider one evening and felt not very good next day. If that is how people feel after a night's drinking, the hangover far outweighed any pleasure derived the night before. I was not keen on doing it too often. There was a working demonstration of all the range of Massey Ferguson tractors especially for us, which was good, for as a rule farm workers are a bit in the background of things. This was a time when TV interviewers made a very poor insensitive job of talking to and about farm workers, so much so, that one of my mates got so het up he nigh on smashed his TV set during one such programme.

May

1st   Flu.

11th   Silage.

June
9th   Hay making.

July
11th   Had subsoiler. (Implement for loosing up the soil below ploughing depth)

23rd   Planting mustard.

30th   Sub-soiling.

August
16th   Combining.

When I went over to driving the crawler, I was without a regular wheeled tractor, other than the one the stockman used for winter feeding, so it was suggested I went over from baling to combining. Not knowing much about combines, other than having driven one a bit, I had little idea how they really worked regarding what had to be altered for different crops and conditions. A second-hand 10' Massey Ferguson was bought through Morris Wargent and Wilde and Michael Thomas from Munderfield put it into working order. All I had to do was grease and set the combine up for the first crop, which was oats in the Castle field. To get there a swath had to be cut off a different crop, so heart in mouth, I set in just through the gateway and the pleasure I felt when the grain came into the tanks was good indeed. "Thank goodness for that," I said to myself. I was alright for about a quarter of the way round the patch of oats, until some flat corn was encountered. The stalks of corn started wrapping around the pick up reel and generally blocking up. As I was at a bit of a loss as to what to do, Roger from the other combine came and gave a hand and explained how to cope. Very little of the field was flat so by the end of the day I had got the hang of the job. Things went well for a few days until up at the Grove Farm I encountered my first soil blockage. By the time I'd realised something was wrong, a fair amount of the field was trying to get through the combine! Lumps of damp earth were coming into the grain tanks and a great mound had built up over the knife, stopping the crop from getting up to the drum.

It was a hot day and I'd stopped facing the sun while cleaning the great mound of soil off the head. The gaffer came on the scene to give a hand. When this was done, I got back on feeling very hot and bothered, having not come across this problem before. But my troubles weren't over, 20 yards further on the gaffer's hand went up, signalling to stop. Apparently most of the corn was coming through the combine out onto the ground. The damp soil had bunged everything up. A fair time later, when I was well into the sweating stage from the hot sun, I vowed not to get into this pickle again if at all possible!

Having the combine with the smaller bed that went through the gateways I left Roger to finish the field and I went to the next to make a place for him to put his bed back on again. While this was happening, I went the first time around the field. This was OK until we started getting high yields and I failed to get around a 12 acre patch at the Brickyards field, Hyde Farm. About 150 yards from the gateway I found my feet skidding about on grain and found I had not looked in the tanks occasionally, as I had been concentrating on not blocking things up the first time round. My first reaction was to jam the brakes on, which caused a lot more grain to be thrown over me, further adding to my annoyance. Looking at the mess I called myself a stupid idiot for not completely emptying the tanks after the last field. The first time I thought I had slipped up, but the next round was the same. So started our high yields of wheat and barley, much I expect to the gaffer's delight.

This was a field that for no apparent reason suddenly started to crop well. Up till then, Brickyards was a below-average yielding patch. What seems to do the land good for other crops is to grow potatoes, the farmyard manure and deeper working does a lot of good. The Quarry field on the Hyde had got rather poor, so much so that one year Mr. Payne came round to see how many lorry loads of grain there were likely to be, but we had already finished the field and it had only yielded about one third of what was expected. A worried

Bait time

113

gaffer walked about the field wondering what had gone wrong. This was one of the very few times we finished combining a field without the gaffer popping up just as we were doing the last couple of bouts. It got to be a challenge to see if we could manage just one field a season without him being there at the finish! We gave up in the end. It was as if he had a sixth sense to within a minute as to when the field was just near the last bit, for I don't think Tom West, the lorry driver, could have kept him so well informed as to be that accurate.

It was Quarry field that caused a distressed gaffer. I have never seen anyone look so lost and perplexed. It was when we were growing potatoes there. The field seemed doomed from the beginning. To start with I was sent packing for attempting to move the soil, to dry, prior to the rotary cultivator or power harrow coming in and bashing it up nice and fine. (The problem was that the potato harvester didn't like clods.) We seemed somehow to be at cross-purposes. This took the wind out of my sails as I was genuinely trying to help things along. It turned out in the end that my instinct about what was going to happen was way ahead of the gaffer's, for come harvest time we got less than a quarter of the crop due to green potatoes and generally poor yield. I don't much want to see another farmer in that state again. He seemed completely unable to believe that he could grow such a poor crop of saleable potatoes on Netherwood Farms, and it was most upsetting to witness this event.

One combining season we had just moved from the Grove Farm to the Hyde, Cow Pasture field. It was just on tea time. The gaffer was on the grain trailer and he'd gone round to Netherwood to meet us at the top of the field, half way round. This was normally OK, but just as we had finished up in Nutwels I picked up several bricks from the water reservoir that had been demolished. These bricks had bent some of the combine, so having arrived at the Cow Pasture, after a quick bite of tea, we set about straightening the bent bits. This took nigh on three quarters of an hour. Meanwhile the gaffer was waiting for us up under the hill, with the grain trailer, not knowing that we were doing repairs. He got a bit het-up when we didn't arrive and began revving up his tractor in his anxiety to get us going again before the weather broke.

One of the things I liked before the gateways were made bigger, (so that we could go back to the farm each night,) was unsheeting the combine in some remote field on a misty autumn morning. It was rather like getting out of bed. After greasing up and doing whatever else was needed, I lay down on my back in a swath of straw, having 9.00 am bait away from the hustle and bustle of the main farm. During this ten minute nap the weather often decided whether we would be combining fairly soon or going back up the yard until things altered. Lying, half asleep, we would listen for the sound of the sun coming out from the mist causing the straw to crackle as it warmed up, which meant we would soon be on the combines. Hearing this I would smile to

114

myself and snuggle a little deeper into the straw, looking forward to a day's harvesting.

For many years when we had finished the last field, Mr. Payne brought out bottles of beer and we all stood around for a while talking. This was a good note to finish on, better than tearing out of the last field and parking the combines in the shed. The farm and fields that produced the crops deserve a little something like this for their efforts.

September

10th   Hauling bales.

11th   Ploughing.

October

23rd   Found my first flint, Nutwels, Grove Farm. Sitting with my back against the crawler, in the middle of Nutwels field, the Grove Farm, having a meal break while preparing the field for corn planting, I was munching away, and looking at the clods I was trying to break down, when a few yards away something kept pulling my gaze. After a bit I got up and satisfied my curiosity. It was a small piece of stone, about an inch long with sharpish edges. Something made me put it in my pocket to look at when I got home. I didn't know anything then about archaeology or pottery or flints or such things. It was just a word I had come across occasionally. Getting home late that night, Maureen wondered what it might be and on looking in a Children's Encyclopaedia found something similar. The possibility of it being of interest and of a fair age was very good for my state of mind at that time. I had been working long hours and was letting something that happened some years before, over which I had had no control, really get me down in the dumps.

Wondering if this flint was a one off and not daring to hope there would be more, over the next few days I spent part of my meal breaks traipsing around the field I was working in. This shook me somewhat as I had always relied heavily on my 10 minutes nap and the three meal breaks a day to stop myself getting too tired. This piece of flint which had the power to make me give up these looked-forward-to naps was a source of wonderment in itself. After several days and a few more rough bits of flint later I really started to get interested and took to looking in books to find out more. Not having had any particular interests other than work, cars and girls up till then, it was like going back to school, this learning about something of which I knew nothing. The sum total of my reading in a year was twelve Readers Digests and one book that I took on holiday. We didn't have a daily newspaper then. Having found several flints one day in Kyre Parks, Grove Farm, I suddenly started to panic. The thought came that later on I would be ploughing the fields again and burying all the flints I had not yet found, never to be seen again. It was several days before I worked out that I had ploughed those fields many times before I found the first flint, so in theory, several years of ploughing and finding could pass when I would still be able to look for them.

In fact, it was about ten years of searching before they became a scarce find again. During these years I came across not only flints but many other things; occasional coins, bones, teeth, chunks of stone, several hundredweights of different-shaped stones, most of which I threw away again. Coming across new sites was wonderful, as these could be visited many times through the winter as the weather kept exposing more bits and pieces. There were a lot of disappointments over things I thought were something interesting, but were not. There is great pleasure to be had finding things, and like mushrooming, the more you look the more you find. One of the daunting parts was finding someone to identify what I had collected. It was Roger Pye who really helped at the start. He was coming to Netherwood in connection with tree planting that was taking place in the woods. He had, unbeknown to me, found a few flints at the back of the Old Piggeries. In my dinner hour he would look at some of my early flints and his enthusiasm gave me the momentum to find more flints and was something to fall back on when I felt I wasn't getting anywhere much.

The local museums were very helpful for small quantities, but when I dumped ½ cwt or so on their doorstep things stopped dead and years went by without my stuff being looked at. Also over the years staff would move on and I would have to get to know different people again. It was not until Mr Fendall at the Worcester Museum took pity on me and agreed to look at my collection in reasonable quantities over a period of several years that I felt I was getting somewhere at last. To begin with, not knowing anything about amateur archaeology, I stored the pottery and other items I was finding in plastic 1-cwt fertilizer bags, unwashed, each site kept separate with newspaper. I didn't look at any of it for about two years and in that time, some of the slips of paper with the different fields or sites written on had rotted away in the damp, so they had to be lumped together under the heading "Netherwood general". Some of the pottery also suffered somewhat. There were two items I remembered putting in the sacks but never found again when I came to wash it all. One was the bottom and part sides of a Roman cup from top Calves Hill site. When I found it there were five little shiny pebbles set in the bottom but they never came to light again. The other was a reddish pink bone from Fealds site, Grove Farm. I never saw that again either. There's a lot to be said for washing and drying finds as soon as possible.

At the height of my enthusiasm, when not working overtime, I would spend 55 minutes of my 1-hour lunch break traipsing muddy furrows in search of finds. Some of the more interesting pieces seemed to find me, rather than me

N. Turner

coming upon them. There was a pull or something that would cause me to go walking in a certain field and after having come across a find I would walk out of the field, no longer interested in looking. One of the two Elizabeth I coins caused me to go for several days running to a certain place until I came across it, but then I had no interest in looking there any more.

The first flint arrowhead I found was the most exciting thing I had ever come across. Its shape is visually pleasing. I came across it accidentally while loading the harrows on to a set of discs ready to move fields. It just sat there on the side where I was busy. I was not even thinking about finds at all, just concerned about getting to the next field. I gave a little jump for joy, carefully wrapped it in my handkerchief and was sneaking occasional looks at it for the rest of the day, just to make sure it was real. This was at the top of Old Roadway, Netherwood. Two arrowheads found me when I had to jump out of the tractor to do some adjustments to the tack on Pensons Farm. Each time I nearly jumped on them without knowing they were there until I hit the ground. At other times I retraced my steps back across a field because of a certain pull. It is as if I have seen something, but it has not registered, as if there are powers at work of which we are unaware.

This was the first year of my finding flints. I only found them in certain fields – others did not appear to even have a single one! "Ah," I thought, "at least I know where to concentrate my looking." But over the next few years this was not a good guide at all. Some of the first fields in which I found them turned out to be the least productive, and others which were barren for several years turned out in the end to be the most rewarding. Most of my field-walking was done in meal breaks as I was rather shy of being found mooching about the farm, except when I was working, so I kept a very low profile about what I was doing. I tended mostly to listen to people when in conversation, not being very good at talking about myself.

Horseshoes were difficult to keep. They tended to rust badly after being ploughed up. After years of dousing them in waste oil the writing on the labels I'd tied on them, to say where they were found, was spoilt, so that did not work very well.

What pleased me most was the variation and time range of the different archaeological finds, which made me feel very humble. I thought of the different people from years past who had lived in the valley, looked on similar sunsets, sunrises and moons and perhaps not very different to landscapes they had seen, as I had, especially in the evenings just before it gets dark, how everything is softened to just the outline of things. These thoughts make one person's life span seem very small indeed. I have often wondered how far my blood goes back, as, putting wars and plagues aside, people possibly never went far away from where they were born. There are five generations of my family who have not been far from the Netherwood area, so maybe some of the pottery may have been used by people in a direct blood line to me. Perhaps this goes some way to explaining the feelings and intuitions in my life.

November
6th   Swiping (or flailing) in woods (cutting briars and grass).

December
7th   Beautiful sunset, Hyde Farm.

8th   Smoke from chimney rising straight up into the sky.

11th   Meteorite (shooting star) going west to east 7.20 am. White turning to brilliant green, lasting five seconds.

12th   Ploughing. Blue tits peeping down stubble.

While ploughing the Middle Meadow at the Hyde, I was sitting in the cab having bait. It was a slightly frosty morning and being near the hedge I was watching the different birds going along it when, after a while, several dozen blue tits were near the stationary tractor. Some were brave enough to investigate the plough, looking into its nooks and crannies. Then many of them started doing something most endearing. The stubble that had been disced some time previously was lying at all sorts of crazy angles and having a coating of dew, the straws seemed to stand out extra clearly. The blue tits were standing on these short bits of straw and cocking their heads to one side, peering with one eye down inside the hollow stems and many were then getting some insect from inside. It was most entertaining watching them flitting from one piece of straw to another. I think what they were finding may have been spiders, for later in the day on a gentle westerly breeze, hundreds of gossamer spiders' threads were floating gracefully along at tree-top height in the pleasant sunshine. Many years before I had known that some spiders moved about in this way for I had been most puzzled one day going up Netherwood drive. It was where the telephone wires were on poles, above ground. These wires in the Roadside Meadows had what looked to me to be streamers of ragged light sticking up at right angles to the two wires, ranging from a few inches to over a foot, solid from one end of the field to the other. There must have been hundreds and thousands of spiders along these wires, as all those tiny thin streamers were touching to give the appearance of a solid block, the length of several telegraph poles distance. I suppose there must have been plenty for the blue tits to feed on if it was indeed spiders that were sheltering for the night in the stubble.

1972

January

The big tin barn at Netherwood burnt down. I think the cause was an electric fault setting nearby straw alight. Someone the other side of the valley noticed it first and rang up the foreman, who tore up Netherwood drive with his horn blowing, rousing the workers in the cottages. This was at night-time and the lowest temperature of the year and subsequently the one or two tractors not stored in the alleyway of the barn that was alight would not start in time to pull a tractor and van out of one of the entrances, as they were starting to ignite. As much of the stock as possible was let out, but many perished in the flames or had to be put down afterwards. The fire engines had difficulty in getting where they wanted to because of the icy conditions. There was a bit of an argument with the gritting lorry called to the scene because part of Netherwood drive was in one county, Worcestershire, and the rest of the drive in Herefordshire. I was living at Bishop's Frome then and knew nothing of what had happened that night, so went to work at my usual time. I started to feel uneasy when going through Collington, I kept catching glimpses of what seemed a reddish glow of some sort. When I got up by Netherwood Cottages I saw the red

119

glow of the hot tin roof which had twisted and partly collapsed. Most of the people had left the scene or were leaving. For a while I wandered around in a daze, unable to take in what had happened. The first job was to round up the stock that had been let out and hear the vet say which ones had to be slaughtered because of burns. The rest were shipped off to someone with room to house them till things got sorted out. Then came the task of buckraking the carcasses of animals that had burnt to death out of the yards in the barn to a large trench dug out by a contractor in the barn field where they were buried. Then generally clearing up. Most of the barn was sold as scrap. Bill Morris of Bromyard had some of the undamaged parts to put up as a shed for his coaches. The grain in the silo in the barn had been set alight and went on smouldering for days. I've hated the smell of burning grain ever since. The one thing that's still about is the glass, shattered from the heat, in what was the dairy, (Now the bait room and wash room.) With the barn gone the face of Netherwood was so altered that it is left to my memory to recall how things were. The firemen said that they thought it was one of the largest farm fires on record, destroying 3 spans and a lean-to with each span having 13 bays all joined together forming one roof! (200 ft x 150 ft approx).

12th   Pheasant shoot.

February
15th   Traying potatoes.

The potatoes that had been in or near the fire could not be guaranteed to grow, so a fresh batch was trayed so they'd go on chitting ready for planting.

March
19th   Flu (Bug).

20th   Discing.

April
1st   A bird that looks like a jay which hops?

Possibly seen False Oxslip. These have disappeared over the years. The last place where some used to grow was by the side of the little pond opposite the Grove Farm, where the frogs used to spawn. This pond was filled in and became part of the field not many years after Netherwood ceased to farm there. I and several other people were most upset about this. That is the trouble when farms keep changing hands, the new owners have no memories or feelings about their new home and so seem to have to make some change or do something to say "I'm the new owner". The farms that stop in the same families for generations suffer less from unnecessary change. When one is a long time at one place, humps and bumps and hollows become so implanted in the mind that they are removed much less often.

4th   Drilling corn.

6th   Rolling corn.

12th   Planting poplar trees. This was in fashion around now and some were planted for several years running in small patches of not very useful land. This generally went well, other than one patch at the bottom of Grove drive where we could not agree on the angle, spacings or which way to have the rows. After digging them up three times and one chap threatening to walk off, leaving us to it, the trees eventually got planted like an apple orchard. About this time, large acres of good farm land were being planted up in the area and seeming to threaten the very existence of farming as we know it. Corn was planted in strips between the rows of trees, but after 6 – 10 years a lot of trees in the locality were grubbed up before maturity and the land put back to its original use.

13th   Curlew with white rump?

18th   First swallow of the year.

20th   Many days are spent each spring rolling autumn planted corn. The smell of the bruised corn over the years has become very much a part of farming, which I am sad to see pass, but it may come round again as lots of things in farming seem to do. I was rolling Kyre Park field, Grove Farm today, stopping for a meal break on this sloping south-facing field, lying on my back amongst the not very high tender corn shoots. It always amazes me how much warmer it is when you reduce your height down to a few inches. It can be quite cold when standing upright, but when down to the height of things growing in the fields it is a totally different world. I have often seen a heat haze coming off a field when I have had an overcoat on whilst tractor driving.

There was a smattering of skylarks around, especially in Pea fields at the side of Netherwood drive and there were several in Kyre Parks field. One nearby flew vertically into the sky, singing nonstop as it went. There was no other distraction or noise so I watched and listened, lying there waiting for this bird to draw breath, but it never did. It went up still singing until it became a tiny speck in the sky, hanging there like a kestrel for a while, then made a quick descent, landing near where it had started. From start to finish this took three minutes, and during the whole time there was no break or falter in this delightful bird's singing. I have only ever found one nest; this was at the side of the lane in the Pea fields.

26th Cuckoo.

27th Muck spreading.

May
11th Rolling corn.

25th Silage.

June
5th   Our family holiday began today in Nolton Haven again. It was something
to measure my life against, a chance to stand back and look at things as an
observer, rather than trying to look at the way things seem from within. I have
been surprised at my unfeeling observance when on holiday, as I watch other
farm workers going about their jobs. Thoughts connected with holidays filled
a fair part of my time while chugging around fields on my own, how they had
been in the past and how they might be in the future, people met and others
observed. We had been there for several years. The caravans were on a cliff-
top then; you could see the sea from the window and keep an eye on the children
playing in the sand, building forts or wandering along looking in the rock
pools as the sea went out. When getting the milk, we would watch to see if

N. Turner

122

Mrs Canton would miss the bucket of water placed in the middle of the milking shed passage, when she slung the udder cloth into it from the far end of the shed. We met each year a family from up North, with their children. The husband went fishing and once gave us a freshly caught mackerel. That was the tastiest fish I have eaten. It was as I imagined the first trout I caught would have been, if the cat had not eaten it!

One day, a girl with 'Chelsea' printed on her T-shirt, riding a push bike, spent the evening and night in a tiny tent on the beach. On going down to the beach last thing before going to bed, the beach had only the girl and me on it, both savouring a little of the magic of the sea in the twilight. Everything was softened, the breeze warm and caressing, the waves gently washing the sand clean for tomorrow's dawn. Two people being a small part of things, each aware of the other; so much so that it was almost possible to reach out and physically touch ones feelings. No word was spoken, just two people caught up in one of nature's nicer times, each going our separate ways after this moment in time. Next morning she was away up the coast, leaving the thought of a vulnerable little tent and a pretty girl imprinted on my mind.

Ricket's Head, just up the coast towards Newgale, was climbable. This was O.K. when I went up with the children, but suddenly, when sitting at the bottom of this cliff, I saw my son David had climbed up without my being aware of what he was doing. Hearing his voice and seeing his head peering down from this shaley piece of headland, gave me a fright! During another holiday, while sitting near this rock, keeping an eye on the children playing amongst the large boulders on the shore one sunny afternoon, I had a feeling of great peace. For a little while, everything was bathed in light that was many times greater than a bright sunny day. This light did not dazzle or blind particularly, it just lit everything nearby so that there was nothing beyond a few hundred yards out to sea. What I normally saw out of the corners of my eye disappeared, so that I was left with just this scene of the children, a part of the sea, boulders, part of Ricket's Head, and the grassy shoreline going down to the water from where I was sitting, all in this bright light. There were no other people about, possibly if there had been, this would never have happened.

July

24th Rogueing (pulling out) wild oats from crops of cultivated corn. This was something I had never done until the Grove and Hyde Farms were part of Netherwood. It was done partly for good farming, but mainly as we were starting to grow cereals to be used for seed, rather than just for stock feed. It was mainly wild oats we pulled out. I had never noticed any before this year, but then I had never been really aware of what a wild oat was. The field in

123

question was the first of many over the coming years to be rogued. It was a small field in the Hyde Farm, Middle Meadow, Bullock field area. (Soon after Mr. Payne took over, as many as four fields were made into one.) The first little field we did was a joyful occasion as pretty well all the farm staff were there, even Mr. Worrell the shepherd, who was not normally involved with the arable side of things. Mr. Payne was in the middle of a straggly line of us walking the field. I don't think any of us had done this job before, so a lot of corny remarks were being bantered about, like whether there were any guns lined up behind yon hedge to pot off whatever we might flush out as we crackled our way through the two-crop field. This pulling out of wild oats by hand was, after a few years, standard practice in all the crops, as it proved a very successful method of keeping Netherwood clean. There was only one field up at the Grove that failed us. In the end we never bothered at all with it as the wild oats had become so well established. When I knew what wild oats were, and before we really got down on them, I watched, when combining, about five single wild oat plants multiply in three years to very significant patches. I worked out that unchecked, in about 7 years, they would have taken over half the field. I spent many evenings and weekends over the years helping to keep them in check.

26th Digging potatoes.

28th Planting mustard.

29th Rogueing corn.

August
2nd Combining.

16th Haymaking.

25th Baling.

September
7th Sub-soiling.

14th Topping potatoes.

20th Ploughing.

October
21st First time I've seen seagulls swimming on Netherwood Lakes.

29th Discing.

November
11th Yellow, grey and black head – blackcap sort of bird.

18th   Brown, owl-like bird with longish tail, seen in evening.

25th   Bird, colour like sparrow, dark brown head and neck, tail like a wagtail.

December
2nd   Sparrow-size bird, greenish-yellow, speckled brown breast.

9th   Fieldfare.

18th   Long tailed tits.

23rd   Wren with bar of gold side of head.

1033 Hours Overtime 1972.

1973

March
5th   Frog spawn was something I took for granted until the latter half of the
1970's. One year there was none at all on Netherwood Farms. In school years
it seemed to be everywhere, in the bits of ponds and boggy parts in fields, but
as farming progressed, draining and filling in wet areas, the spawning places
disappeared. The pond at the Grove, before it was filled in, was one of the only
places where I would guarantee to see frog spawn.
   It was at this pond that in school years we used to catch newts with worms
tied on the end of a piece of string. The newts would partly swallow the worm
and could then be pulled out and their pretty bellies admired. The frogs spawn
seem to be one of the first things to happen in spring. I've seen the spawn up
the Grove some years with a covering of ice after a hardish frost overnight.
Other times the pond has been flooded during heavy rain with the spawn
disappearing in the muddy brown water. We would sneak up to this pond
about spawning time and peek down by the bullrushes to see the first blobs.
Generally, there only seemed about 3 days a year when it was possible to hear
the frogs purring, when I got to the side of the pond and, keeping well back,
watched the dark top halves of the mating frogs. During the couple of years
when I never came across any, I had a conversation with a workmate who said
his children were still finding some from somewhere and bringing frog spawn
home in a jumper to watch it grow into baby frogs. This place was just over

Netherwood brook, at the bottom of far Sallybeds field, in Jones' the damson people's farm. For several years this was the only place where I was sure to find frog spawn. In a wet season, I have helped the water find a way to the brook by making a way for it with my foot, and in a dry time I have made little dams to keep the area from drying out and scooped mud out from under the blobs, so letting them down into what water there was. For several years I took some bits of spawn blobs home to the goldfish pond in the garden at Bishops Frome. Eventually frogs did spawn here, but the fish ate them as soon as they turned into tadpoles, so another small pond had to be made without any fish in. The Bishops Frome frogs seem always to spawn later than Netherwood ones. With the decline in the frog population was an almost parallel decline in the snakes at Netherwood. For a few years I could walk about without ever thinking about where I was stepping. At the time of writing this, the frogs and toads are getting established again as are the snakes.

(1993 – approx 1,000 blobs found on Netherwood Farm, in 20 years they have increased from less than a dozen blobs of frog spawn.)

11th   Black headed seagull.

14th   Peewits' nests have declined over the years on Netherwood and for several years I've not found any at all. Whether it is the change from mainly spring planting to nearly all autumn planted cereals that has contributed to their decline or the sprays and fertilizers, I do now know. Perhaps a mixture of both. About 15–20 years ago, there was a fair chance of finding a nest in several of the ploughed fields each year. We'd got the preserving of the many nests we came across to a fine art when working the fields in the spring. Initially we would work as close to the nest as possible, but leaving it untouched. This was fairly successful. The best method turned out to be to gather up the eggs, usually four, and a bit of the nest, which mostly was a few pieces of last year's stubble, move them over onto the land which was already worked or planted, then when the bout was finished, make a depression in the ground about where the nest was, and place the eggs and nesting material in it. Then keeping fingers crossed, we would keep an eye on it to see if the peewit returned to continue sitting, which nine times out of ten it did. It gave me great satisfaction to see the anxious bird walking hesitantly to where the new nest was and finally wriggle and settle back on the eggs. The biggest problem is seeing the eggs in the first place. It was alright if the bird was sitting well and flew straight up in front of the tractor. You knew then exactly where the nest was. Otherwise, if the peewits were flying about the general nesting area, it was often impossible to spot the nest at all as the camouflage was so good. The two fields with the most nests in were usually Top of Old Roadway and 40 Acres, Pensons.

(One year there was five nests in one corner of the 40 Acres,)

(1990's – Lucky to find one nest a year over the whole of Netherwood Farm where as there used to be at least a dozen.)

March 12th–**April** 2nd   Discing and harrowing every day.

March

15th   Primrose out.

16th   White violets out on Old Park Cottage site.

19th   Lots of starlings flying north in the mornings.

April

3rd   Rolling corn.

8th   Silage.

12th   Barn owl, Bank Street, on dusk.

15th   Bird, slate grey back, pinkish underneath, mistle thrush size, flying low along hedge, Hays Meadow, Grove Farm. Sparrowhawk – my first siting of one.

16th   Pair of kestrels. The first ones I saw nesting were in a broken off hollow limb of a beech tree by the side of Top of Old Roadway, a part called Grandstand Patch, from the days of Netherwood Races – Point to Point. This tree had initials and dates carved in it from when the races were held. It fell down a few years ago. It seems that there was a more varied selection of birds on Netherwood after most of the big woods were felled and replanted again with different species of trees. When ploughing, or grass cutting, a kestrel will often swoop down and grab a mouse that has been exposed, then return to a vantage point in a nearby tree. One year a kestrel, somewhat down on its uppers and very apologetic looking, took to eating worms that were being ploughed up. Kestrels have remained fairly constant since this date.

17th   Ploughing pheasant patches.

18th   Swallow.

22nd   Small greenish grey bird, grasshopper warbler.

24th   Spreading pig muck.

25th   Spreading fertilizer.

26th   Cuckoo.

27th   Rolling spring barley.

30th Bird with white rump and white edge to wings, blackbird size, sparrow colour, by lake, common sandpiper.

May
7th Small brown duck.

11th Scuffling potatoes.

12th Swift. First one.

14th Bird with white rump, grey blue black and head, dark round eyes, pinky brown breast. Wheatear? One, sometimes two, have for many years turned up when working land for spring planting. To see this distinctive bird on the freshly worked land looking for food was a sight to look forward to.

19th Moulding potatoes.

20th Seagulls floating on strong east wind.

June
2nd Rotavating spud headland.

5th Silage. Small grey-white bird, nest like a wren's on the floor in grass in the woods. Plaintive sound. Wood warbler.

15th Swiping.

23rd Holiday. Newgale, Wales. For several years we spent our holiday in a chalet belonging to Mr. and Mrs. Larcombe, relations on father's side who kept a shop there. This was O.K. as the charge was very reasonable and having found some flints in the cliff face at Penycwm, I liked to pick a few out each year, as the weathering kept exposing fresh ones. This was alright, as long as no-one was sunbathing down below, for they got very upset when bits of stone and soil that I dislodged showered down on their uncovered bodies. I took what I had found one year to the local museum. It seemed deserted, and after wandering about for a bit, I stood by a counter place and gave a few 'butler's' coughs. This produced a rather tousled, heavily breathing fellow from a door at the side. I started to show him what I had found, and then out came an attractive young lady, looking rather flushed, a bit of a smile on her face and apparently straightening her clothes. It seemed that I may have chosen the wrong moment to bring my finds in. For all that, he was very helpful, but said the person best able to help me was Jean. Someone who was not available at the time.

The first year we took the twins, they were fascinated by the soft wet sand, and would spend the time just poking their fingers in it, not wanting to be moved on any account. While keeping an eye on them one day, a well-dressed girl of about 21 came walking by. She had trousers, boots, and a three-quartered jacket and hair tucked under a wool hat. Being a sunny day with most people in swimsuits, I thought she was best suited to be walking through fashionable London. Later on, I saw a man pushing a bike with no seat, tyres, chain or pedals, and I said to myself, "You won't get anything worthwhile out of that by the time you've carted it home", thinking he'd fished it out the sea. Then I saw the girl again. By now she had taken her hat and boots off, rolled her trousers up a bit and by doing so, looked a couple of years younger. "That's better," I thought, "more in keeping with the seaside." Meanwhile, I had been idly watching a man and woman wandering about the rocks as the tide went out, seeming to find an interest in the seaweed or something. On coming round a large clump of rocks a little later on, I started to do a quick about turn, as the girl came into view again. "Gosh," I thought, "she's got no clothes on – must be in the act of changing into her swimming costume!" But before I had completely turned, I saw she had on a pale green bikini, so it was alright. Being interested in what the couple were doing on the rocks, I went over and watched for a bit, and getting into conversation with them, found they were collecting seaweed for larva bread.

Meanwhile, the bikini girl had come up and started helping with the seaweed collecting. I had not realised they were connected. Seeing this girl close up, I realised why I had thought she had nothing on. The bikini was transparent in certain light and position. This apparently 21-year-old, sophisticated girl who had walked onto the beach a while earlier, had now turned into a vulnerable, pretty 16-year-old Welsh girl, who was helping out in school holidays until going on to college or university. While helping her to fill and move the sacks of gathered seaweed, I learned that it was sometimes done with a covering of snow on the rocks in winter time. The hardest part apparently was getting all the sand out before the seaweed could be used for human consumption. The bike turned out to be for carting filled bags to a place a vehicle or pick-up van could reach, by putting the sack on the crossbar and pushing. The one vision or scene that stays in my mind, is of the girl shaking a bucketful of gathered seaweed into a sack and seeing the cheeks of her bottom through the transparent cloth, gently moving about in a relaxed and to my eyes, most pleasing manner.

July
9th   Silage.

10th   Swiping. This was cutting briars, grass and small trees along old pathways (rides) in the woods with tractor and swipe and creating new rides where possible. This took several days owing to the steep slopes and boggy areas. It was at times a rather hairy job. Lots of care had to be taken, otherwise when driving through undergrowth as high as the tractor, you would suddenly come to a halt, wheels spinning madly, either because of a wet hole or straddling a tree stub, which usually jammed under the tractor, stopping all movement backwards or forwards. Most of the rides were done with a tractor before safety frames came in. The first year I went swiping with a safety frame on, I was alright until going across a steep slope, through a narrow avenue of trees. I found I could not get where I normally did. The trees were growing upright and the tractor, being at an angle, caused the safety frame to wedge behind the tree trunks. Much heaving and levering was done before I was able to reach the end of the ride. This safety frame caused someone else a bit of bother as well, for over at the Hyde Farm there was a fairly low loft, built above sloping cattle pens. When spudding, after the muck had been cleaned out, we used to drive the tractor under this loft without any bother. This one chap, Tom Panniers, the first time we had the safety frame on, was used to going underneath; he had been doing it for years. The Dexta, being a nippy little tractor, was mostly driven about in top gear. So, only doing what he'd been doing for years, Tom tore under this loft, going in under the bottom side, where the gap was the greatest. He got about halfway through, when the top of the safety frame started to catch the floor joists. Going at such a speed, he was unable to stop in time, so ended up wedged underneath with the engine stalled. Unable to pull it back out with another tractor, the air had to be let out of the tyres before it would move at all!

Back to the woods and swiping!

There were two places in the woods that did not like me going into them swiping. One was Rabbitbury Coppice and the other was the far top corner of Netherwood wood, near to Hyde Hill. For years, each time I got to these parts of Netherwood, within the hour, I'd be limping back to the farm, something broken, bent, or fallen off. The first time, at Hyde Hill corner, was when there suddenly seemed to be a lot of water about. "Didn't think it was this wet," I said to myself. Pressing on, avoiding branches, briars and flying sticks, it was not until the tractor seemed a bit lop-sided, that I found what had happened. A stick had ripped the valve off the tyre, letting the air and water ballast out. Unable to get another tractor up to where I was, I had to back all the way out again, so as to keep the flat tyre on the highest side. The next year, same place, the front wheel fell off. The stub axle had sheared. The same problem. How to get back to the farm on level ground. After a bit of head scratching, I found all the rotten stumps and bits of logs from around and about, piled them on the swipe, until it was heavier than the front of the tractor. Then, using the hydraulics and steering brakes, I made my way back to the farm on three wheels – much to the amusement of my work-mates.

The next time I did not get such a direct hint to keep away from that neck of the woods. What happens is that on steep ground, unless the oil in the back end of the tractor is slightly above level mark, the hydraulics will not lift the swipe right up, so with the combination of sideland ground and plenty of oil, the seals let the oil through onto the brake linings. This means the brakes never work at all, so when it happened I had to make sure I was in the right gear before getting anywhere near a hill or obstacle, and I was able to finish the day off like this. I told the foreman about the lack of brakes and parked it in the shed, swipe taken off ready to put on another tractor. Next morning, as we were going about our various jobs, Tom Panniers, the stockman, was on his way down to the diesel tank to fill up before going round his cattle, and out around the farm. As he was going down the gaffer, Mr. Payne, walked by, "Mornin' boss," said Tom, "lovely day." Mr. Payne smiled, "Good morning," nodded in agreement as to the nice morning, which it was, for about a second and a half, then came an almighty crash. Tom had jumped on the Dexta with the oil on the brakes. He must have been the only one on the farm who had not been told. It was downhill to the diesel tank, and when the brakes were applied, Tom just kept on going straight into a large electrical junction box, where the underground cable branches off to the various buildings. The result was a mangled junction box, dented tractor, bewildered Tom, thinking that the nice morning had been short-lived. Gaffer looked irate, no doubt thinking unkind thoughts about "tractor drivers." After this I stopped swiping up the far corner of Netherwood wood, leaving it in peace.

The junction box was to feature in something else a year or so later. I was digging a trench with a mechanical digger, between the bait room and piggery site. It was in preparation for a new farrowing house. After a short while, I cut through an underground electric cable. Having had this cable leaking at some time or other, by the handling pens that had made the stock a bit jumpy, I knew where we used to switch it off. So I sent my work-mate down to do this. When he came back, nodding his head, I got down in the trench and had a look at the damage. Parting the ends of the cables with my bare hands, I then got a spade and started to clean around better, when all of a sudden, the spade disappeared! Looking at my empty hands and the spade a few yards away and me rather dazed, I went over and picked it up. Seeing the bent twisted metal end, I turned on my mate and started to cuss him in some form, saying he had not switched the right box off. He said he had, so I walked down and had a look, and found he had indeed switched the right one off. Thinking something in the fuse box had come adrift, I took the cover off and had a look. What had happened was that after the farm fire a lot of electrical work had been done, and unbeknown to us, the switch-off point had been moved down to the box by the diesel tank. The cable, when we looked closer, went behind the box we had switched off, but was not now connected to it in any way. All that had saved me down in

131

the trench, when I was handling live wiring, was the fact I had on wellingtons and a rubber mac!

The other area that disliked me, Rabbitbury Coppice, had it in for tractor exhausts three years in succession. Each time I shamefacedly went back to the farm, making a horrible noise, with silencers broken or missing. The fourth year I told myself, I would take extra care. Any bough that looked as if it might swoop down and have a fight with the tractor exhaust, I would chop off or avoid altogether. In my care over watching things head height, I subsequently shot off at an angle, down a fallen tree and poked a stick through the radiator! The next year, I decided to go downhill, where I normally went up. This would save half an hour or so instead of going a long way round to get to a point not many yards away. All went well until I came to a sharp turn. I knew I was not going to make it long before getting there, but there was nothing I could do. With the one wheel locked and steering hard round, I went straight into a tree, half thrown over the bonnet on impact. With this came a cloud of steam from the crumpled radiator and the noise of the fan blades, catching parts that had been pushed out of true. After lots of digging and levering, I got myself out and made yet another unscheduled journey back to the workshop. I was beginning to lose my enthusiasm for this job. I had worked it out that it was the hardest job in farming for me with the mental strain of keeping a map in my head of all the places where I could and could not go in the woods on Netherwood, Hyde, Pensons and Grove Farms. All this, combined with the physical side of constantly trying to stop a tractor from taking the shortest way down to level ground, plus the hostility of some of the woods to my presence there each year, made me decide from then on to ease back a bit. Anyway, the plantations had grown up to the extent that they largely kept themselves free of undergrowth. Amongst all the aggro of this job, there were better moments of seeing butterflies and birds' nests which I would not normally come across, and once seeing two fox cubs playing in the Jones Brothers, Freeth Farm, mowing grass. This grass gave me pleasure to walk through; it never grew too high and was full of all sorts of flowers, rattle grasses and what have you, like the mowing fields of my school days. The hay that was made from these fields smelt so nice that I often fancied having a bale in the porch at home, just to sniff at occasionally. It seemed to trigger off something in me that perhaps has been passed down through generations of people connected with the farming countryside.

16th   Potatoes.

29th   Mustard planting.

30th   Hospital. Face operation. Hereford County Hospital. This came about

132

because a large freckle started to grow and swell up. For a couple of years my sister, who is a nurse, had been saying I should go and have it looked at. I had never got round to it. It was something that never bothered me. One chap at work thought it was from me getting oil on my hands in a morning and somehow getting it on my face. I finally went to the doctor, who sent me to the hospital to see a specialist. I had partly worked out that by going at this time of the year, if anything had to be done, it would be around winter time before I would need time off work. I was wrong, for the hospital put a letter in the post saying they wanted me in Hereford on the next Monday morning. This gave me just 2 days, so I did not have much time to think about it. I was not in hospital long before I was operated on. Owing to the nature of the operation, they took some skin from behind my ear and stitched it in the place where the freckle had been. This meant that my head was swathed in bandages with a bit of hair sticking out the top, which caused one of the nurses to refer to me as "Turnip top." Having my head so covered made me very hot and I spent the first couple of days with very little on in the way of clothes. It took me a long time to come round after the operation. The chap in the next bed, who went in after me, had come round, had a meal and was as right as rain long before me. One supper time later on that week, the nurse was asking what we would have to drink. Whether I did not like the choice, or had been thinking of something else and just happened to be looking her way, she broke off in mid-sentence and said in a most agitated fashion "DON'T YOU DARE LOOK AT ME THAT WAY." I still wonder what she had interpreted from the look in my eyes!

The chap in the next bed was from a farm as well. A log had flown up off the saw bench, knocking one of his cheek bones in. Being normally active people, we behaved rather like caged animals, wandering about a lot. It was alright at the start, going down by the nurses' quarters and having things shouted at us, and on down to the far end of the grounds. We made the mistake of then taking walks out towards town. This was past Matron's office, so on getting back to the ward we were firmly told that the Matron was not having us wandering around in pyjamas and dressing gowns. We then confined ourselves to watching the rabbits coming out from under the hospital building, nibbling the nice short mown grass and occasionally varying their diet by having a go at the rose bushes.

By the time I went back to work, harvesting had started and the gaffer was driving the combine that I normally used. He would not let me do any for at least a week, partly perhaps because the dust mask I wore came where the operation scar was. He managed to cope with both the drying side and driving the one combine before I got back into things. I felt an outsider watching someone doing the job I normally did. We never grew oats again after that year. The gaffer had had to combine some badly laid fields of oats while I was out of action but whether this had any bearing on why he went out of them, goodness knows.

August
24th   Combining.

September
5th   Finished combining.

6th   Discing.

17th   Potatoes.

23rd   Ploughing. (Grey brown, large, sparrow size bird, white rump with black tips to tail).

30th   Kingfisher, Collington Lake – single cheep sound. Dived into the water. This was the first kingfisher I had seen since schooldays, when one used to perch on a bit of tree by the bridge at The Knowle. After a couple of years I used to see one along Kyre brook on Grove Farm. One summer, about this time, something unpleasant must have got into the stream opposite Kyre School, because I saw several fair-sized dead fish by the bridge up to the Grove. I had heard talk that there were fish in the brook, but always took it with a pinch of salt, as I had never seen one myself. I only hope that there are fish back again now.

After that I never saw kingfishers for several years, but one was sighted again up at Collington Lake in 1986. Also in 1989 one has been seen on Park Lake, and small fish in a pond by Netherwood buildings.

October
3rd   Swallows still here.

5th   Swallows gone.

7th   First mink seen by me on Netherwood Brook, bottom of Castle field. This is the first wild mink I have seen on Netherwood. I was having tea under a sloping, knarled oak at the bottom of Castle field, my feet more or less in the brook, reclining with my one elbow in the little patch of dry soil at the base of the tree that the pheasants used for rusling in. On seeing this black shape, I thought "That's a funny looking rat." Then I noticed its tail was different. I'd only once seen a proper water rat, in my early days at Netherwood over at Tee Baune Lake, and it was quite a pleasant looking fellow compared to the rats around the farm buildings. This thing was definitely not one of those either. On getting home that night, I looked it up in a book and found what it was – a mink. In a few years they had spread up to Netherwood Lake where several

134

were caught. When we farmed the Hyde, they were up Perry Wood brook. Collington pool has them now, and I have seen one on and off up Netherwood brook since that first sighting. They are quite brave animals which do not seem to take much notice of people. In 1987, I watched one diving in the swollen brook, stop under water a minute at a time and often coming back out at the same place where it had submerged.

14th   Sub-soiling.

18th   First snow on Clee Hill.

25th   Thousands of spiders floating by on their home-made kites and thousands more spinning veils over the recently ploughed furrows.

27th   This October morning, I ploughed the Quarry field, Hyde Farm. It was a misty morning with the first hard frost of the year. Some of the leaves were changing colour, but not many had fallen. Stopped for bait at about 9.00 am by the side of Perry Wood and leaving the cab, with overcoat and woolly hat on and sack to sit on, I went and parked myself just by the edge of the wood, amongst last year's beech leaves. (Once, while lying under these beeches and looking up at the small patch of sky coming through the tops that curved towards one another, I thought how similar this was to standing in a cathedral and looking up at the graceful columns and arches). Having had my two sandwiches, slice of cake and flask of tea, I lay down on my back to have ten minutes nap. The sun had not yet come out properly, there was no movement of air, so it did not feel as cold as it might have been. Having had years of practice at snoozing, I was in the land of dreams very quickly. Just before normal waking time, I became aware of something disturbing the dead crisp beech leaves. "That's a heavy-footed pheasant," I thought, as in the stillness of the woods some sounds come through extra clear. The footsteps seemed rather uneven, then started to quicken in pace, causing me to open my eyes and sit up abruptly, wondering what on earth was going on. While I'd been asleep, the sun had come out properly and was catching the trees in this top semi-circular part of the field. The leaves on the not very tall hedgerow trees at the edge of the wood, were covered in frost, making them stiff and heavy. The sudden warmth and slight movement of air coming out of the awakening steep dingle, was causing the leaves to come crashing down in ever quickening succession. To see these many coloured leaves from elm, a willow type tree, hazel, elderberry and ash, covered in ice, reflecting the light as the frozen stems let go, was to me a remarkable occurrence. From start to finish it was not more than a minute.

28th   Stoat (or weasel?) on the scent of a young rabbit, this rabbit eventually took refuge in the fresh disced land at Collington's.

Most leaves still on the trees, just turning colour.

November

27th   Thrush-like bird, reddish breast – fieldfare or redwing.

30th   Hundreds of peewits with frost on their backs – some lasting all day. Forty Acres, Pensons. When ploughing in winter time for a month and a half from December to January for seven days a week, weather permitting, the birds get to know where they can get an easy meal, especially when the ground is frozen. These are flocks of rooks, crows and jackdaws, seagulls and, a little more shy, the peewits. When seeing the peewits land on the stubble or when ploughing, I am reminded of the kestrels. Both birds, when touching down, one on the land, the other in a tree, do so in such a way that it is impossible to tell when their feet actually make contact, it is just one graceful movement from flying to stationary; unlike the rooks; when they land I can almost feel the ground shake. This frosty, foggy, winter's day was fairly dry. The surface of the field I was ploughing was also fairly dry and crumbling with no ruts, so I was able to carry on even though it had been a hardish frost during the night. By middle morning, the fog had not yet lifted and the windows in the cab were constantly misting over. Only the one at the front was kept clear by the heat from the exhaust. No birds were feeding yet on the fresh turned furrows. On and off for most of the morning, I had kept seeing some movement out the corner of my eye but had not taken much notice, thinking the movement of the tracks was the cause. I stopped for dinner at 1 o'clock, halfway up a bout of ploughing with the plough still in the ground. Over the years I had found that it was best not to sit in the seat for mealtimes, unless I put the crawler and plough at right angles to the furrow, for with everything in the working position, part way through eating and just as I was starting to relax a bit, one hand or the other, would suddenly make a dive for the steering levers quite of their own accord. This would make me jump, cup of tea or sandwich being lost in the process. I suppose it is a hangover from ploughing at nights, when one is trying to fight off sleep, and sometimes getting to the stage when in the state between wakefulness and sleep movements become jerky and erratic. Getting fed up with disturbed meal breaks, I found that by sitting crossways in the cab, things were much better. Not having a heater in the cab, it was usually rather cold, unless the sun was shining on the glass, so I sat in an overcoat and jerkin, with woolly hat on my head, and for the winter months another safety-pinned over my right knee. There must have been a draught from somewhere, for after about 5 years driving the crawler, the knee had become very sensitive. The extra hat made all the difference. A small patch of ice would form in the cab roof above my head in cold weather. When this melted, I knew it was possible to remove my overcoat.

136

During this particular meal break in the 40 Acres, the sun eventually broke through, clearing the fog. I was curious to see how much of a bend I had got in the ploughing, for I had not been able to see one end of the field from the other, so I cleaned the condensation from the windows. This action caused a few birds to fly up. "Ah, peewits," I said to myself, "that's what's been catching the corner of my eye all morning." As the plough got near them, they would move over a little. "Nice to know there's one or two keeping me company," I thought. On gazing out across the frozen stubble, I found it was not one or two, but hundreds of them. I had stopped smack bang at their night-time resting place. The ones that had flown up from near the crawler had left little patches of unfrozen ground. No wonder I had not seen them before, because until they moved their camouflage was so good, with the patches of frost on their backs, that they blended in very well indeed with the surroundings. The insulation of the peewits' feathers was so effective that at about half past 3 o'clock when it started to get foggy again, a good many of the birds still had patches of frost on the feathers between their shoulder blades. It was marvellous being so close to so many of these normally shy birds. They did not bother to feed this day, nor did any other birds that normally came in large numbers. The freezing fog must have put them off.

Sadly, this joyous occasion was to be turned into one of sorrow. The fog next morning cleared early, leaving a sunny day. When I continued ploughing, the birds, starved from yesterday, were jostling with each other for a while, until each had taken the edge off their appetites. Rooks, crows, jackdaws, seagulls and peewits were all mixed up. When things settled down, crows were one end, seagulls in the middle, and peewits t'other end. Being more hungry than normal, the peewits were taking no notice of me, gobbling worms just a foot or so away from the crawler tracks, looking like people who were eating with their arms tied behind their backs. Never having been so close to so many before, I was watching one that appeared to have only one leg. It looked a healthy bird nonetheless. Thinking, "Poor thing," I started looking closely at the others. The more I looked the sadder I became. Among the 200 or so peewits, only about a dozen had two good legs and feet. All the rest had some deformity, just like leprosy or as if they had stood in acid and it had eaten various parts away. Some had one good foot and a stump the other. Most just had a blob a bit bigger than the leg itself where the foot normally was. One had just one leg with a blob a bit below its knee. This bird could not walk or stand so had to use its wings all the time and in the process of getting worms from the moist furrows, was getting in a sorry state with mud starting to build up on its wing tips. Whether the birds had been like this from birth, goodness knows, anyway most seemed to be coping alright in spite of their afflictions.

137

December
3rd   Nut tree still with green leaves.

1117 Hours Overtime 1973

1974

February
22nd Frogs getting ready to spawn, nice purring sound.

March
22nd Discing.

25th First butterfly.

26th Skylark, floating down to earth singing, wings outstretched.

27th Shoveller ducks on Tee Baune Lake.

30th First wild bee.

April
1st   Three little rabbits in ploughed field.

4th   Lime-green-yellow brimstone butterfly, Perry Wood.

6th   Discing and harrowing.

15th First swallow.

20th Cuckoo.

21st Nice smell from poplar catkins in Far Sallybed.

26th Finished corn planting.

29th Mist on fresh planted field.

30th Rolling corn.

May
1st   Saw two cuckoos, Netherwood Lake.

4th   Oak leaves out before ash.

Oak before Ash, we're in for a splash
Ash before Oak, we're in for a soak

5th   Bird size of a house sparrow, black/white head, white feathers in tail. Reed bunting? Tree sparrow?

13th   Bees. Top Calves Hill in ash tree, with orange bags on legs; some with yellow bags on legs; some with nothing on legs.

19th   Flint arrowheads.

28th   Silage.

June
5th   Flu.

13th   Swiping rides.

July
16th   Potatoes.

26th   Planting mustard.

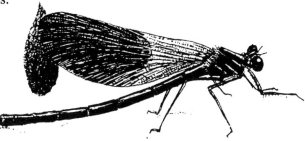
Damselfly – *N. Turner*

August
2nd   Discing.

13th   Combining.

September
4th   Ploughing.

8th   Lots of daddy-longlegs.

10th   Kingfisher and dragonfly, Grove Lake.

22nd   Small brown duck that keeps diving. Tufted duck? Netherwood Lake.

23rd   Ploughed in mustard. Swallows perched on fresh turned furrows.

24th   Rolling grass seed.

29th   Bird like a sparrow with bar side of head, badgerlike, whinchat?

October
13th   Pheasant among red leaves of cherry tree in sunshine, very pretty.

21st   Moving corn.

November
2nd   Sub-soiling.

10th   Sunrise – the sky reflecting autumn colours. A beautiful morning with only sounds of nature.

24th Trees good for having a nap against, especially those with big roots; like an armchair.

December

1st Squirrel's dray in holly tree.

8th Start of winter ploughing.

15th Evening trees, top of Calves Hill, silhouetted against clean sky, topped with pink-red clouds.

21st Crows and jackdaws flying north east as dawn breaks, returning at 4.15 pm from the south west, in long straggly line, to roost around Wall Hills camp area. Jackdaws, crows and rooks. I've grown very fond of these birds over the years; they belong to the area as people do and have to take the rough with the smooth. They come back home to roost each evening in winter time. The rooks nest together in their rookery. The crows and jackdaws spread out for spring and summer nesting and keep in the background of things then. I find it most endearing when the jackdaws pair up in late winter and several pairs sit in the branches of a tree with only one nesting hole. This used to happen at The Knowle before the hollow apple trees fell or were cut down. The straggly long line of these birds in winter, going and coming each dawn and dark, becomes a precious sight over the years, especially after not noticing them for a couple of seasons, perhaps because I was not in the right place at the right time. To hear their chatter out of sight somewhere on Netherwood on a cold foggy winter's day is comforting. I can quite understand how ravens became a part of the Tower of London. Seagulls and some of the other birds are not loyal at all, coming and going when it suits them. Although I like to see them, the feelings they evoke are not the same.

A pair of crows nest each year in an oak tree, top Old Roadway, near the small pond. It is a very windy place with a good view. To see them plonk down for a meal just under their tree when I am working the field seems the proper way of things. But farmers look on them differently and today returning to this field, I found dead bodies of these crows under the tree where they had been nesting. They had been blasted with a 12-bore shotgun. Several times over the years this has happened to things I have become attached to. A gnarled old pollarded elm tree at the top of Hyde Hill, (that reminded me of the trees that looked like people's faces in children's picture books) was cut down. Also an ash tree which housed a swarm of wild bees. They were cut out, and put into a hive. It hurt me for years afterwards to see this disfigured tree, empty and sad, on the skyline. When ploughing the Parks in winter time up towards the Freeth Farm, silver birch trees without leaves against the evening sky, took on the shapes of dodo birds. They were cut down one winter for no apparent reason.

I was getting to the stage of making a point of not liking anything in case it disappeared. The selling of the historic part of Netherwood Manor hurt me, as did the closing of the footpaths on Netherwood. I don't suppose the then farmer even thought that anyone would be attached to any of these things. On the other hand it could be said he had done good things which balanced out, like planting up a lot of the woods and making lakes, that brought us many different birds.

Pied wagtails: The resident pied wagtails are very loyal to the ploughing. There are always about half a dozen of them, though several years ago, there were about 50 one autumn in Collington's. When ploughing daily for a month at a time, the wagtails fly up and down the field with the crawler and plough, flying as if suspended on a piece of elastic. They hang around in the mornings when I am greasing and filling up. At meal times they walk about on the cab roof with their muddy feet as if to say "What have you stopped for?" They get so full from eating the tiny grubs, that after rushing to pick one out of the furrow, they often stop after getting it in their beaks, hang their heads and drop it down again, tummy unable to cope with any more. It gets to the stage that whenever the crawler is moving, the wagtails expect the ground to be ploughed over. While moving from one field to another, going along a stone roadway, the birds will land a few yards behind, look sideways down at the ground, then up at me and then back again to the stones, just like humans when they think a thing's being done wrong. Pied wagtails are the most happy-go-lucky birds I've come across.

I grew up in the days when boys didn't wear pants, they were things only girls used. After we were married, it was thought that I should start wearing some, but habits of a lifetime die hard. I waited till winter time and one cold Monday morning went to work with a pair on. After 3½ hours, that was it, I'd had enough. Overcoat off, trousers off, pants off and up till now I've never tried the things again. I started off again . . .

22nd Flocks of chaffinches about. Two hares following each other in the dusk at 4.30 pm, Collington fields.

23rd Sunny spring-like day; even the skylark tried a few notes. Greeny coloured wren – grasshopper warbler? But wrong time of year.

25th Strong winds most of the month.

27th Rainbow around the moon for a few minutes at 5 pm.

28th Lots of mice in ploughed fields.

1077 Hours Overtime 1974

1975

January

1st   Ploughing. Bramblings.

2nd   First peewit.

3rd   Beautiful early morning sky with clouds of varied colours, no wind, mild, birds singing, foxes barking – it was like spring.

5th   I ploughed up acorns in the middle of the fields, I wonder what carried them there?

12th   First wild primrose out.

14th   Spiders web tunnel below surface of water in Collington Lake, leading into roots of grass with enticing-looking entrance.

16th   Blue tits at bait time, hunting for food, peering down into the stubble. Very entertaining.

20th   Still ploughing. Birds like geese in beautiful 'V' formation were flying south – 26 of them.

21st   Lots of crows, rooks and jackdaws. I would be sad without them.

22nd   Wild white violets out, Grove Lane.

23rd   White shape of barn owl, Grove Farm. While ploughing Turnpike field, after tea this moonlight night, the barn owl from Grove buildings came hunting once down the verges at the side of the lane towards Kyre brook. I had seen it do this several times before. This particular night was near full moon and very clear. After a while, the barn owl came back along the brookside working its way along the rough grassy bank that rose steeply up to where I was working. The lights and noise of the crawler did not seem to put it off at all. As I turned, at the same time the white ghostly shape became stationary in mid-air, hovering a few feet above a patch of rough grass on an updraught of air in clear, beautiful moonlight. I had not seen a barn owl do this before. The fresh westerly wind was hitting the steep slope up from the brook and the owl, like a kestrel, seemed to hang there motionless, 10 – 15 feet above the ground. It was still in the same position when I dropped the plough in to go back up the field – so, leaving the engine running and lights on, I sat in the warm cab looking at and savouring the scene. Time stood still for a while as I watched broken clouds rushing across the sky, the bleached dead grass stalks waving about in the wind, the outline of Kyre School in the background and, the centre of

142

attention, the barn owl, a vibrant living thing spanning the time between daylight and darkness.

24th Kestrel – hunting in strong wind, keeping same height and forward position.

28th Finish winter ploughing.

30th Frog crossing the road on the way to work at Batchfields.

March
19th Frog spawn.

20th Discing and harrowing.

April
25th Cuckoo.

26th Grove Farm. Bird singing like an elf tapping rapidly on a glass anvil – grasshopper warbler?

27th Trees burst into leaf in matter of hours.

May
2nd Ash and oak came out into leaf on the same day.

3rd Harrowed over and killed two baby hares, causing me to weep in frustration at having done this.

4th Rolling corn.

7th Fertilizer spreading.

9th Rolling spring barley.

14th Chipped a nice piece of worked flint by dropping it on tiled floor.

19th Working and planting pheasant patches. They were small bits of land in the woods about ten at one time, planted up with barley, kale, maize and, for a year or two, a mixture of seeds that provided cover and food for the pheasants. Part of this mixture was sunflowers and to come across these in full bloom in the woods was quite startling, a complete contrast to the natural surroundings. Once when the gaffer, Mr. Payne, was fiddling seed on one of these patches, the bow of the fiddle jammed in the tractor wheel and snapped in half. I only wish I could remember the words the gaffer used when this happened. They impressed me greatly, summing up the situation and feelings most accurately. What I marvelled at, was that not one swear word was used in this torrent of abuse.

143

June

4th   Swiping rides.

28th   Thornbury Fete at Netherwood House.

July

3rd   Bales.

13th   Perpetual motion. This is the only time I have noticed it in nature. Going into the wood at the top of Coverfield, I sat amongst the young red oaks that had been planted here, to have a meal break. It was a calm still day, and a dead leaf, suspended on the end of a long slender twig through a hole slightly off-centre caught my eye, being the only leaf moving at the time. The action of the leaf moving from side to side in a twisting fashion, caused the twig to move up and down slightly. The action of one upon another kept things swinging non-stop for half an hour or more. During that time, it never altered pace at all. It was quite strange going back to work, leaving this solitary leaf, on its own, swinging away.

21st   Potatoes.

August

7th   Combining.

15th   Silage.

24th   Finish combining.

30th   Rolling grass seed.

September

1st   Discing.

13th   Ploughing.

16th   Badger crossing road, Summer Pool.

21st   Swallows still here.

25st   First heavy rain since summer.

26th   David Brooks left.

29th   Few swallows still left.

October

5th   Ploughing.

10th   Sub-soiling.

14th   Bees on ivy flowers in the sunshine. I had never seen so may bees before on ivy, humming with noise and activity.

20th   Autumn colours in the hedgerows. These were at their best along the road from Bishops Frome/Munderfield, in the last half mile before the main Bromyard/Hereford road. The hedges had not yet been trimmed and the leaves were still on, in vivid contrasting colours. Often one farmer on one side of the road will cut his hedge, the other not, so the balance is gone; but just this once the colours worked together, and I felt as if I was driving between a pair of twisting multi-coloured caterpillars as the morning sun shone on the dewy hedgerows. It was about this time that I started to experience the hazards of working long hours on my own always accompanied by noise, vibrations, dust, heat, fumes and pressures just to please other people – parents, gaffer, wife. Human nature seems always to worry about something, even if only whether to wear socks for one day or one week. With a fairly big worry, the general day to day living is hardly noticed. When working 7 days a week, 12 – 14 hours a day, for a month or so at a time, there isn't much time for anything other than sleep, so there is no problem as to what one does outside work! An advantage in one respect!

December
1st   Bird like kestrel, smaller and browner, flying close to the ground.

3rd   Startling sunset. All that was seen of the sun all day was when it shone on the west-facing tip of the valley, bathing it in brilliant orange-red. The sun at that time out of view behind the other valley ridge.

7th   Lime green sky between the clouds. A brand new moon. Trees on the skyline very clear and sharp. I blew the moon a kiss in appreciation of this scene.

1096 Hours Overtime 1975

145

1976

Year of the summer heatwave.

March

2nd   Rolling corn, winter wheat.

5th   Spreading fertilizer.

6th   Discing and harrowing. First primrose. First baby hare.

10th   Along Grove Sling brook, wild duck, heron, moorhen, kingfisher, grey wagtail, barn owl.

29th   Watched kestrels mating.

April
1st   Elizabeth I coin 1569, found in Barn field.

20th   Rolling spring barley.

24th   Rotavating pheasant patches.

26th   Cuckoo. No frog spawn found by me this year.

28th   Swallow.

May
2nd   Swifts.

16th   Swiping rides.

21st   Silage.

23rd   Robin-size nest or smaller, made of grass and dried nettles; eggs whitish covered with light brown speckles and black spots at large end of egg. Deep in long grass and nettles in conifer wood.

31st   Bullfinch's nest on conifer tree.

June
2nd   Tennis elbow injection.

6th   May flies hatching out from pieces of stuff floating just under the surface of the water at Netherwood brook bottom, near Salleybeds. Five or six grey mice with white bellies playing in the brook, same place, with flat roundish noses catching the emerging May flies. Water voles.

7th   Netherwood Lake. Small blackish duck with red-brown head. Pochard. Holly Blue butterfly.

13th   Red Admiral butterfly.

14th   Three or four mice like creatures climbing trees, top corner Netherwood wood, against Hyde Farm, with long tails same width along whole length, blunt-ended. Dormouse.

July

3rd   96°F in the shade, 115°F in the sun. Hot days bring swimming to mind. Over the years Mr. Payne re-dammed two lakes, and jointly, with Mr. Edwards, created one, and then a smaller one below the reservoir called Peter Rabbit Pool. The two redammed were Park Lake and Tee Baune Lake. The bottom one now belongs to the Hyde Farm. The joint one made over at Collington Meadows, later went into the ownership of Mr. Edwards, Underhill Farm, with Netherwood retaining shooting rights. When this lake was created, the stone bridge over the brook was at the bottom of the new lake and the right of way now goes over the dam. Les, who worked for T. J. Read of Hereford, with a Taskavator, was one of the main people in the making of these new dams. Beside the pleasure of helping build them, carting trailer-loads of soil back and forth, I have, over the years, had many pleasant dinner hours swimming in the wake of these clean new areas of water.

For the first couple of years of their life, the lakes were relatively free from weeds and seemed to warm up better. Whenever working and weather permitted, one would have a dip, usually without a bathing costume, as most people on the farm went home to dinner. The chance of getting caught with no clothes on was a bit remote and there is a certain pleasure to be had from swimming naked, an added freedom and closeness to nature. If I was feeling extra modest, I would use my pullover as trunks. This was not all that successful because two legs didn't fill three holes and when wet, the pullover did stretch rather. It was a rare feeling I got from lying on my back in the middle of the lake, with the sun beating down, just moving an arm or a leg occasionally to keep myself afloat, with no people about, and just my mouth, nose and eyes above water, not a ripple disturbing the surface and no sounds as my ears were submerged. Closing my eyes for several minutes, all sense of direction was soon lost, the sun shining warm on my face and body the only connection with Mother Earth, the world that I experienced. Time itself ceased to exist, like being in a mother's womb.

The lakes are not always an even temperature. When swimming from one end to the other, an occasional cold patch will be encountered. When the water is calm and the sun shining, swimming along without disturbing the surface, with just my nose out enough to breathe and eyes almost at water level, I could see thousands of tiny flies spreading over most of the lake. After the swim, drying was done with my handkerchief and the sun finished off the job. I did once make the mistake of taking a dip when potato picking was in progress in the Parks adjoining. I wore my pullover on this occasion, but it was next to useless, being old and thinly woven, and stretching down to my knees after I'd been swimming a while. Being a very hot day, three of the 15/17-year-old girls who were picking on the farm, came down to the lake to cool off, which made me feel rather hot, for, to be able to reach my clothes, I would have to climb out in full view of them. The spare hole in my makeshift trunks showed rather a lot of what is normally kept out of sight. Putting off the moment of emergence, I just kept swimming around. The girls, not satisfied with just paddling about up to their knees in the water, and perhaps encouraged by the sight of me swimming, decided to do likewise, going in just as they were, clad in T-shirts, shorts, blouses, trousers, bra and pants. While they were thus occupied, I got out quickly and proceeded to dry myself the best I could and get back into my trousers, while trying to hide behind 6" high grass. What stuck in my mind about this incident, was when I was dressing I could hear and see the girls frolicking about at the edge of the water, one of them saying, "Ooooo . . . it's lovely," as she splashed the cool water on her sun-warmed thighs. How many thousands of times this sort of scene must have been enacted going back through the centuries!

Even when not swimming, it is good to sit at the lake's edge as the mere presence of the water has a calming effect on body and mind. For several years in two of the lakes, I would spend dinner-time tossing little bits of my sandwiches to the occasional hungry trout which could be enticed right up to the water's edge, "swimming" on its side in an effort to get the tasty bread from the shallow water.

The lakes seem to be a place where people go for pleasure but also when things are not going well. A young girl, very conscious of her long legs, would, when meeting me, stand behind her companion, tugging down her short skirt, trying to hide her long thighs. Another time when they were were sitting on a tree stump, I was walking towards them. I was both amused and embarrassed for as soon as she saw me coming, she arranged and rearranged the position of her legs and skirt at least half a dozen times before I got to them. This girl, later when I was working by the lake, irrigating potatoes, sat under a tree, all on her own, which was unusual. After a while she came and sat down by the overflow amid the noise of engine and pump. I knew something was wrong, for normally she kept her distance in a friendly kind of way, and suddenly to have this girl almost sitting in my lap, was a strange feeling. My heart went out to her but also I became angry at the same time, sensing the hopelessness she was experiencing, for I had had a taste of that. Her parents were going through a difficult time in their marriage. It is distressing for a child to witness arguments between father and mother, as I know when my parents had occasional rows. All sorts of fears go through one's mind but there is very little a son or daughter can do about it. I've always thought it would be better if parents could stay together until the youngest child was about 16, for at that age the whole world is opening up and one's head is full of thoughts outside family life. The break up of parents, should, at that time in life, be the least traumatic for the children, but then we don't live in an ideal world. I decided not to pry but give her some physical support. I asked if she would like to drive the tractor up the field to spread the load of water, and so take her mind off things a bit. This she managed after a fashion, not having driven before and getting back to fill up again she seemed to have gained enough confidence to go back home. Thank goodness I said to myself, as I was getting worried as to what she might do if unable to face up to the situation. Getting to the first bend in the farm track, she came to a halt, seemingly unable to go any further. If she was feeling as I think she was, her legs had gone to jelly and an awful gnawing feeling was at the middle of her. Slowly turning around, she walked back to where I was in an expressionless robot-like fashion, not knowing what to do. She hung around for a while, then went and had a wee under a nearby tree and eventually set off again, this time able to keep going in the direction of the splitting-up home.

Another time I came across the same girl and a friend. They were sitting in the corner of a cornfield, trying out their first cigarettes. They made a pretty picture, the two heads of hair set against the corn crop nearly ready to harvest. I have seen the girl again recently and found she is now a very attractive young woman.

5th   Planting mustard.

6th   Potatoes.

18th   Swiping rides.

25th   Combining.

August
6th   Finish combining.

17th   Topping seed potatoes.

22nd Eight buzzards circling together above Rabbitbury Coppice.

September
19th   Hot day. Ploughing in the Parks field with cab doors open, a hornet flew

in one side, hovered for a few seconds at eye level 6" from my face, letting me get an eye to eye view of it. Thankfully, it flew out of the other door.

26th   Swallows gone.

October
3rd   House martins still here.

13th   First frost.

November
12th   Planting corn.

24th   Pheasant shoot.

December
5th   Sub-soiling.

12th   Grove Farm, bird, whitish front, black head, slate grey back, slightly smaller than kestrel, flew along 2 feet above ground, sparrowhawk.

13th   Goldcrest. Heron eating worms from the ploughing.

16th   First snow.

679 Hours Overtime 1976

1977

January
3rd   Beautiful, multi-coloured sunrise, 8 am, crows flying between me and the sunrise, sharp contrast. Many birds when ploughing in frosty weather. Approximately 80 crows, rooks and jackdaws, 80 seagulls, 80 peewits, an assortment of smaller birds, redwing, starling, mistle thrush, pied and grey wagtails. Peewits still feeding on worms when dark, looking like people with their arms tied to their sides.

5th   Rising moon, orange-red.

10th   Crows and jackdaws taking off for the day as daylight dawns.

11th   Vixen screaming early morning.

12th   Pied wagtail sleeping in briar patch.

13th Snow and winds. Rough weather, snow 6" deep.

19th Ploughed up mouse store of acorns and maize.

February
14th Curlew calling.

April
4th Started planting spring corn.

13th Potato planting.

17th Swallow.

27th Fencing.

29th Cuckoo.

May
1st Swift.

2nd Planting maize.

Ploughing the Barnfield

151

5th   Hawk, slate grey back and wings (sparrowhawk) carrying full grown blackbird.

16th   Oak out before ash.

June
20th   Several stone slabs visible at crossing of Old Footpath through brook between Bullock field, Hyde and Forty Acres, Pensons. Impressions in clay, found when building dam, Middle lake between Netherwood and Hyde.

August
21st   Lots of peacock butterflies.

22nd   Netherwood Lake, bird (one or two), seagull-like, black back, white front, dives for long periods and swims a long way under water. Cormorant.

September
13th   Small speckled owl, bright eyes when close to it.

15th   Sub-soiling.

24th   Owl calls echoing in Perry Wood.

26th   Barn owl, Hyde.

27th   Double 'V' of seventy three Canada geese.

28th   Hyde – dingles full of biting midges.

October
14th   Debbie Adams and Michelle Halling from Netherwood Cottages. Over the years many children have had rides in the crawler cab, sometimes half a dozen at a time would come running across the field and pile in. I smiled as they stood and sat around, their heads bobbing in time with the motion of the crawler. Debbie and Michelle had had one or two goes on their own, and I had given them a go at steering. Debbie, being the eldest, could just manage to sit on the seat. Michelle, younger and smaller, had rather a job. The only way she could manage was by sitting on the end of my boney knees, putting one foot on the dashboard and grasping the steering brake lever with two hands, managing to have strength enough to guide the crawler down the bout of ploughing. While one was steering, the other sat on the toolbox at the side and would nod off to sleep, with the warmth and shaking of the cab.

This Friday, after Barry's mobile van had been to the cottages, the two girls came over to where I was ploughing and both sitting together by the side of me, showed me their purchases from Barry. They each had three different bars of chocolate. Neither looking at the other nor speaking, they each laid their purchases on the toolbox lid, admired and fondled them, decided in what sequence they were to be eaten and, each in a world of their own, staring into space, munched away until none were left. By this time it was getting dark and the crawler lights were on. Nearing the top of the field, the gaffer came into view, I stopped when I got to him and he opened the cab door, dazzled by the lights and expecting only me to be there. His eyes opened a bit wider as he saw three faces peering down instead of one. Taking it in his stride, he discussed what he had come about and left me to it. The two girls seemed to be settled in for the night, so it was just as well that someone came for them before they finally nodded off to sleep. I've never seen two people extract so much pleasure from a few sweets as those girls.

When working behind Netherwood Cottages, a cup of tea would be brought out by one or other from the cottages. One girl, Christiana, instead of going to sleep this once, would each time I came up the field, put a different doll in the window behind her bedroom curtains for me to see in the headlights. Next morning a sleepy head peeped out and gave me a wave before going off to school.

19th   Finish autumn corn planting.

November
14th   Grove Farm, Canada geese flying from lake to lake as it got light. Two barn owls softly screeching by the crawler while I was having tea in the dark.

16th   Grove Farm: grey hawk, skimming down the side of the hedge. Sparrowhawk?

18th   The robin seems to do its feeding at dusk, shyly popping back and forth to the nearest hedge from the ploughing. This is often the last bird that I see feeding each day. The seagulls mostly set off when there's still plenty of daylight left, invariably taking off and flying south, possibly to the Severn Estuary. I have never seen any gulls go north in the evening in the whole of my time at Netherwood. A few of the last seagulls would have a last minute meal, seemingly to overdo it a bit and become front heavy, their crop taking on a distorted shape from the last worms gulped down. Flying then appears to be hard work with a very laboured take-off, resulting in a low circle of the field. Then they come back into land, have a few minutes of neck stretching and away they go again, flying very low, just clearing the nearest hedge and keeping treetop level till out of sight. I wonder how many tons of worms they have eaten in my time of ploughing on Netherwood Farms, as often there are several hundred at a time on many days throughout each year.

Jack Spitting Feathers. This man has spent most of the past year fencing on

Netherwood Farms. He has worked on his own, dug post holes with a long-handled worn out spade, driven a big Vauxhall car around the farm with his tools in, lived in a caravan, parked in the alleyway of the barn, only going home for weekends. Pigs were kept in the empty cattle yards over summer and fed out of hoppers that had metal flaps at the bottom, which they lifted up with their snouts and each time they withdrew their heads, the flaps came down with a bang, so all day and most of the night, there was constant banging coming from these yards. Asking Jack (never knew his other name) how he slept at night with all this noise a few yards away, he said it wasn't too bad as he was a bit deaf in one ear, so he lay with his good ear on the pillow, so keeping the noise at bay. Jack had worked out what time of year flies became active in the hedgerows as his job most of the year was a warm one and flies do pester when a person sweats. Asking him one hot day how things were going, he said he was that hot and thirsty that when he spat, it felt like he was trying to spit out a mouthful of feathers. Hence the name I'd given him.

22nd   Canada geese and mallards landing on new lake by moonlight.

24th   Frost brings nature closer.

25th   Moon seems extra big as it balances on the rim of the valley and as I looked at the stars through the branches of a big oak tree.

28th   Large 'V' of Canada geese silhouetted against the evening sky. Most impressive.

30th   About three hundred seagulls whirling around the crawler while ploughing. It was like being in a snow storm.

December

2nd   A few fieldfares. No peewits yet.

3rd   Two peewits today, Tee Baune Lake frozen over. Ice covered with fresh fallen oak leaves.

4th   Seventy peewits today, many with deformed legs.

5th   Evenings now getting much darker, plough lights on 4.40 pm.

6th   Hare, crouched in stubble, nose twitching, bulging eyes, able to see behind without turning its head. A pleasant looking hare.

7th   Fox carrying off dead piglet from muck tump, 8 pm. Seen in lights of van.

9th   Small blackbird size bird on boggy ground bottom of Roundcots field. Two yellow stripes down head and back. Jack Snipe smashing little bird, and

154

the only one I've ever seen. The tolerance of this bird to noise and movement was quite exceptional. It stopped as close as 2 feet from the moving squeaking tracks and roaring engine of the crawler. Its camouflage was so good in the worked stubble land that I was afraid of running it over. The ploughing had to suffer a bit as I was keeping an eye out, breathing a sigh of relief each bout when I came to a spot in the field where it was feeding and caught sight of it moving unhurriedly out of the way.

12th   Shoot.

15th   Mild sunny day, birds singing, lots of spider gossamer floating by on a light breeze. In the evening, smoke from chimneys going straight up.

20th   Cock bullfinch and two hens feeding on nettle and dock seeds.

882 Hours Overtime 1977.

1978

January
5th   Ploughing.

12th   Finish winter ploughing, except for sixteen acres for pig slurry.

25th   Pheasant shoot. Sunny with a touch of frost, cold out of the sun; the cold fresh air in the woods on a hot body most invigorating. Poor shoot for pheasants but lots of woodcock. Woodcock seem to have increased considerably over the past few years since planting up of woods.

February
22nd   Rain freezing as it hit the ground.

24th   Lambs' tails and silver pussy willow out; first warm day.

28th   Found arrowhead on top site, at top of Old Roadway.

March
3rd   Wild bees active in oak tree, Tee Baune Lake.

11th   Started spring planting.

14th   Frog spawn found at Grove pond; none last year.

15th   Snow.

April

3rd   Pair of butterflies mating, and blue tits nesting in hawthorn trunk.

4th   The sweet smell of the woods breaking into life.

12th   Wheatear.

14th   Barn owl: Bank Street.

May

1st   Oak out before ash. Sparrowhawk caught blackbird, five yards away from me.

4th   Wild cherry blossom smells like marzipan tastes.

7th   Swifts.

9th   Trees coming into leaf.

10th   Stopped crawler 9 pm and as I got out of the cab was surrounded by birds, singing all around from the different dingles, having a last burst before going to bed.

13th   Two bluebells left in van by Debbie and Michelle. Planting maize.

14th   Strong smell of wild garlic coming from Perry Wood in the dusk. Most of the trees came out in leaf during the past week.

24th   Stung by bee – puffed up and itched.

29th   May blossom coming out.

30th   Start silage.

June

2nd   Thunder. Smell of May blossom mixed with honeysuckle coming from the dingles.

4th   Ridging potatoes.

19th   Swiping rides. A moorhen on Peter Rabbit pool, fetched a water lily leaf and gave it to the one sitting on the nest of eggs.

July

When stopping to say "hello" to Joanna Payne, who had spent several days on her own pulling wild oats on one of these hot days, I was struck by her eyes. I'd never seen them so alive before. I expect she was physically tired but the intensity of feeling shining out from those brown eyes seemed to reflect the cornfields that she was working in.

156

7th Silage.

August
19th Start combining.

23rd Ninety five house martins and swallows on wire, Vicarage Cottage, early morning.

27th Frog in corn field.

30th Six herons flying in 'V' formation.

September
4th Finish combining.

5th Sub-soiling.

10th Hazel nuts ripe, hawthorn berries very red. Seems early.

15th Tom Panniers left Netherwood.

16th Came to work this morning feeling that I had only been away a few minutes, as if I had never been home. I was ploughing Flints field, Grove Farm and there were days when I never spoke to anyone. I was out of the way at work, and left to get on with the job. Going home late at night the children were in bed, so I rarely saw them, unless they were ill. Maureen was sometimes in bed or, by the time I'd relaxed enough to talk, she was feeling too tired. Sometimes several days went by without conversation. This Saturday morning must have been one of these times, for on greasing and filling up the tack (crawler and plough), it seemed as if I had been ploughing until a few minutes ago, had a bite to eat and was starting another tankful of fuel's work. Hard as I tried, I was unable to recall going home, going to bed, getting up and coming to work. I could recall the previous day's ploughing up till the time that I would have gone home. The crawler was still warm, as it often is when working late and starting fairly early. After several more minutes of moithering over the apparent loss of memory, I half thought I had fallen asleep in the cab and had not been home at all! Then reason started to set in. I always bring enough food and drink for three meals a day, so if I had not been home I would not have any food or flasks of tea. After a little while telling myself not to be stupid, I eventually scrambled up into the cab to check. I had been home, for the flasks had been filled and fresh sandwiches cut . . . For the rest of the day I tried to remember some small detail from the previous night, but I never did. It was a complete blank. This had never happened before, nor has it happened since, other than when going into a deep sleep during my ten minute nap after meals. When awakening, I was not always sure where I was, whether at work or home until I opened my eyes. Then came the problem as to which meal time I had just had, bait, dinner or tea! This, I

157

soon twigged, was easy to solve. Just look in the bait bag and see what food and drink was left!

October

3rd   Over one hundred Canada geese circling Netherwood pools. Swallows gone.

7th   Two swallows seen today.

8th   Rabbit reclining between furrows after ploughing in mustard. Nice to see a few rabbits again.

11th   Fallen leaves on bare earth, very beautiful.

15th   Midges about on a beautiful morning with leaves turning colour; misty in the hollows; no wind; birds twittering; sun shining, a little cloud and sounds carrying a long way.

23rd   Cutting maize.

31st   Strange sunset, thin white bands of clouds.

December

3rd   Ploughing.

4th   Clouds looking like balls of cotton wool in the moonlight and the fresh-turned furrows glinting appreciatively in return.

8th   Heavy rain in morning, very cold. Cleared up in the afternoon, became mild, clear and very beautiful. Such contrast; everything looked as if it had been spring-cleaned. Clouds in the evening sky being drawn as if by a vacuum, at an even pace in relation to each other, no cloud going faster or slower than another. Some were shaped like animals. One was like a cow being drawn backwards. All this happened in silence, for where I stood, there was no wind nor movement of air; everything was still and quiet. To see the clouds rushing across the sky with this absence of noise was as if it were happening on another planet.

23rd   Peewits floating on a sea of ploughing. When ploughing at a certain angle and in the right light, the peewits sitting or standing, seemed to be part of one living, breathing world.

I ran off the road into the hedge where The Well Head lane joins Collington Road on the Ley-Line.

31st   Van bump where ley-line crosses road. Bitterly cold east wind, soil freezing on exposed plough boards before reaching each end of the field.

821 Hours Overtime 1978

158

1979

January

1st   Diesel fuel waxing. Spent a long time chipping brakes free, soil had frozen on idler and rollers. One front idler did not want to turn for a long while. Sunset over Calves Hill with trees silhouetted against the sky.

3rd   Small redwings.

March

2nd   Saw a curlew.

4th   Silver pussy willow out. Two buzzards circling in clear blue sky, very low and very sharp, top Tee Baune Lake.

6th   Lambs' tails out. Ploughing, Cow Pasture, Hyde. Ash tree just below Hyde Hill looks coated in silver.

April

15th   Sally leaves burst open almost in one day. Usually the hawthorn or elderberry come into leaf first.

17th   Spring planting.

22nd   A pair of pheasants or wild mallards sums up spring.

24th   The smell of things growing and buds bursting open is hard to define. Poplar trees are coming into leaf.

May

1st   Saw a fox chasing a hare in bright sunshine out of the wood and across the ploughing.

9th   Swallows, swifts and house martins, skimming low over the dam between the two lakes came closer to me standing there than any wild birds had ever done before. Many more were lining up on the wire fence in the rain a few yards off, chatting away between themselves. Perhaps it was their first landing in this country this spring that made them act as if I was not there. They reminded me of a coach load of humans at the seaside.

10th   Oak out before the ash.

13th   Small greyish bird flying a few inches above Park Lake, making a piping sound. Common sandpiper?

14th   Exceptionally hot day and fir cones popping at The Knowle. Queen

159

wasp scratching something off old dead cow parsley, a surprisingly loud noise in the stillness of the woods.

15th   Planting maize.

19th   Rolling corn. The woods top of Coverfield smell sweet in the evenings. I can be working in the Coverfield all day and then as the sun starts to go down, this extraordinary smell rises – a mixture of the trees and plants and damp boggy things I can't identify. It comes rolling down into the field as the movement of air takes place on a still evening. It is a haunting smell that seems to trigger off something in my brain, programmed, it seems, from ancestors of long ago, even coming through the dust mask when combining. All that I want to do is to breathe in as much as possible, for it triggers more emotions and feelings than even the smell of a woman seems able to do. The only other place I have come across anything like it, was at the bottom of the Grandstand Patch of woodland, but even this lacked that special something that Coverfield wood possessed.

June
25th   Maize planting.

Coverfield with Haunting Scent Wood in background
Photo: Roger Halling

160

July

1st   Sparrow-like bird, brown cap, brown cheeks, brown throat, plaintive cheep call. Reed bunting?

5th   Trimmed weeping cedar tree at the front of Netherwood House, planted 1850. It was said that it is difficult to grow, so we workers took bits that had been trimmed off and stuck them in the ground, but the only person to have any success was Tom West, the lorry driver. He got a piece to grow for several years, but it eventually broke off at ground level one windy day. The piece from ground level to the base of the bush was only the thickness of a pencil, so it seemed that something was wrong with it, or had been chewed by voles.

26th   Watering potatoes.

August

2nd   Canada geese started flying around.

11th   Holiday. Molegrove, Cardigan, with family and wife's parents. There were gales this week and the sea was very rough, but it was on the way down the lane to the sea that I saw the tidiest farmyard I've ever come across. Hardly a wisp of straw was out of place. This walk down to the sea was by a narrow lane with high bank hedges, very pleasant walk at dusk, with a haunting aroma of decaying fungi. Where the lane is near the sea, a couple used to park and sleep in the back of a small van, where a tump of land between the lane and sea had a springy, grass surface. This evening, when standing looking at the rough sea, a young girl with red hair and wearing green did a few handstands. Catching me watching she then treated me to a series of cartwheels and this small red and green figure, tumbling over and over on this spit of land, in the half-light reminded me of the elves and fairies of my childhood. It is not only the sunshine and sandy beaches that give us memories of a place.

28th   While combining Nutwels field, Grove Farm, a teenage girl who liked driving various farm machines had a go at combining. It was easy standing crop so she was able to cope alright. As the evening drew on and the light faded, the combine lights were switched on, and working in a small pool of light, brought a new atmosphere and feeling to the job. The combine had no cab so there was still a contact with the work and the weather. As she got off later that night and went home, she looked at me and said, "I feel just like a Queen." It is good to know that I was able to make one person happy for a while once in my lifetime!

Later in the year, down by the small pond next to Kyre Parks field and Flints field, whenever I had a meal I sat on the dam and a robin would sit on the nut bush by the side of me and eat crusts of bread thrown to it. It seemed to

161

think it should keep an eye on strangers. For many years, in summer and winter I had my meals there, because I liked the feel and friendly air of the place. It was possibly the nicest area of all Netherwood Farms at that time, and not once was I able to sit down without the robin being there.

Narrow-lipped hellebore grew by the side of Tee Baune Lake, adjoining Coverfield, and meadow saffron or autumn crocus used to be in the small ashbed at Bullock field, Hyde Farm, and early purple orchid or common spotted orchid at Kyre Parks field, below little pond.

We used to feed the ducks on the lakes at Netherwood in the 1970's. There were several hundred in the winter months and, if disturbed, the winter sky was filled by them flying between the lakes.

September
1st   The autumn song of the robin is so full of meaning for me as if nature itself had been captured in its notes, a reminder that the seasons are constantly changing and that summer does not last through twelve months of the year. Mr. Worrell, the shepherd, did not like this song when the robin sang from the farm buildings. It reminded him that winter was coming round again.

2nd   Several quail flushed out when combining; they just flew a few yards then dropped back into the corn. Seen a couple of times in White Meadow and Big Orchard field, also once in the corn at Hyde Farm. They have only been seen for about three years and I had seen none before.

12th   Finish combining.

22nd   A little owl was hunting in bright sunlight; I watched it catch a mouse I had ploughed out, then it ate it in nearby hedgerow. In my father's day, at Netherwood, poles were stuck in the ground, with traps on top to catch little owls, as they were considered a pest at that time.

28th   Grove Farm. Warm sunny day. Trees just starting to change colour and are beautiful with the sun on them, casting strong shadows. About a hundred Canada geese flew over.

30th   Harebell flower, Tee Baune Lake. This is the only place where I have seen any on Netherwood. Odd ones grow on some very poor marly soil, facing south, between the orchard and lake, and a few were seen once at the top of Hyde Hill.

October
6th   Swallows left. When having dinner, sat by the side of Park lake, and half way through my sandwiches, the lake was invaded by many swallows and martins, wheeling and diving about, almost coming to a standstill as they drank

from the surface of the lake, dozens of them at a time. Then, after about five minutes, they all took off high into the sky, out of sight, leaving me a little breathless from watching such an unexpected happening. I'm sure there are fewer swallows around Netherwood now than there were in the 1970's. One time walking up past Little Netherwood Cottage, I saw the tiled roof covered with the still black and white blobs of swallows or martins catching the warm afternoon sun. This was the only time I had seen a roof covered like that, though people do say it's not uncommon. Sand martins in my school days nested in Low Hill gravel pit, Hall Farm, but no longer.

9th   Lay on my back amongst falling wild cherry leaves at Brickbarns Cottages, Netherwood, nuthatch overhead, and the comforting call of a crow in the distance, a pheasant nearby, spiders trying to drop their webs on my face and midges biting, I thought that this is one of the best places I have seen for a house. It is sheltered in a south-facing position set in the fold of higher ground, so north and east winds should blow straight over the top. There are two small streams joining at the bottom of the garden, and wooded dingles on three sides. Since the tin was taken off one half of the stone double cottage roof, they have fallen into decay fast. The brook that runs down to Collington's Lake in a big curve, runs over rocks in places and is bounded by beech trees. Fencing up the side of this brook one warm spring, just as the delicate beech leaves were coming out, is one of my happy memories of Netherwood, with the water rippling over the slabs of stone. It was an interesting fencing job, full of twists and turns, and ups and downs, across and back across the brook. In such a setting at a time of year when the pace of things is speeding up after winter, with the pleasant relaxed company of Colin Beaumond who worked at Netherwood for a couple of years, some of the less pleasant aspects of farmwork seemed worthwhile. Once, while fencing, I threw a metal handled bowsaw back on the ground, because it was too hot to hold in comfort. It had been lying in the sun for a while and on picking it up, I immediately dropped it again, it was so hot. I have never known this before or since. Whether it was the angle it was lying at, in relation to the sun, goodness knows.

13th   Coverfield. A still evening, sounds are very clear and carrying a long way. I can hear people talking from a quarter of a mile away.

15th   Coverfield. Redferns timber people from Bromyard, went along the top of Coverfield, from Hyde Hill. The timber wagon was loaded with tree trunks, behind a four-wheeled tree loader, followed by the crawler, without a cab on, the driver carrying a long ladder, crossing the fresh furrows of the part ploughed field. A lovely sight. The timber was from some magnificent mature beech trees from Hyde Hill, a few of many that died in the 1976 dry spell on

Netherwood Farms. In about two years, they changed from things that were beautiful, to leafless, partly boughless skeletons, sad to look upon. When the dead beech trees were being cut down on Hyde Hill, I heard the timber faller calling out in anguish, "Fall, damn you, fall!" These trees were very unstable, with great dead boughs, ready to fall down at the slightest jarring.

December
9th   When ploughing Nutwels field, Grove Farm, near the centre of the field that sloped south west, I saw half a dozen or so partridges. The red sun was just going down and shining on their breasts, so that they turned a pinky hue. It must have been the place where they spent the night for they were very loathe to move out of the way of the crawler and plough, only begrudgingly moving a few inches each pass I made. Thank goodness, just before it got completely dark, I saw them scrambling over the furrows and settling down in the spot that was now ploughed, where I first saw the pink warm bundles of feathers.

10th   Night lightning in the west. I have seen this on several occasions over the years, usually when walking back to the farms at night after ploughing, without a torch. Flashes come off the skyline without thunder.

Charcoal patches, for want of a better word, areas of burnt soil that I have kept ploughing up in the same spot ever since I've been at Netherwood, about ten yards across. Two in the big Hopyard, one at Collingtons, one at Parks and one at Stable meadow and one at Coverfield. Several also in the woods above Netherwood on small levelled patches.

Carving in beech tree (now gone), top end of Park lake of a figure of an old-fashioned soldier in uniform.

825 Hours Overtime 1979

1980

The old historic part of Netherwood was taken down and shipped off to America. The high stone foundations from this mainly timber part of the building, called the Essex room, were re-used, together with stone from some cottages at Bringsty, near Bromyard, to build an extra wing and additions to the stone manor house. The foundations were already second-hand stone. By the shapes and dates that fit the worked blocks of stone, one assumes it originally came from the early Netherwood Mansion and chapel c.1300. The corner stones used in the new wing must have been used before because they are curved and sooty on the inside, so must once have been part of a square or oblong stone chimney. Some of the stone part of Netherwood House that was left, was found to have been built on made up ground. There was a five foot layer of red marl on top of ten feet or so of blackish soft soil. This possibly was the moat that once surrounded Netherwood Mansion. Wooden piles four feet long, four to five inches in diameter, now gone to dust, had been driven in about a foot apart. These acted as foundations for some of the walls of the new (1700's) three-storey house.

February

11th   A pleasant warm day, several birds singing well.

16th   Spreading pig slurry.

21st   White violet out, Park Cottage site, and pussy willow.

April

7th   Discing for spring corn.

10th   Migraine.

13th   Poplar trees' beautiful perfume as they come into leaf, carried across several fields. It comes only from the trees by the side of Stable Meadow, near Netherwood House and some up by Brickbarns. The other poplar trees around the farm lack this special smell of spring.

16th   I found about thirty pieces of flint to-day in bottom Collington's.

17th   Planting Potatoes.

18th   Sun setting in a cloudless sky.

19th   Hawthorn leaves out first.

24th   Planting maize. Oak out before ash.

25th   Swallows, martins and cuckoo all seen or heard by me to-day. Good to have them back.

May

2nd   Rolling spring corn. Scent of bluebells coming up from Rabbitsbury Coppice, near Grandstand Patch.

June

2nd   Ridging potatoes.

3rd   Sitting quietly under a hedge, one realises with how many creatures and things one shares the world.

5th   Thunder storm. Magic of the clouds clearing, cooler air, birds singing, cuckoo changing its tune; so much around if only one stops to look and think.

10th   Migraine.

22nd   Canoe Rally, Hereford to Ross. I remember going with brother-in-law, Martin Bolton, several years ago for a trip up the River Wye in his double canoe. It was a sunny day in summer, the river was low and the water warm. I sat in the front of his canoe paddling, though I wanted just to admire the scenery, letting Martin do the hard work and the steering. That was really the first time I had been on the water since I was a teenager and I enjoyed it very much, so I decided to get a second-hand single canoe. This I tried out with Martin, who had also bought one. One January day, at Brienton, just above Hereford, it was very cold and the river was swollen. The double I had been in previously was quite stable; the singles were not so good. When I got in, I was taken downstream before I had any sort of control over the boat, Martin nearly made it to the other side, but put his paddle in too deeply and turned himself over and had to swim the last few yards to the bank. I was still trying to stop going round in circles, which was bad enough, but I was near the end of a fisherman's line, which was doubly embarrassing. He just sat there hunched up with the cold, his face expressionless, no doubt thinking, "Why doesn't that stupid pillock go away and leave me in peace". I eventually made it to Martin, who was shivering from the cold water. Because of the cold, I had put on two pairs of trousers, jumpers and such so, giving Martin one of each, we continued up the river, until running out of energy, we floated back to where we began, and then packed in for the day.

Brian Vaughan, another brother-in-law, got a single also and we three spent many weekends exploring the local rivers. Canoeing is about the only thing I have done with my five children over the years. We went on some of the smaller rivers, the Wye, Arrow, Lugg, Teme and Frome because Wye Kayaks and others had taken the trouble to find out which were suitable for canoeing, legally and otherwise, so we were reaping the benefits of their time and hard work. My pleasure comes from the scenery, more than the challenge of the water itself. Parts of the Wye are very beautiful and memorable. The Arrow had many weirs and stretches remote from houses. The Lugg, in parts, looks like paintings where the river runs level with the surrounding fields, with cattle grazing nearby. The Teme is pleasantly average and the Frome is a small personal river. There are always memories of a kingfisher, or of shoals of little fish in shallow sunny water, herons or a colony of black-feathered cormorants.

166

Then, below Tintern Abbey, the reflection of the autumn colours in the mirror-calm waters, between Tintern and Chepstow, make it impossible to tell where the water ends and land begins. This was before the speed boats got established and water skiers disrupted the waters.

The smells of different parts of the rivers call you back the next year, though others, carrying outlets from factories and farms, are very different. Then there is the occasional clash with fisherman, water bailiff or landowner, but generally these are not too daunting, and are part of the human scenery.

23rd   Swiping.

24th   Silage.

29th   Watched baby moorhens swimming underwater.

July
12th   Haymaking.

14th   Frank Hatton, gardener/handyman, washing car, hissing at the same time. This puzzled me for quite a while. Why did he make this sound? It turned out that in his younger days he worked as a groom, spending a lot of his time brushing dried mud off horses and the hissing, between clenched teeth, was something that was commonly done in those days to help cope with the dust created by this brushing. The washing of a car used the same actions, so the hissing unconsciously accompanied what he was doing!

Similarly, a chap at Netherwood, who liked using a chain saw would, when working in the workshop, using an electric grinder or drill, switch them on and off in rapid succession, simulating the revving up of a petrol 2-stroke driven chain saw.

23rd   Combining.

27th   Two possible ley-lines cross, one from Garmesly Camp to Edvin Loach Church. The line crosses the road up by the garage, Collington, on the bend with the junction that goes up to Well Head Lane. There have been numerous accidents there over the years. I have been off the road three times myself in icy weather at this spot. A lad from Netherwood suddenly found himself in the ditch with one of Netherwood's new vans. He could not explain how he came to be there, and the dent in the van caused by going into the ditch he was able to push out, so no-one knew about it. In my early days at Netherwood, it was round this corner I went with a van load of potato pickers when the tyre went off with a bang. The other line goes from Garmsley Camp to Stokes Hill, through Bannalls Farm moat. Both these lines in summer and winter on the longest and shortest days, are each opposite to the other at sunrise and sunset.

167

Edvin Loach Church – built on Ley line   *N. Turner*

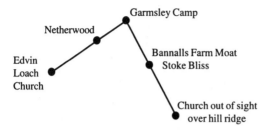

Where the line runs through Flints field, Grove Farm, several things have happened over the years. A top link broke between crawler and plough; another time a track pin came out and spread the track out in front of me. It took some time to get it back together in the dark. Once the crawler clock broke, and then the clock started up again for a few minutes, eighteen months later, at the same spot, and for several years running, it always seemed to rain when combining this patch. Another time John's power harrow broke after one bout and was useless for the rest of the day and Roger ran out of oil with his tractor and had to walk two miles back to the farm for more.

29th   Hyde Farm. Wind suddenly changed to the opposite direction, heralding strong thunder storms; weaned lambs nearby stood like statues. A young barn owl started hunting in the suddenly reduced light.

August
3rd   Birds seem to talk rather than sing at this time of the year.

23rd   Watched hedgehog looking for food by fish pond in bright moonlight; no other sound except a dog barking in the distance.

25th   Owls are noisy at this time of the year, listened to three different owl cries.

September
1st   Swallows and martins gathering on electric wires in the early morning. Soft colours of seeds and berries on the trees.

7th   Finish combining.

15th   Ploughing.

23rd   Top Calves Hill, young poplar tree leaves contrasting against the natural tree greens.

27th   Planting winter barley.

28th   White Meadow – ploughing. After stopping work, about 9 pm and setting off home, I stumbled along until my eyes got used to the dark (I still haven't got round to carrying a torch). Part way along the Little Hopyard field, which was grass, some animal got up, having a pee at the same time. Unable to see what it was, I plodded on, ignoring the funny feeling going up the back of my neck, when all of a sudden there were a hundred or so getting to their feet and peeing. It was as if hundreds of taps had been turned on in a matter of three seconds, then all abruptly turned off after another three seconds, leaving an electrifying silence. This happened in total darkness, but coming to work next morning, I saw what it was! The field was full of sheep!

October
7th   Night lightning from the south.

9th   A green meteor 7.45 pm in the north-west. Swallows have gone but still a few house martins left.

11th   Fifty Canada geese grazing on stubble with about 150 seagulls, 100 jackdaws, crows and rooks on the fresh ploughing in Big Orchard.

12th   At least 300 seagulls today in frost, mist and sunshine with the leaves turning colour.

13th   What sounded like a burst of laughter came from the crows and jackdaws, somewhere in the woods over by Collington meadows.

19th   Saw wild mink at bait time, Perry Wood, Hyde Farm, three quarters of the way up a sloping ash tree. They were being mobbed by crows, jackdaws and magpies, with jays screeching encouragement in the background. The brook that runs up Perry Wood was the last in the area where I watched fish play around and eels going in and out of tree roots, lit up by shafts of sunlight which came down at an angle through the trees.

21st   The smell that you only get from fresh ploughed old turf, Pensons sling.

22nd   Thirty pied wagtails looking like swallows, perched on electric wires, Bullock field, Hyde Farm.

27th   Watched stoat kill rabbit below Rabbitbury Coppice. The rabbit was squealing as it came out of the wood, running in a slow crouching fashion, down across the Little Hopyard grass field. The stoat was about thirty yards behind, loping along. The rabbit could easily have out-run the stoat, but instead it got slower and slower, letting the stoat catch up. It's as if the stoat was somehow willing the rabbit into submission. On catching up, the stoat appeared to be biting and sucking just above the rabbit's right ear, this went on for quite a while, perhaps one and a half minutes, the rabbit just sitting quietly, letting it happen. They were only about ten yards away. The stoat then looked at me, moved away from the rabbit as if to go for cover, hesitated, went back to its prey and started to drag it towards the hedge where I stood. It did this by pulling it backwards and rolling it over as the rabbit was four times its size. This was quite a feat of strength, taking several minutes to move it the seven to eight yards almost to my feet. It then darted through the hedge and down a dry culvert under the road, came back and somehow by pulling and running through and pushing a bit, managed to get the rabbit through the hedge and into the safety of the drain, apparently ignoring that I was there. (When father was rabbiting on Netherwood with Frank Briscoe, they used to sell the skins of the stoat that they caught).

30th   Watched kestrel catch a mouse two feet away from where I was ploughing. Kyre Park field, Grove Farm. Lots of jays about. Distinctive smell of fallen oak leaves.

November
3rd   Movement seems to be associated with noise, so it seems almost unreal seeing the clouds rushing across the sky when no wind is blowing near me.

10th   Bullock field. There is a purple sheen on alder and silver birch without their leaves.

11th   Flints field, Grove. The second time nature let me in on her beauty was a scene that stands out above most others. It was bait time one frosty, misty morning. I was starting to plough after maize, and was parked where a few maize stalks with their cobs on had been left because of a fallen bough. Sitting crossways in the cab, with the windows partly steamed up, I became aware of a rustling noise. Carefully turning my head to look behind I saw a spotted woodpecker, working his way round a cob of maize corn. This red, black and white bird stood out against the dull frosted maize leaves, and to complete the picture were three hen pheasants a few feet away, catching the red of the early morning sun.
   A five day old moon was setting over Garmsley Camp, like a pillar of flame on the horizon from where I was ploughing above the ley-line in Flints field.
15th   Beautiful changing sky after heavy rain in Nutwels field. The oak trees are keeping their leaves on the longest; next are the hazelnut trees.

16th   Perry Dingle has the most ferocious midges I have come across. Father endorsed this by saying when he used to check Kyre Hospital spring water supply, further along towards Kyre Bank, he and Tom Corbett had the same problem. Tom used to come out in bumps from these midge bites. I have gone down into the woods of Perry Dingle to have a meal break, and on sitting down

171

by the brook, have been attacked within a few minutes. I would cover my head with a sou-wester rain hat, with handkerchief hanging down over my face, poking bits of food under. They would then start crawling up under my trouser legs. When I tucked my trousers into my socks, they then wriggled their way through the fibres of cloth. This was too much for me, so I would gather up my part-eaten meal and move to the field at the edge of the wood. They soon found me again, so I moved back to the crawler, sitting in the cab to finish off my meal, until it was time to start work again. They were active at all times of the year, even in winter time, if it was fairly mild. The only time I was able to sit in the dingle free of them was when a strong wind was blowing. This they were unable to tolerate.

Ivy snuggling up to a sally tree.

17th   Nutwels. Kestrel eating large robin-sized bird, while streams of feathers flew in the wind as it plucked its prey and ate it.

19th   Watched crow or jackdaw having a long wash in Tee Baune Lake, seeming quite happy sitting in the middle, dipping its head under water and throwing droplets over its back. It had no problem flying off again.

20th   Coverfield. The wind made music in the tress which mingled with the sound of birds and the rustling of leaves and was spiced with the smell of decaying autumn undergrowth.

21st   With the leaves off the trees, the dingles have a new dimension.

22nd   When mild, the birds sing and when cold they twitter.

23rd   Clee Hill seemed very clear and close to-day and I was able to count houses there, 11 miles away.

27th   First snow.

30th   Working Forty Acres, Pensons. Hard frost, kestrel sat on a furrow surrounded by 12 or more pied wagtails, untroubled, searching for grubs.

December
1st   The seagulls did not stop to feed, they soon flew away again; the worms can't taste right.

3rd   Saw the birds moving about in the dawn of a frosty clear morning; pink sunrise over Little Netherwood. I see the faces of different people in the expressions of the birds.

7th   Frosty. About 400 seagulls on the fresh ploughing. Field had been mulched so perhaps worms are tastier.

8th   Twelve peewits today, first ones seen this winter ploughing.

10th   Goldcrest wren, Stoney field.

893 Hours Overtime 1980

1981

January

1st   Rabbits a pest again for the first time since myxomatosis; they ate quite a lot of the winter barley off eight acres, top of the drive. Four hares in the Barnfield, Netherwood.

7th   I felt a welling up of loving feelings for Netherwood inside me when going up Netherwood drive. This feeling came at the same place where, years ago going up through the roadside meadows, now called Peafields, I made a vow not to fight over women and not to worry about money. It was totally unexpected. I wasn't feeling any different; just looking up towards Netherwood House and the woods behind. The feeling was like being in love with a girl and you see her coming towards you and want to put your arms around her, and hold her tight. This was the feeling I had for this place; only for a second or two, but enough for me to imagine I had great long arms and was able to hold the whole of Netherwood close for a while. Other things happened at different times of a similar nature. One was when I was walking up over the site of the old mansion, by the two walnut trees, to the north-west of Netherwood House, going to the woods to continue swiping rides, having left the tractor up there for some reason. It was one of the few times when no-one was at Netherwood at that particular time of the day. The owners were away. No stockmen, foreman, gardeners or anyone else was there. I was the only person working on Netherwood for these few hours till feeding time for the stock in the evening. Just before the walnut trees a voice said: "I'm really getting my money's worth out of you". Half stopping and shaking my head in disbelief, I knew this voice was that of the farm itself; it had come through plain and clear inside my head. It is at times like this that I wonder just how much we humans have lost real contact with the world we live in.

The other thing was again in the Peafield. This was a taste, or an ability to feel or grasp in a very real way, just for a split second, the atmosphere and way

173

of life of the peoples at Netherwood over hundreds of years. This, strangely enough, came through to my mind via someone else. Perhaps having a deep affection for this person and because she had lived at Netherwood and loved the place, somehow this happening was helped to come about.

8th   Blackbird or thrush started singing at Bromyard/Hereford road junction, at the top of the by-pass. It's still dark but, coming to work, I can hear it singing, even with the van windows closed, 7.15 am. For several years this happened and really set me up for the day, but after the stone cottage on the corner was demolished, I hardly ever heard it with the same intensity.

11th   Ploughed up part of cobbled road or yard in Middle Meadow, Hyde Farm, adjacent to existing asbestos farm buildings. This fits in with finding medieval pottery in the same spot one foot below ground level.

12th   While ploughing long periods by oneself, one develops an affection for the birds and animals that one sees and hears.

15th   Large sun rose this morning, with a few snow flurries. Ploughing last field at the Hyde.

17th   Snowdrops coming out.

Thornbury Fete held at Netherwood Manor
10. 06. 89

18th Birds starting to sing a little.

23rd Hyde. Mild day, several different birds singing and twittering. Buzzard meowing in the background. No frost.

27th Bishops Frome – dawn chorus started 7.15 am.

February
3rd Blossom out at Mr. and Mrs. Barbers, The Castle, Collington. This blossom is one tree only it must be something wild the the cultivated fruit had been grafted onto. When this and the witch hazel near the council yard, just beyond Bromyard, on the Hereford road, are out, it seems that spring is not far away, even if it snows later.

The orchard at The Castle was pushed out in about 1985, and with it went a little bit of what I used to look forward to each year.

11th Barn owl hunting in the orchard at The Knowle.

March
1st Thunder and lightning.

2nd Curlew calling, Netherwood.

Sid Battenham said that in the Norfolk area the farmers would test the warmth of the soil before spring planting by sitting on the ground with bare bottoms. We in the Netherwood area were not so sophisticated. If the time of the year was about right and the land was dry enough, we just got stuck in and did it.

23rd Heavy rain.

24th Buds starting to burst in the hedgerows; some wild cherry blossom out.

27th Nature's life is a series of gifts to be enjoyed but not to be taken with you, except in the mind.

30th Two clumps of oxslips (officially called false oxslips), Grove Farm.

31st The purple black of the rooks against fresh-worked land, a very pretty sight. Elderberry and hawthorn leaves out first.

April
3rd Two blobs of frogspawn, Grove House pond.

4th Spring planting.

5th The fine gentle perfume of spring in the air.

14th Ploughing, Grove.

16th   Rolling and discing, Grove.

17th   Spreading fertilizer, Hyde and Grove Farms.

20th   Oak before ash. Swallows at Monnington Falls, River Wye.

21st   Wheatear in Barn field.

24th   Snow.

26th   Many swallows dead in this cold spell, many perishing hunched together in the boathouse at Park Lake. (They never really got back to pre-1981 numbers as only once have they nested in this boathouse in the years up to 1993). Professor Lawrence found that one of the dead swallows had a ring on its leg.

May
7th   Swifts.

8th   Rolling spring barley.

9th   Curlew standing on top of another curlew, gently flapping its wings (mating?), in front of The Knowle. Perhaps a curlew's nest, Forty Acres, Pensons; the only one I know of, but grass will be cut for silage before it has chance to hatch eggs, so is doomed from the start.

12th   Planting maize.

19th   Shearing sheep.

25th   Smell of winter barley coming out into ear.

June
1st   Silage.

3rd   When working at the Hyde Farm, near the buildings, a shower of rain had damped a patch of silt on the road that had been washed there by a previous rainstorm. The house martins that were building on the farmhouse seized the opportunity of this handy building material before it dried up in the sun. About a dozen of them were to-ing and fro-ing from mud to house; so intent on what they were doing, that they took very little notice of me, and I was able to get close enough somehow to catch the feel of what they were doing. I have never seen such gentleness in anything before, there was no squabbling or fighting over this small mud patch, each in turn hovering, then quietly getting its beakful, hardly seeming to land on the tarmac. I am very pleased to have witnessed these few minutes filled with kindness and gentleness, unlike nature that is mostly eat and be eaten, which has to be, for the survival of things as we know them.

176

9th Maize cultivating.

13th Watering potatoes.

22nd Redstart in Quarry field, Hyde.

24th Got up before dawn (3.30-ish) to catch the sun coming up along Grove Farm ley-line. A slightly cloudy morning and not a clear sunrise, but the sun appeared to come up in about the right place. Stopped for a little while at Kyre School, watching the swifts feeding, very low, very noisily and dominating the scene there. The odd car parked and mobile at this time in a morning, makes one wonder what some people are doing. That evening watched sun set along the other ley-line from up at Edwin Loach church. It seemed to set in about the right place over Garmsley Camp. I was the only person at the church, which is one of the few left about that does not lock its doors, so it was nice to walk inside, and then explore the ruins of the earlier church on the east side. I really appreciated the quietness and the view from this church, as such places seem few and far between. The only sound was from a harsh-voiced crow that seemed not to like my presence.

29th Migraine.

July
21st Combining winter barley.

24th Spreading pig slurry.

August
4th Irrigating potatoes.

21st Combining

September
4th Sub-soiling.

7th Ploughing Big Hopyard. It was here that I saw my longest-legged hare! Perhaps it was getting on in years for it didn't seem particularly worried by my presence. It would spend most of the day squat down with occasional bouts of nibbling at small tussocks of grass in the stubble. When I got too close to it with the plough it had to move over a bit. On the morning of the second day's ploughing it took the huff and instead of moving across the field, bit by bit, as I got close, it got out from its well-camouflaged squat behind a tussock of grass, still in the same part of the field as yesterday, stretched, looked disdainfully in my direction and ambled up to the hedge at the bottom of Calves Hill. Its legs then looked really out of proportion to its body compared with other hares I'd seen. It settled itself at the base of one of the ash trees, got hold

177

of a small branch of ash leaves that the hedgetrimmer had cut off and for the rest of the day sat there nibbling at this branch, watching me, perhaps thinking, "There goes another of my favourite patches of grass!" As dusk fell, it went back over the furrows to the centre of the field, where I suppose it had its home.

13th   Stinkhorn covered with bluebottles by badger set, top corner of Collington Meadows.

15th   Netherwood. Heard the sounds of the valley awakening in the still early morning; smelt hops being dried across the valley from Underhill Farm.

18th   Found Elizbabeth I coin, Middle Meadow Hyde.

20th   Night lightning.

23rd   Found first field mushroom this year. Some years it is a job to find any on Netherwood; other years enough grow for everyone to have a meal after the stockmen have had their pick. Perks of their job, I suppose! We tractor drivers don't have the same opportunities to walk the grass fields and orchards. The most mushrooms I have seen was in the 1960's when the Big Hopyard was ploughed up from grass. This was the first time this field had been ploughed since I had been at Netherwood. The following autumn, having grown a crop of winter wheat off the field, just before ploughing again, the field was white with mushrooms. It was impossible to go from one end to the other without running over some. It was quite a sight – these white caps contrasting with the bare, red-brown earth.

25th   Found a baby hare a few weeks old while ploughing mustard in Coverfield. Seems rather late but I have seen small ones in other years at this time; hares seem to have a breeding range over most of the year. Pigeon sitting on eggs, Collingtons.

October
6th   The sun shining under the clouds after a storm at evening time, made everything clear and sharp, as I ploughed Castle field, Netherwood. Magic sight of sand or house martins flying high under a double rainbow that curved over Castle Farm on the other side of the brook, while the last of the day's sun slipped below the horizon.

Swallows still here. Seventy Canada geese flying between Netherwood Lakes.

9th   Three old oak trees on the skyline at Brickbarns, seen from Roundcots field, look like a cat running or a human from the waist up, leading a child by the hand, both appear just to be coming over the brow and waving "hello" to

178

Kyre Valley. Viewing this from many parts of Netherwood over the years, especially at dusk, these forms seem to dominate, ever watchful. It seems to me a few hundred years ago they might have dominated an area, reminding people of their roots.

19th   While sitting having dinner in the wood above Coverfield, a bird like an elongated pigeon alighted in a tree a few yards away, sitting perfectly still. I watched for half a minute while it scratched the base of its beak with a claw on its left leg. Then flying in a quiet relaxed way, wove its way through the branches of the trees, on through the wood, unlike a wood pigeon that seems to crash its way through branches. Male hen-harrier. They are well-established in Radnor Forest not that far away.

24th   Mother died.

26th   Sitting in the crawler having tea under the solitary oak tree in the middle of the field, where the big orchard used to be, a little owl came down out of the tree and proceeded to investigate the crawler, walking along the tracks, peering about as he went. It then caught sight of me through the cab window, stopped and, head slightly moving from side to side and round and round, body perfectly still, it looked at me for a while. It had the most enquiring eyes I've ever seen in man or beast.

November
2nd   Spreading pig slurry.

14th   Snipe on Park Lake overflow.

17th   Ploughing maize ground.

20th   About 200 crows, rooks and jackdaws enjoying the strong blusterly wind soaring up and around the sky in a great mass of black dots.

14th   Grey wagtail in Sallybeds.

December
13th   Hardest frost recorded at The Knowle, −23°C and bad blizzards.

15th   Maple seeds blowing across the surface of the frozen snow.

657 Hours Overtime 1981

1982

January

3rd   Oak tree in the west corner top of Parks, Netherwood, has a spread of branches of thirty one paces, ninety three feet.

5th   Nature never stands still, everything seems to be growing or dying. Nothing stands still.

7th   Animals spend a lot of their time just looking at the world around them. It is a satisfying thing to do oneself; just empty the mind and look and listen, especially when the wind is blowing, so that you are looking at an ever-changing scene of grass, trees and crops, swaying back and forth.

21st   Ridge and furrow, ten paces apart, running parallel with the road from The Knowle to bottom of Netherwood drive.

25th   Ploughing again. Weather has been too bad for over a month. Saw two hares chasing each other, top Calves Hill and a buzzard over Collington Meadows.

28th   Pair of partridges, Big Orchard.

29th   Mice have been making runs under the snow, leaving grooves in the snow flattened grass in the dingle, Sallybeds.

February

1st   Owls hooting well into dusk, echoing along Netherwood wood.

2nd   Two peewits returned to Forty Acres, Pensons today, to the only field where I found a nest last year. Evening sky like October.

4th   Twenty peewits on stubble turnips. Peafields.

5th   Found, "May 1931", carved in beech tree at Grandstand Patch. Point-to-Point races.

8th   Canada geese on Park Lake first thing in the morning.

11th   Many rose bushes killed off by hard frosts in the last couple of cold spells; some of the ivy on the house also caught, and some of the evergreen bushes and trees killed.

19th   Six blobs of frog spawn, Jones', damson people's site.

22nd   Wild white violet out by Netherwood House pond.

26th   One heron and three swans flew over Netherwood today.

March

1st   Came in like a lion, windy-wet with thunder early in morning.

5th   Coltsfoot out, Park Lake dam.

16th   White fencing between Parks and Coverfield, there was a solitary clump of coloured primroses, jutting out of the bank of the small stream. It was in full bloom, making the days spent fencing there a pleasure, walking back and forth past this pretty sight.

18th   Many leaves on the ground under the holly trees.

21st   They say, "As many frosts as there be in March, you will have in April also".

22nd   Pigeons started cooing.

23rd   Blackbird's nest in roll of pig netting.

24th   Pair of long-tailed tits, one with feather in its beak.

25th   Came in like a lion, going out like a lamb. Started working land for spring planting; third warm, sunny, and calm day. Dawn chorus going well, many trees showing green and a ladybird emerging from a spruce cone, and poplar tree buds smelling sweet.

27th   Elderberry leaves out, closely followed by hawthorn, willow and larch needles.

29th   Scuffling for potato planting.

30th   Blue tit tasting a pussy willow blossom.

31st   Wild damson (or plum) at the Castle Farm out late this year because of the colder winter. (Last year out 3rd February).

April

2nd   Misty morning; a few minutes of hot sun then a swirling patchy mist coming down again for a while. Birds singing well.

6th   Two house martins at Netherwood.

8th   Cuckoo heard, Bishops Frome; swallow seen Netherwood.

9th   Heard curlew, Bishops Frome.

12th   Wheatear. Ash-bed, top Calves Hill speckled with wood anemone and lesser celandine.

13th   Pair of tree creepers, one going sideways along a branch, bottom of Big Orchard.

17th   Finished potato planting.

18th   Two baby hares, Forty Acres, Pensons. Park Lake – first toad spawn I can recall finding.

22nd   Fresh smell of things growing as I walk into the woods out of the hot, dusty tractor.

29th   Oak before ash.

May

4th   Lime green of the poplar tree leaves, top Calves Hill. Bluebells out. Frosts at night.

6th   Delicate smell of crab apple blossom, top Calves Hill. Ash trees still bare of leaves.

9th   Ten swifts, Bishops Frome (Vicarage Cottage).

16th   May blossom out.

17th   Silage.

31st   Canoeing, River Lugg.

June

1st   Orange-tip butterfly above Netherwood House.

6th   Some of the oak trees coming into leaf, very uneven; the cold winter must have affected them.

10th   Slow worm, The Knowle.

13th   Second cut of silage.

July

18th   Several Small Tortoiseshell butterflies on white thistle heads, Barn field.

19th   Combining winter barley.

20th   Cornflower in barley crop this year, Barn field and Collington's. These pretty, lonely patches of blue in a sea of golden ears.

23rd   Black beetle hanging onto a brown-grey moth, took a bit of separating; moth still alive after. Barn field stubble. Seagulls looking for worms behind the baler.

28th   One thousand bales of hay.

August
1st   Sub-soiling. Strong smell of stinkhorn going past badger corner, Collingtons. Several Red Admiral butterflies.

2nd   Very warm weather, peewits circling low over Collington's Lake. Pigeon landed in water, had a drink and flew off again. Dragonfly on Collington's Lake.

7th   Baby hare, a few days old, in Big Hopyard. Seventy seagulls and 70 peewits, seeming to mingle in together well.

12th   Planting stubble turnips. The ash in the hedgerow has grown up twice the height of the rest.

14th   Combining winter wheat.

21st   Quail, near Sallybed.

26th   Foxgloves come where rides have been bulldozed through the woods, I have not seen them there before this.

29th   Some sort of poplar tree leaves have gone brown two-thirds of the way up tree.

31st   Coverfield, small bird in stubble, no tail, greyish, with yellowish head with two or three black stripes running through, robin size. Young quail?

September
4th   Baling. Hazel nuts turning brown; seems early.

5th   Swallows and starlings lining up separately on electric wires. Wonder if animals and birds get as much pleasure watching us humans, as we get from watching them.

8th   Canada geese starting to fly around in formation.

9th   Some of the holly and laurel trees are starting to shoot from the bottom after seeming to have been killed by the extra cold winter.

12th   Started ploughing. About 500 peewits on worked stubble, Coverfield.

13th   A real hop-pickers morning, with early mist. Young Christmas trees, Rabbitbury Coppice. Grandstand Patch covered with cobwebs, all shapes and sizes standing out with the dew on them.

14th   Strange evening. A long time between sunset and dark; it almost seemed to be getting lighter for a while; a gentle mist about.

15th   All peewits seen this time seem to have good legs and feet.

16th   Lots of nuts this year, but not many blackberries. It must have been quite something when most of the farms around had hops and many had hop kilns; the smell of the drying hops hanging in the air must have been haunting and nostalgic.

16 – 17th   Very hot still, and misty in the mornings. Wind blows from the south-east until 6 pm, then changes round to the west for the rest of the day. The new plantation at Grandstand Patch smelling the same as Coverfield, only mixed with the sweet smell of cider apples.

18th   Far Sallybed. Two buzzards eating worms from the fresh ploughing, getting as close as ten yards before they fly into a nearby tree. One has a whiter breast than the other. When I started work at Netherwood, I only saw buzzards along the banks above the farmhouse contour. Over the years they have moved down to the lower part of the valley, and it is now possible to see more of them flying over the low ground than along the banks and woods on the higher parts of Netherwood.

19th   Flock of crows landing just like a pack of cards falling down.

22nd   Saw a few martins and swallows today.

24th   Swallows gone.

25th   First seagulls this ploughing.

26th   Large numbers of martins catching flies above the mustard. They make frenzied attempts to catch the last few flies as the mustard patch gets smaller under the plough. They look just like a swarm of bees changing their position over the field as the wind gusts, almost as if they were on an elastic band. They kept coming back over the mustard in tight-knit groups after each gust. Were they having their last meal before flying abroad?

Another year ploughing in mustard after the early potatoes in front of Netherwood Cottages. It was a sunny day when the last few acres were being ploughed. This year an extraordinary number of bees were feeding off the yellow flower heads. The field at the finishing side ended up in a point just in front of the cottages. As the afternoon wore on, each bout caused the bees to become more concentrated in this ever-decreasing triangle. In the last bit of an acre there were more bees than flowers, so the ones with nowhere to go, were landing on the crawler, trying to get something from the yellow dust that had been knocked onto the bodywork from this six foot high mustard over the last few days. As the field finished in late afternoon, I saw Chris Woods looking up at his house where thousands of bees had spread themselves over the wall of the building. Suddenly deprived of their source of food, the bees seemed to be taking stock of the situation before going back to their particular hives or trees, and the slanting yellow rays of the evening sun shone on their bodies, putting the finishing touches to an unusual scene.

One misty cold September/October morning in my early twenties, when having bait over Collington Meadows, where the lake is now, and sitting in front of a clump of wild flowers and grasses with the damp dew over them, I saw two bees clinging onto the limp flower heads. What a shame, I thought, they have died in the middle of their work! During the half hour break, the sun came up, drying up the dew and putting a bit of warmth in things, and to my surprise, the bees moved. After another five minutes they seemed none the worse for their night out!

When potatoes were on the Big Hopyard and the mustard was planted on half the field, I went and sat at the edge of the crop for dinner just to watch the bees, flies and butterflies feeding there. In the main there were two sorts of bees, one, a soft grey-brown bee, the other black or a very dark colour. The difference between the two types was obvious. The black bees were coming and going from the south-east, flying very purposefully, straight onto the flower heads and departing at high speed, always in the same direction with no hanging about. The soft grey-brown bees were just the opposite. They seemed to wander in from a northerly direction, casually fly around a bit before alighting on the yellow flower heads. Then, still taking their time, they eventually meandered back the way they came, at a leisurely pace.

30th   String of crows and jackdaws, heading across the middle of Netherwood, going south-west towards Hyde Hill.

October
1st   Planting winter barley. Four partridges sleeping in the middle of Roundcots field. October seems to be the month of beautiful evening skies.

2nd   Trees just starting to change colour. White Meadow; wheatear-type bird, robin size, pale underside; sparrow colour on top; speckledy, browny-orange strip side of head, shortish tail, spent several hours just sitting on wire fence. Whinchat?

5th   While potato harvesting lots of spiders ran across the rows out of the way of the digger; top Calves Hill. This month birds flying are easier to see with the sun that much lower and shining more underneath them.

9th   Crows, jackdaws and rooks come back into their own at this time of the year. It is very comforting to see and hear them as winter approaches.

10th   Eleven partridges eating gravel, bottom Netherwood drive.

Grove Farm – early morning start

13th   Four martins today.

18th   Possible remains of peewit's nest on potato ridges, top Calves Hill.

24th   First frost.

25th   The unusual sight of nine adult cock pheasants together.

26th   Saw two buzzards circling, anti-clockwise, in a clear blue sky, drifting east on a fresh west breeze, getting higher as they went, shadowed by two crows flying a few inches above them.

November
1st   Top Calves Hill, very wet. Large ruts in the potato field made by the tractors, children almost disappearing from sight as they try to cross over them. Two potato pickers caught me and smeared mud all over my face. It was too muddy to run fast out of their way, but it ended alright. I rather liked the feel of one of the women's hands on my face as she wiped it carefully off again.

3rd   Fieldfares heard.

5th   Twenty skylarks down drive at Netherwood.

17th   More crows, jackdaws and rooks than usual in the gang that is about.

23rd   Sub-soiling.

December

7th   Thunder and lightning. Blue flash over Bromyard.

14th   More hares than usual taking to the woods this winter.

600 Hours Overtime 1982

1983

January

2nd   Crows and jackdaws waking with a deafening clamour just before 8 am up by Brickbarns. Nine Canada geese flying towards Collington Lake from Netherwood, 9 am. Sunrise along ley-line over Edwin Loach. Pair of partridges middle of Roundcots.

3rd   Pair of nuthatches seen.

7th   Few snowdrops out, two primroses out top of Park Lake, mild; up to 54°F. These animals have been caught on Netherwood – fox, badger, pole cat, hedgehog, stoat, weasel, squirrel, mink, domestic cat, hare, rabbit, rat and dog.

10th   Ploughing White Meadow. Hazel catkins have started coming out; very plain in the headlights of the crawler against the other gaunt shapes of trees.

12th   Mild, still day, no frosts for a couple of weeks.

13th   Fieldfares on the field where stubble turnips have been grazed off, Collington's.

14th   White Meadow. Two hares standing on their hind legs boxing with each other – a lighter grey, slightly smaller one of the two then followed the bigger, more sandy one, a couple of feet behind, in a zig-zag fashion, out of the field, occasionally having a scuffle on the way.

16th   Only one seagull today while ploughing, and that soon went. Dawn chorus at 7.30 am. Still, mild and dry.

20th   Bees out on mahonia by Netherwood House.

23rd   Dry weather for a fortnight. Planting winter wheat top Calves Hill.

30th   Collington's: A bird with brown back and pale underside skimming about four feet above the ground – large, fieldfare size – sparrowhawk? Ivy tightly wrapped around a dead elm tree; looks like a swarm of bees hanging on the branch of a tree.

February
3rd   Possible crossbill seen Netherwood wood.

13th   Rabbit runs showing up in the dry freezing weather, patches about two feet apart, looking as if a person has walked about with weedkiller on his boots; where the grass thaws they show up very plain. In places they go in straight lines or wiggle about between the trees in the apple orchard, above Netherwood House, like a network of small motorways. Some are in graceful curves like one that went first in a dead straight line then curved off around the dovecot, keeping exactly the same distance from the walls. A human could not have done any better with a measure and string. The rabbit went up in my estimation after seeing this. In all my years of work, I have never seen these runs as plain as this before. Most of the two foot apart patches had rabbit droppings by them. Father used to know where to put rabbit wires in relation to these patches so that the rabbit's head went through the noose. Roger Hallings had to point these out to me. I suppose I have spent too much time looking for bits of flint and pottery. My eyes get tuned into seeing certain things. Dan Hill, pigman, could not understand my interests, he being interested in living birds and animals. He said my bits of pottery and flint were dead things so why bother with them. I can see his point of view, that we should try to live our lives in our own space and time while we're on earth, "Be where you are now as much as possible".

20th   Brooks around Netherwood seem to have cut two feet or more deeper into the ground in the past couple of years; in places where once the water was at ground level, there is quite a drop down it now.

22nd   Far Sallybed drain head used by bird for smashing snail shells, mostly yellow and brown-striped, with a couple of pink ones.

25th   Several white violets out, Park cottage site. No frog spawn yet.

March
1st   Coming in like a lamb, first spring-like morning, slight frost, no clouds, sun strong, filling the woods before the leaves come; birds singing, pigeons cooing.

3rd   Mouth ulcers.

4th   Some of the hazel catkins have come out, some early ones have gone brown and shrivelled and fresh ones have come out by the side of the others.

7th   Many robins about now. Working land for spring barley.

8th   Pair of little owls flying around in daylight, Big Hopyard.

12th   Daffodils coming out.

14th   One blob frog spawn in Vicarage Cottage fish pond. Wild damson out, Mr. Barber, The Castle.

15th   Water-rail Park Lake.

18th   More blobs frog spawn, Jones', damson people's site. Wagtail-type bird with flash side of head, meadow pipit. The beech tree in Grandstand Patch, had fallen. EM or FW 14 or 4 May 1934 had been carved in it. From Point-to-Point time.

28th   Wheatear, White Meadow.

April
16th   Hawthorn leaves out first.

18th   White Meadow, little owl standing in its doorway, legs spaced wide apart in entrance of hole in ash tree, four feet from ground. It watched me skuffling potato headlands, adjoining Hopyard.

May
1st   Very wet. Oak before ash, many leaves coming out in the past couple of days.

5th   Swifts back, and swallows.

6th   Nick Adams' funeral.

13th   Scented poplars by Netherwood House coming into leaf.

14th   Working land for maize planting.

21st   Very wet month, rain almost every day.

24th   May blossom out. More bluebells showing this spring than ever.

26th   Potato planting.

June
4th   Dawn chorus started a few minutes before 4 am. Start first cut of silage.

3rd   Hauled timber from Grove Farm. Mr. Payne has had oak, mahogany and cedar seasoning in cowsheds round foldyard for several years. This was then re-stacked in old lorry shed.

5th   Scent of elder flower heavy in the air around Netherwood the past few days, mingled with occasional whiffs of white clover.

13th   Very warm, 91°F in the shade, 114°F in the sun.

14th   Getting combine ready.

15th   Baling hay.

16th   The extra dark green of the leaves on the trees this year must be due to the extra hot sunshine.

18th   Quail, Brickyards, Hyde Farm. Combining winter barley.

22nd Kestrel caught six mice while baling straw, top Old Roadway.

24th   Many butterflies and insects when filling tanker from Park Lake for potato irrigation.

26th   Warm day, no wind. Took shirt off in morning until nine at night.

28th   A short-tailed water rat type mouse, piggery buildings, Netherwood.

29th   Hottest month on record.

30th   Very hot today.

31st   Far Sallybed, discing stubble while a fox sat in the middle of the field in broad daylight, surrounded by 200 peewits and 50 seagulls who seemed to take no notice of it.

August
2nd   Painted Lady butterfly.

5th   Several people's ripe gooseberries disappeared overnight; none left; first time it's happened as I know. Birds of some sort must take them before people get up in the morning. One day there is a full crop on the bushes; the next not one solitary gooseberry. The extra hot weather must have upset the normal food supply.

6th   Combining spring barley.

7th   First Clouded Yellow butterfly I'd seen; it stands out from a long way off, when flying with a hedgerow in the background, it's brilliant colour unlike any of our butterflies.

9th   Around Park Lake speckled wood butterfly. Small white butterfly.

190

10th   Green dragonfly, Collington's. After harvesting the corn in the Big Hopyard, there was a strip of thistles two feet wide by about ten yards long at the drain head, between White Meadow and Hopyard. (Many years ago someone bled to death from a knife wound, while working in the hops there). These thistles had come because a hollow on the corner had been filled up with soil from building work at the farm and the sprayer just missed this small strip of land. While baling the straw, my eye caught a lot of butterfly activity on these few thistles, I stopped to look, and was fascinated by the variation, so decided to have my next meal break early in case they weren't there at normal dinner time. I sat down with the sun behind me, a few feet away from these thistles, had my sandwiches and tea just watching. It was like a local agricultural show! A gathering of people that are not normally seen in each other's company! The Gatekeeper, Wall Brown, Small Skipper, Peacock, Small Tortoiseshell butterflies, plus bees, flies and wasps. Several of these species, all mingling together made one of the prettiest moving pictures I have seen for a long time. This corner of land has witnessed sadness and happiness for man.

11th   Blackberries getting ripe. Wasp beetle? Collington's.

14th   One field left to combine, winter wheat.

15th   Harebells, Tee Baune Lake, nice clump, also Clouded Yellow, Holly Blue, Small Blue butterflies, on this sunny warm area of short poor grass. One good thing about Netherwood, is that it has so many dingles and woods, which act as a buffer against the sprays and fertilizers, so giving insects a chance to survive.

21st   Robin started to sing his winter song.

28th   The eye of a wren peeped at me over a leaf, while having bait in Ashbed, top Calves Hill.

29th   More dragonflies than usual about this year. When I was by Park Lake dam one came flying across in a sideways motion, and hovered about a foot away at head height, just in the corner of my vision. Slowly turning my head, I tried to get it into focus, but as my eyes moved a fraction, so did the dragonfly, just keeping to one side and slightly above my point of focus. This was not a coincidence, for I tried several times to look at it properly, and the same thing happened. The dragonfly seemed to be looking right into the back of my eyes, as if playing with me in a superior mocking way, completely in charge of the situation. Eventually it zoomed away across the lake, seeming to be laughing as it went and saying "I beat you".

30th   Fewer swallows about than usual.

191

September

1st   Started autumn ploughing.

8th   Jackdaws sitting in pairs in the tree at The Knowle, staking their claim to the nesting site for next spring.

9th   Planting winter barley.

10th   Mouse on top of my bait bag hung on the fence, top Calves Hill; a gift from the kestrel that was catching mice that I was discing up in the stubble? This was not a one-off coincidence, for the same thing happened when working in the Parks field. My bait bag was again hanging on the fence with a dead mouse carefully placed on top. I suppose the kestrel had seen me many times get this bag off the fence, sit down and proceed to eat out of it. Maybe it was its way of saying "thank you" for making many mice available over the years of ploughing and such!

18th   Ploughed up little hoards of acorns in Coverfield, one hundred yards from the nearest oak tree. Had mice or something been very busy?

19th   Plenty of mushrooms on Netherwood this September.

20th   White Meadow, ploughing in mustard while it was raining. Suddenly a host of swallows and one martin appeared to feed on flies that were loathe to get off the flowers into the rain. The swallows had to follow the plough up and down the field, so as to get the flies as they were flushed out into the rain. Some of the swallows came almost to a standstill, plucking the flies from near the sodden yellow flower heads. Others acted like humming birds, actually hovering and taking the flies from off the plants themselves. When I stopped for dinner, they perched on the furrows for about five minutes, and after this they all disappeared. Halfway through dinner they re-appeared, lining themselves up on the barbed wire fence adjoining the Hopyard field, a dozen or so sitting between each fence post, nine feet apart, and facing east, ready to start feeding as soon as I started ploughing again.

25th   Tee Baune, Clouded Yellow flying, and two Comma butterflies feeding on blackberries.

30th   Many young squirrels about in the fields. Myxomatosis still about.

October

9th   A bird slightly smaller than a kestrel, speckled brown, darker top when flying than the kestrel. It flies about eighteen inches above ground, hardly flapping its wings, being mobbed by crows. Sparrowhawk, Pensons; similar

192

type of bird, only slightly larger and pigeon colour, sat hunched in an ash tree for a quarter of an hour.

11th   A white light hovered just above the horizon, south-east of Netherwood, stationary some of the time, about ten times as bright as a star, fading and moving about then flashing and disappearing over the horizon, about 8.30 pm.

20th   Holly berries, very red, in big clusters, stand out well.

22nd   Many large seagulls when ploughing, but not many of the smaller type of gulls. First real frost.

23rd   Robin, hedgesparrow, blue tit, great tit, and chaffinches feeding early morning where the maize had been cut.

24th   The time of the year that the wind starts to go through me, instead of around me.

30th   I came upon a buzzard while driving the tractor near where the culvert was blocked, which had created a small fresh water pond from the overflow from the reservoir. The buzzard was just dragging a moorhen off the edge of this water. I braked the tractor, leaving the engine running at the same revs and just sat there looking. The buzzard did the same, staring in my direction for about a minute, standing on the poor moorhen, stamping one foot repeatedly down on it, beating it into submission, or trying to claw out feathers, the moorhen seeming to get all the time flatter and flatter, until it looked like a strange shaped piece of board. The buzzard then flew up with the moorhen in its claws, but, only a few yards off the ground it lost its grip, allowing its prey to drop. The moorhen then made its way back to the water, and didn't seem too flattened after its ordeal. Ten minutes later when I came back by, the buzzard was still hanging about.

December
4th   When I was taking Christmas trees to Tenbury market, having a little time to spare, I went to look at the river from off Teme bridge. Leaning over looking down at the water, I encountered one of the most peaceful scenes I have experienced. Just where the water swirls through the archways, some mallards and a couple of farm ducks, one white, were swimming against the current, and generally meandering about. Gradually the noise of the traffic disappeared into the background and ceased to exist. I was in a world with ducks, the river, me and nothing else, and was able to look down on the ducks quietly winning their battle against the current, and one of the ducks looked up at me as if to say, "Quite something, aren't we". The next year I went to the same spot and found the ducks and everything were just the same. No matter

193

how long I stopped and looked, nothing would change. It seems these scenes are completely out of man's hands; there is another force somewhere that creates them surely for pleasure or wonder. In earlier years the Christmas trees were sold on the farm to travellers or dealers. One family spent the winter locally earning money where they could this way, then moving to the coast for the summer months. This year I was buckraking the trees out to where they could load them on their wagons. It was early and a wet cold morning when they arrived. The man and a couple of his family went straight to work for about three quarters of an hour, while the wife set about getting their breakfast. First a fire had to be lit, this was done with any wet bits of sticks she could lay her hands on. I admit I looked on in amazement at this feat, done with so little effort and in a short time. How she ever got the sticks to burn I don't know, I might have achieved the same results but with the aid of a couple of gallons of waste oil and diesel or a car tyre. She then proceeded to cook bacon, beans and eggs. All this was done out in the open in drizzly rain. I shall look on this woman with great respect after this, and remember the picture, on this cold raw day, of the family sitting around the fire getting stuck into this tasty, mouthwatering breakfast.

18th   Stoat seen twice, catching a rabbit near Netherwood House.

19th   Moths about after dark. Saw spiders' webs floating by on a light westerly breeze, mild and sunny today.

702 Hours Overtime 1983

1984

January
1st   Ploughing.

28th   Blackbird/thrush singing, Hereford road junction, Bromyard 7.15 am.

February
2nd   Lambs' tails out by Brickbarns Cottages, few elsewhere yet.

8th   Lots of small ladybirds where the wire touches the stakes at Rabbitbury Coppice – Calves Hill fence, one-eighth of an inch long, black, with up to five red spots all same size and colour. There were four or five at each point of contact where barbed wire is stapled to the thirty old stakes.

10th   Ploughing. Just warm enough to have dinner sat in Rabbitbury wood. Curlew calling to another, also owls and buzzard. Jackdaws squabbling over nesting site; oak tree Calves Hill.

12th   Six long-tailed tits flying and feeding in hawthorn bushes near Salleybed.

13th   Freezing fog froze on the trees. Lambs' tails very pretty when the sun came out and they shone from silver nut branches. It was in this place near Salleybed field, that I was ploughing one foggy Saturday. It was only possible to see a few yards down the field as the fog was thick. Having half an hours' bait at 9.00 am, I was part way through my snooze when the sound of voices, very close, awoke me. Looking around, I could not see because of the mist, then, within a few minutes the sun came through chasing the mist away, and lo and behold, the voices of the hunt then came into view! Several people on horseback were near me on the headland. They had come up in the sound-deadening mist, unknown to me. It was a shock to my system to find myself surrounded by horses and people after thinking I was alone and unlikely to see anyone that day!

14th   Saw Great Spotted woodpecker, the first for some time, Rabbitbury Coppice. The winter home of the Green woodpecker which was seen most mornings when going fencing.

22nd   Rabbit paths in the winter corn Castle field, like motorways crossing.

26th   Came to work without car lights. Netherwood brook seems deeper by one and a half feet than a few years ago. There had been a culvert at brook level that used to keep getting blocked up, but now it runs freely owing to the level of the brook sinking this past year or two.

27th   I saw a kestrel knock two doves off a branch of a tree, at Netherwood. It knocked one off then turned around, swooped back, knocking off the one that was still sitting there, rooted to its perch. The kestrel then caught sight of me and flew off.

March
1st   I saw frogs on Jones', damson peoples' site, getting ready to spawn. (Came in like a lamb.)

2nd   Came in like a lion. Curlew calling.

3rd   Four blobs frog spawn, Jones' site.

6th   Twenty-one blobs, Jones' site. First smell of grass growing.

9th   Planting spring barley.

14th   First primrose out.

30th   Wild white violets out, Netherwood.

31st   First butterfly.

April
2nd   Planting potatoes.

4th   Pussy willow showing golden.

9th   Elderberry leaves out.

15th   Fox behaving like a hare, lying in between the furrows of the ploughing, moving over a few yards when the crawler gets too close. This happened for several hours during daylight, middle day; black tips to its ears, red looking legs, white bib and end of tail, ginger grey on back with a lighter ginger band over shoulders. Its tail is two-thirds the length of its body. When it lies down, it wraps its body around its tail in a clockwise direction.

17th   Planting maize.

19th   A pair of wheatears arrived. Most years I see only a solitary bird on the fresh worked land.

22nd Cuckoo.

25th   Martin.

26th   Weather very warm, leaves on the trees coming out very quickly.

29th   Saw small blue butterfly, Bishops Frome. Several house martins, no swallows yet.

May
2nd   Oak before ash.

9th   Swifts. Possible Adder seen near Pensons sling. Orange tip butterfly, Netherwood.

June
10th   Birds start singing 3.55 am.

13th   Lots of willow seeds, or something off willow trees, blowing about.

14th   Tadpoles in new little pond where culvert blocked up Park Lake, near what was a dump in Mr. Payne's time. How quickly the frogs found this new patch of clean spring water for spawning. We humans are not so clever as we think we are.

17th   Dawn chorus, Bishops Frome, 3.45 am. Jackdaw followed by blackbird or thrush. (I haven't yet sorted out their different songs). They are first to start the morning.

18th   Silage, second cut.

July
1st   Not many swallows this time. Sandpiper, Park Lake.

2nd   Irrigating potatoes, Park Lake. Raining hay! A whirlwind had picked up some of a neighbour's crop and had deposited it over the lake, the water ending up with a thin covering of hay over it.

4th   Green and yellow dragonfly, Park Lake. A rainbow, surrounding the tractor, caused by water spray while irrigating potatoes. (A long while ago I remember a rainbow made from redshank dust while combining in the same field).

5th   Damsel flies seem to hatch and mate in one day, for next day Park Lake is deserted.

6th   Park Lake. Saw snake, light green smooth body. Perhaps smooth snake,

N. Turner

197

though I did not see its head. A green algae in the lake seems to come up in the heat of the day and sink overnight. Speckled Wood butterfly.

8th   Park Lake. Several birds singing today; they have been quiet for a while. Very hot day. Strong smell of elderberry blossom. I saw a black hairstreak butterfly on the dusty potato headland in Parks Meadow, while watering potatoes. The water of the previous load had damped down a bit of headland near the wood, adjoining Stable Meadow. On coming down to fill up again, I saw this small solitary butterfly in the middle of the flattened headland. I stopped to see what it was, crept carefully up to it, hoping to see it with its wings spread open, so I could see what sort it was. To my surprise it never flew away, I bent down to get a closer look, gently poked my finger at it, but still it did not budge, keeping its wings tightly closed. Kneeling down, I put my finger right up close to its tongue which never moved from the damp dust. The end of my finger was almost as big as the whole of the butterfly and all it did was to pick up its left front leg – the thickness of a hair on my head. And put it against the end of my finger as if to say, "That's far enough". All this time it was still getting moisture or something from the ground. Thinking, "That's an exceptionally brave act for something so small", I got back on the tractor, made a detour around it, flattening a few potato ridges in the process, a thing one did not normally do and so left the black hairstreak in peace. Next load it had gone.

Dipper seen Park Lake.

15th   Blackcap singing, Park Lake. Family of ten young mallards and their mother walked single file over the dam to graze on the half-ripe wheat up a tramline in Peafield. They came back later in the day, one hesitatingly going first until it reached the safety of the water, the rest following.

21st   Hauling bales.

22nd   Park Lake. Black and green-grey caterpillars feeding on nettles. Dragonfly with blue body.

23rd   Park Lake, Common Blue butterfly.

24th   Park Lake, Gatekeeper butterfly.

25th   Park Lake, Meadow Brown and the Ringlet butterfly.

27th   Park Lake, Holly Blue butterfly. Wild black cherries, very ripe and sweet to eat, near boathouse.

29th   Park Lake. Lent my tractor seat sponge to an artist sketching by the lake. Lowered the lake six inches with water for potatoes.

30th   Park Lake. Six queen wasps feeding on wild angelica flower.

August
2nd   Small copper butterfly near Salleybed. Dan saw a pair of sparrowhawks exchange a mouse in mid-air.

3rd   Sub-soiling top Calves Hill stubble. Six hares together, their heads and ears just showing above the stubble, all facing the same way on the skyline of this sloping, curved field; also an old looking toad with one eye.

5th   More than usual amount of Gatekeepers and Common Blue butterflies to-day.

8th   Ploughing, Grit Hill.

10th   Two foxes behind Pensons in corn. One got through the square of pig-net fencing fire.

18th   Finished combining.

20th   Several half grown toads in potatoes, Parks field. Still very hot and dry.

23rd   Thunder and rain.

29th   Bale hauling.

September
1st   Daddy-long-legs everywhere, wild ducks on Park Lake, scattered like leaves over the water; two herons and many more dragonflies than usual this year.

6th   Ploughing for winter barley. At least 300 seagulls, one with club foot.

7th   Birds twittering, 6.30 am.

9th   Far Salleybed. Young, year or so old, cattle were lying peacefully in the centre of the field when a rain storm blew up. Suddenly, the field was empty. All that could be seen of the cattle was white faces peering out of the wood on the far side of the field, just like people. Later I watched them following three herons around the field. Hawthorn bushes are the first to establish on a new fence line after about twenty years.

10th   Most impressive bright yellow moon came up over the horizon as darkness fell. Watched the herd of cattle chasing a lone pheasant around their field.

13th   Brilliant Clouded Yellow butterfly, Roundcots.

17th   Ploughing, White Meadow. First serious rain for months. A storm was passing, blown by a westerly wind as the sun was going down behind Rabbitbury Coppice. The field I was ploughing was already in shadow and the sky black-grey to the horizon. To the east the sun shone from underneath the clouds, so that Coombs wood, The Castles Farm and the trees at the bottom of the White Meadow were in bright sunshine. The red-painted barns of Castles Farm, stood out in bright contrasting colour and a large rainbow curved over the whole scene. Starting back down the field, heading straight for the centre of the rainbow-edged picture, I got out of the crawler to have a better look. I was so enthralled by it all, that I stopped the engine to enjoy things better. Standing on the squelchy stubble field I said smugly, throwing the question to nature – God the Creator, "Improve on that then!" To my amazement and everlasting humbling, they, or it, did just that, for into the scene, high up in the sky, came a formation of birds, as if they had been poised there, ready to come on when summoned. This 'V' formation of birds coming through the edge of the rainbow, were like two laser-straight lines coming to a sharp point. There were perhaps 40 birds in this big 'V', with three little 'V's' of about 20 birds below and behind. They flew in formation against the black clouds, with the sun reflecting off the underside of their wings, like lights winking, in turn. It was as if a series of waves ran along the lengths of the 'V', from the front to the back with two more waves of winking lights in quick succession, like the movement of millepedes' legs along the ground. Were they seagulls on their way home for the night, putting the finishing touches to this superb scene, and perhaps saying "Thank you for all the food over the years". They flew south-east towards Bromyard, and their slow progress across the sky was easy to watch, picked out by the sun for a long time. I vowed never to challenge my Maker/God/ Nature again!

19th   Three different owls hooting echoed along the wood, back of Netherwood House an hour after dark.

20th   A feel of autumn in the air this evening.

October
4th   Fieldfares and redwings seen, Dan Hill – also about 40 pied wagtails in a flock.

12th   End of Mr. Payne as gaffer and start with Lord and Lady Darnley. Before Netherwood was sold, when building alterations were being done to the house, some bees were found living in the wall of the house, I think above the kitchen. The builders, under the guidance of MERV, were unable to work because of these bees, so a length of pipe was put to the entrance of the nest to try to guide them away. This did not work, so in the end they had to be destroyed because it was not feasible to take the stone wall to pieces. I have read that when something happens to bees, it often affects the people involved. By getting rid of the bees in his house, did Mr. Payne somehow set the seal on his leaving Netherwood?

October

When working down Tee Baune orchard, something jumped over the fence nearby. Thinking a dog had scared George's sheep and one of the ewes had leapt the fence in panic, I walked down the orchard to round it up. As I got closer, I thought, "That's a funny long-legged sheep; it must be somebody's goat." I followed it along and came to the conclusion that it must be a deer of some sort. When it reached the other end of the orchard, the deer, without any effort, jumped the fence into the Parks field and disappeared from sight. This deer was seen by several people in the next few days, and is the one and only time I have seen or heard of a deer on Netherwood, except that it was a deer park several hundred years ago. It was as if it were welcoming titled owners back to Netherwood.

One other thing struck me as strange, which was that a couple of years later the dovecot in Netherwood garden, which had been empty during the thirty-odd years since I had started work on the farm, suddenly acquired occupants. Several white doves started living and breeding in it, as they had done originally. Perhaps it is all coincidence, but it gives food for thought all the same. We humans think we are the be-all-and-end-all of everything, but perhaps birds and animals have an affinity with things and places and a past that has in one form or another been handed down to them. One evening at dusk I was walking down the side of Rabbitbury Coppice under the tall overhanging ash trees, and I had the feeling that the trees with their roots deep in the soil belonged more to the earth and the world than ever we humans. We seem such temporary, fragile things, scampering over the world like a lot of ants. Having found what could be Neolithic quern stone in the Coverfield at Netherwood, I began wondering how much corn this acre of land might have produced between the years 2000 BC and 2000 AD. Calling it, for easy reckoning half a ton per acre, this patch of soil has been very useful. It can nowadays produce four tons per acre! Clearly this soil then has been for the benefit of humans and other forms of life for centuries. It should then be for all intents and purposes, pampered and mollycoddled, for as long as possible, by those of us who have the loan of it for a while.

14th   Lots of hazelnuts this year.

15th   Ploughing.

17th   Dan watched a hobby feathering a young dove by barn.

18th   Watched fox hunting in Barn field on dusk, white tip on the end of its tail.

31st   Twenty to thirty long-tailed tits cheeping their way through the apple trees we were shaking for cider, Little Netherwood, some of them only two yards away.

December
4th   Voices carrying a long way today. Small orle (alder) grove of trees silhouetted against wintery sky with pinky-orange clouds.

9th   Ploughing Coverfield. The moon going down over Garmsley Camp as the sun rises over Edwyn Loach Church.

December
While walking back up to the road after ploughing late one night, was greeted going past Little Netherwood house, by the sight of the sheep standing in a pool of light from the low, uncurtained, cottage bay-window, all looking intently at the television on in the room.

780 Hours Overtime 1984

1985

January
Three hares chasing each other over White Meadow, in the snow.

14th   Barn owl, Collington.

18th   While burning tree tops, top of Park Lake with snow on the ground, four robins sat in a holly bush with the fire between me and them. They were after food from the thawed ground and decaying logs of wood.

23rd   Hibernating hornet found in a dead log, in a circular hole burrowed out of the rotten wood. It was one and a half inches deep with the entrance filled in behind it, it was only just able to move its legs in the frosty weather.

31st   Birds singing a little in the morning, 7.15 am. Snowdrops came through and showed white in two days.

February

1st   Fieldfares in Hopyard.

13th   Dead barn owl on snow on the roof of Netherwood barn.

March

1st   Came in like a lamb!

11th   Frog spawn on Jones', damson peoples' site.

12th   A tawny owl sunned itself in a small oak tree by the side of far Sallybeds on this frosty, sunny morning. While having lunch a small hawk zoomed a few feet from the crawler, just above ground, brown back, mistle thrush size.

13th   Barn owl sat on the garden fence of Parsonage Farm, Collington.

16th   More snow.

17th   Heard curlew.

18th   First primrose out.

19th   Watched by a golden brown tawny owl sitting bolt upright on a bough of tree, between Sallybeds.

20th   Discing.

26th   More blobs of frog spawn in ditch above old dump, Netherwood.

27th   Wheatear arrived.

29th   Wild white violets out.

30th   First warm day.

April

10th   Deer in Tee Baune orchard.

12th   Frog spawn hatched, Netherwood.

15th   Cuckoo heard.

16th   Sally trees first in leaf.

17th   Planting potatoes.

24th   First two swallows. Brimstone butterfly, Pensons Farm.

30th   Canada geese chicks on Hyde pool. Discing maize land. Peewit chicks at Grove Farm.

203

May

1st   Small wader-type bird by Park Lake; blackish head; whitish underneath; blackbird size, flies with legs dangling, water rail?

3rd   Swifts at Bishops Frome.

4th   Taking down fence for pheasant pen.

6th   Oak before the ash.

7th   Planting maize. Orange Tip butterfly, old dump, Parks.

18th   Went on a bus trip to Stonehenge for the day. It was interesting, but I did not catch the mood of the place. Perhaps it is something one should visit several times a year in different weathers and seasons to catch the flavour of the past. Or perhaps be there for a night, to give oneself time to feel the spirit of the stones. Not mixing often with people, I find that, suddenly being surrounded by strangers, I am so aware of them that I am unable to concentrate on viewing the likes of Stonehenge. My main memory of this day was of when I sat in the bus waiting to come home. A bus a little way up the park slowly pulled out in front of where I was sitting. It was about one-third full of people and a girl was standing in the passage in the middle of the bus, as if she was looking for someone to share her excitement at being there. Catching sight of me looking in her direction, she smiled, then waved and eventually was standing there, two hands waving, as if saying, "I've seen Stonehenge, it's great! Don't you think so too!" Then, this girl, about eighteen years old, just stood there looking at me in rather a startled way, as if the strength of feelings had surprised even herself. As the bus drew away from sight, I was left with the memory of her haunting, dark, wide-open eyes that seemed to be saying, "It's a lonely world, please don't forget me." They conveyed a feeling that made me want to chase after the bus and give the girl a hug, saying "I understand how you feel."

This instant mutual attraction conveying meaning between two complete strangers I find is mostly, if not wholly confined to girls in their middle to late teenage years. Younger girls' eyes seem not to know what's happening. Older women have a guarded look, as if to say, "I understand what's happening, but nothing is going to happen here and now, this minute!" I remembered vividly some years ago, when Bromyard horse show was held just over the river on the side of the road, towards Tenbury Wells, half a mile out of town. (It was the year Pat Smythe rode at Bromyard). Three girls came in a lorry with their horses. I had the pleasure of standing by one of these girls for most of the show by the side of the course. Every so often we looked into each other's eyes, in a relaxed way, the girl seeming quite happy, knowing what was happening and never attempting to move away or spoil what was going between us. I remember, too, how some years later, when Bromyard Gala was held on the Hereford road; out of town at Mintridge Farm, I went again to the show. There were fewer horses and more steam engines this time. I spent several hours walking round everything, and was about to go back home, when out of the thousands of people there, one person suddenly stood out from all the other people around me. Whether she had been looking at me first or not, goodness knows, it was as if someone had joined two invisible life-threads together, that connected each of us, making it impossible for us not to want to be closer together. The people and the show around, seemed to fade into the background. She was, at a guess, seventeen; slightly on the small side; brownish complexion; short blond hair brushed back off her face; blue eyes. We looked in a confused way at each other and I found that my desire to go home had vanished. The girl was now joined, presumably by her mother, and they went into a nearby tent. I discreetly followed, wanting a closer look at the young lady, who was wearing a pair of well-fitting jeans and a blouse. She eventually spent some time looking at polished stones to hang around one's neck, and eventually finding one she liked, she tried it on and bought it, but the chain was too long to match the heart-shaped locket that she already wore. The salesman said that if she waited ten minutes, it could be shortened. I then went over to watch some glass blowing and shaping, and the girl came and stood by my side. As the minutes went by there was an edging closer together, we hardly dared look in each other's direction now as we felt so close. But that was as far as things got, for her mother came over with the now shortened chain and polished stone, taking her daughter out of the tent and into the crowd.

27th   Hot springs, Netherwood Hill, showing.

June
3rd   A lot of May blossom this time.

13th   Swiping rides in woods.

25th   Building new pheasant pen.

July
1st   Cuckoo still shouting.

3rd   Great Crested grebe, Middle pool, Tee Baune. Also a dark-coloured duck with ducklings.

4th   Cuckoo has not changed its tune yet.

7th   Haymaking.

9th   Black Hairstreak butterfly on privet, The Knowle. Cuckoo usually

205

changes its tune around 15th–18th June and flies around The Knowle before going away until next year.

15th   An oak limb, a foot in diameter which I cut off twenty-five years ago has taken till now to heal over, leaving a vertical join up the middle of the scar.

17th   Spider web in crawler cab has forty-one cross strands an eighth of an inch apart, a very neat construction.

19th   Cleaning pond by Netherwood buildings.

24th   Combining winter barley. Comma butterfly, Castlefield.

29th   Hauling bales.

August
6th   Canada geese on stubble at Roundcots. Robin started its winter song, hanging around the buildings.

8th   Planting stubble turnips.

23rd   Rain! It has rained almost every day this last week or so.

24th   Draining.

28th   Conker tree starting to change colour at Munderfield.

September
1st   Combining.

2nd   Draining.

3rd   Ploughing. Mice in the cornfields and grass and in amongst the corn.

10th   Small hawthorn bushes overgrown with goose grass and covered with the upside down parachutes of spider webs laden with mist droplets. Beautiful, with the sun shining down through them. A real hop-pickers' morning.

14th   Bales. A dull reddish-brown toad and a small frog, normal colour, in stubble, top Old Roadway. Toads seen in several corn fields this year, making a comeback after many years of absence.

18th   Several small flocks of sparrows flying to and fro in the hedgerows this autumn.

23rd   Dragonflies, Collington Lake.

24th   Saw my first blue butterfly this year, Collington field.

25th   Ploughing. On slatted footbridge that spans a narrow part of Collington

Lake, lying on my back, eyes closed, I was disturbed for a while by what I thought was an angry squirrel, making an unusual noise. Not bothering to open my eyes, I just lay there wishing it would shut up and let me doze off. This it did eventually. Just before going back to work, I went for a walk for a couple of minutes round the lake, leaving my bait bag and what I was lying on, on the slatted bridge. When I got back, I saw something nosing about my sandwiches and flasks. It sensed it was being watched and a black shape turned towards me, then half starting to go on across the bridge away from where I was standing, it changed its mind and stood snarling at me. It was a mink. This presumably was what had been making all the noise a little earlier. Standing there facing one another, it was obvious the mink was not going to back off, so I stood there watching it make its snarling way towards me and the edge of the lake. Thinking back to the time when I had a mouse up my trouser leg, I was not very keen to start kicking at it if it got too close. The edge of the bridge was a yard from where I stood, and when the mink got across, it popped down a small hole in the lake bank. It seemed unafraid of man.

(No mushrooms so far this year).

While working in Collington Meadows, now one field, there were two days with no wind and cloudless skies and I had my meals at 9 am, 1 pm and 5 pm, sitting on the same footbridge at Collington Lake. One morning at bait time, the sun was breaking through the mist and warming things up a bit. I was sitting there admiring the scenery, keeping one eye open for any birds that might show themselves, and looking at the reflection of the trees in the calm surface of the water. On the surface itself, and under the surface, I became aware that the leaves and bits and pieces floating there were moving in the wrong direction under the bridge and not heading, as I expected, towards the overflow. If there had been a breeze to move the surface it would have been expected, but as it was, it had been a calm night and there was not even a hint of any movement of air. Looking deep into the water near where I was sitting, I noticed that it was only the surface of the lake that was moving, below the surface all was perfectly still. The movement of the floating leaves was fairly rapid and as I looked more carefully over the whole surface I saw that there was a general movement all over, as far as I could see. The surface water was moving from the centre of the lake towards the nearest bank or shoreline. It was as if, in the cold, calm night, the lake had contracted, drawing all the easy floating bits on its surface into its centre and now, responding to the warmth of the morning sun, relaxing and spreading itself out again. It seemed a living, breathing thing, responding to day and night, heat and cold. (When ploughing, the earth always seems to turn over more easily about an hour after it gets dark). Not wanting to get too excited about something that perhaps always happened, but which I had not noticed before, I decided to check again at dinner time, and if all was still calm and sunny, at tea time as well. I was well aware that lakes have different characters. Park Lake seems to catch the westerly wind which turns it into a miniature sea, with waves and a swell. Tee Baune Lake does not catch the wind so much, has more weed and turns brown after heavy rain, and when swimming in it I find it has cold and warm spots.

At 1 pm, middle day, Collington Lake was still calm and sunny, so I studied it again for half an hour. There was no surface movement in any direction. Tea time, 5 pm, came. The weather was still the same, so I sat and had tea on the little bridge. The sun by then was going off the lake and, as I was half hoping, the leaves and bits of stuff on the surface started to move back towards the middle of the lake from the outer edges, where I was sitting. The surface bits were speeding in the opposite direction from where they had been going that morning when the sun started to break through. For me it was a thrilling day, for I had seen something I had never seen before. I began to realise how close water is to the way human life and death appears. Water, as far as I know, cannot be killed or got rid of. If boiled, it turns to steam, then comes back to water. We humans, and other animals, drink it, some is passed through the body, some is used up in breathing and so on, but it is still around to be drawn up by the sun and let down as rain again. I suppose so long as there is gravity and nothing escapes into outer space, there will always be water in some form or other, just as life, human and otherwise continues in some form. Perhaps it is the same when a person dies – the spirit, or life force is drawn up, as the sun draws up water to turn it into clouds, later to fall back to earth, to the human life force. When somebody dies, that life is available to enter another body, perhaps when a baby takes its first breath, or perhaps as a man's sperm fertilises a woman's egg.

Water in its different forms, becomes something different at each stage. The drop of water that falls to earth is not the spring as it comes out of the earth; neither is it the stream that runs into lake or river; neither is it the sea. The fields and woods on the farm have taken on a similar role, but each part is individual in its own way, especially for me, as memories are built up over the years of things seen, done, experienced or heard about. On occasional visits for tractor spares to local firms, I get great pleasure from the mixed feelings and emotions as I walk round the back of their premises and look at the old tractors that have been traded in for new models. If no-one else is around and everything is quiet, there seems to be something left of the people that used to drive them. To stand close to these used, battered machines and pick up the feelings coming from them, is strange. It is not something I can do for long, perhaps because I don't understand what is happening. After a while I have to walk away, back to the reality of the day and what I am supposed to be doing. When walking between new tractors, no feelings come from them. They just seem to stand there waiting to acquire a spirit of life and feeling. I now say "Thank you" to each individual field after I have taken a crop of some sort or another off it, and "Thank you" to the tractor after a day's work. It is somehow a token of my awareness of all the different people that made the machine, from the men who dug the iron ore out of the earth, to the people who made all the individual parts and those who put it all together in order that I may jog up and down the fields and observe the changing seasons in pleasant surroundings. The valley breathes like the lake too, when the wind is still. The mist in the morning will roll up out of the hollows and disperse as it gets to the rim of the bank above Netherwood. Then, in the evening, cool air will come down from the rim, bringing the scent of the woods with it. I feel this strongly from the banks above Netherwood looking in a northerly direction towards Clee Hill, with the sun behind me, which gives a wide, clear view. Someone else I know also has this awareness of things and says "Sorry" each time he cuts a bough off a tree.

The North American Red Indians of years ago seem to sum up for me the way I view the earth and place where I work and live. Their attitude to, and relationship with, their surroundings make a lot of sense, for they see everything in harmony with everything else. Man to-day seems to be trying to do too much, too fast, without thinking about the consequences of his actions on his surroundings. On the farm where I work, I fear that if the year's work could be done in a month, the farmer would still not be satisfied; he would then want it done in a week, and so on and so forth, until it was done so fast that there would be no point in doing it at all! Today people pay to go places to take exercise, when years ago it came free with the job!

Was my experience of the lake's breathing something I had to discover for myself, or was it something lost from years ago which had always been deep inside me, like the smells of Coverfield wood? Then, when in the right surroundings and frame of mind, I was to become aware of it? Or is there some force that only allows us to experience things when we are capable of appreciating them?

October

2nd   Went to Gainsborough for crawler parts.

5th   Forty-eight Canada geese, one wheatear, Parks field.

6th   Ploughing in mustard behind cottages. Baby hare ran out across the

209

ploughing into the front gardens of the cottages watched by Bob's dog, who neither moved nor blinked at this close encounter with a chaseable, edible form of nature.

7th   Some swallows and martins catching flies over mustard flowers.

9th   Hornet, top corner behind Pensons. The sun reflected off the spiders' webs, strung across the tops of the stubble (Big Orchard).

12th   Grass heads covered with spiders' webs, filled with dew, caught by the rising sun, down at eye level. Like being in another world, Forty Acres, Pensons, ploughing.

21st   Fox, Calves Hill, mooching about where the cattle had been fed, surrounded by pheasants that were picking up the bits of corn the animals had left, neither taking a bit of notice of the other, just a magpie who kept flying near the fox this sunset.

23rd   Leaves still on the trees and mostly still green. Twenty-one consecutive dry days this October.

November
2nd   Fieldfares. Jackdaws pairing up on Ernie's chimney, Pie Corner.

6th   Only one or two mushrooms this year, at Tee Baune orchard.

13th   Small, half-sized duck diving and swimming a long way under water, light grey, Park Lake – dab chick?

18th   Cutting maize.

20th   Sub-soiling maize ground.

27th   Ploughing. Oak trees' leaves ranging from green to attractive brown. Oaks one of the last to lose their leaves.

December
23rd   Crows, rooks, jackdaws, when windy, fly in a tight group in a column high into the sky. Generally, crows, rooks and jackdaws when flying together are a very higgledy-piggledy lot, not neat as the peewits when they fly around.

24th   Working for days on end in one field with no leaves on the trees, and only the different colours of the wood. The branches look drab except for a few minutes during the day when the light is right and it is very beautiful.

1027 Hours Overtime 1985

The slatted bridge – Collington Lake

1986

As I get older, things of childhood start to become important again, like the hedgerows, birds, flowers and the time to look around.

January

14th   White Meadow. Bird on its own, like a starling but with the colour of a hedge sparrow, feeding along the bottom of a fence, corn bunting? skylark? snipe?

15th   Three pairs of eyes in lights while ploughing on the brow of White Meadow. As they ran off, the eyes seemed low to the ground and did not move up and down when the animals ran; perhaps they were badgers.

16th   Kestrel, eating what looked like a starling. After a quarter of an hour all that was left was the feet, beak and a few feathers.

17th   Hen chaffinch perched on the plough when I greased up this morning. We had a bit of a natter, me talking and the bird putting in a few appropriate churps, quite at ease with me. Saw mink heading downstream at the bottom of Castle field. Seem to be more yellow hammers and greenfinches about than ten years ago, but fewer blackbirds. The other side of the valley from Netherwood seems to have different birds. Perhaps because there is less arable that side the brook. Ploughed at night in the White Meadow, I felt extra tired and found myself seeing things. One was the shape of a woman lying in the furrow in a pale long one-piece dress. I was about to plough this apparition in within the next couple of seconds, which was not a good feeling. Later I found I was looking down on a man walking on a flat place on a mountain with two people at his side. Was I half-asleep and dreaming?

19th   Spider caught fly in crawler cab. Unusual to see a fly active in the middle of January. One autumn at crawler driving time about eleven spiders set up home in the crawler cab, each in their own part. The boss ones had the front window, usually three big ones. They all left lines of droppings down the windows. Nothing much was seen of them all day except when a fly got in one of the webs or one of them decided its web was too dusty to be efficient and would robble it up, bit by it, then drop down and set about putting a new one up again. At dusk they all got active, just before I put the lights on. They would all hang about an inch down the windows and were silhouetted against the fading sky. Strange to see all these forms bobbing about because of the vibrations of the crawler. Then the darkness hid what they were getting up to. Last evening two small spiders hung down between the three big ones. I thought it seemed presumptuous of them as they were treading on dangerous ground, so I made a special point this evening of seeing if they were still there. As I feared, they weren't, and I'm sure the one boss spider looked twice as large as it had the previous evening. I suppose it had eaten the two foolhardy upstarts. There was one extra black, slim, large one that had its home outside, in the windscreen wiper. It seemed to have a set up that allowed it to drop straight down on any part of its web, so it was very successful in catching anything that landed. This spider would make dummy runs when nothing was in its web. Just keeping in practice, I suppose!

Where a fence had been put through a level field 25 years ago, the soil has dropped on either side of it by three to four inches, through ploughing and working the land.

March

1st   The main appreciation of winter seems to be when it ends and spring comes, for without this change from unpleasant to pleasant weather, spring would lose much of its charm and effect.

3rd   The grass that has been scorched brown by nearly a month of freezing east wind, smells, now it is warmer, like the smell of grass that has been "gramoxoned" – sprayed with weed killer.

4th   The frog spawning place by the old dump is still frozen over. Saw moorhen there.

5th   Wild white violet, much battered, came out down under the snow at Park Lake.

8th   No frog spawn yet; ground not yet properly thawed out. Mink, bottom of Sallybeds field.

13th   Planting spring barley.

14th   Hazel catkins coming out.

15th   Frogs spawning, old dump. About twenty males, black-ish on backs and white-ish underneath, and about five females, slightly larger and more orangey-brown.

19th   White violets out, Park Cottage site. Forty blobs frog spawn, old dump.

27th   March in like a lamb, out like a lion.

April

5th   Planting new hedge sides of Netherwood drive up from main road.

7th   Snow. Curlew.

11th Planting potatoes.

14th Primrose out.

18th Planting garden hedge, Netherwood.

20th Wheatear.

21st Toads spawning, Park Lake and Hyde Lake.

24th Three swallows.

25th First spring-like day. Till now it has been cold and damp.

26th Yellow wagtails.

27th Started planting potatoes again after wet spell.

28th Most of the trees are coming into leaf at the same time this year – hazel, wild cherry, elderberry, thorn, poplar.

May
3rd Finished planting potatoes.

4th Discing for maize planting.

18th Spotted flycatchers.

26th Some yew trees and evergreens scorched on the east side from several weeks of cold east wind in the winter.

June
2nd Silage.

4th The farm ducks find lots of tasty food in the loads of silage brought in. Very entertaining to watch them clambering up over the heaps and disappearing out of sight between the loads. I have to be careful not to bury them when buckraking into the silage pit.

6th May blossom coming out.

8th Hundreds of tadpoles, Park Lake, going over the top of the dam overflow and being washed down the brook. More cowslips than usual about this year.

July
7th Baby frogs or toads moving away from Park Lake and Tee Baune Lake, heading up into the woods.

16th Irrigating potatoes.

24th Combining.

August

9th   Combining oil seed rape.

11th   One sandpiper, Netherwood farmyard and about twenty dunlins, Park Lake.

15th   A feeling of sadness when half the small conventional oblong bales in Parks field had been hauled, the rest just sitting there waiting forlornly for people to start gathering them too, for they were spoilt the longer they were left. The field should have been full of workers at harvest time as soon as the field had produced its crop and not left in a half-finished state.

24th   Sub-soiling, Roundcots. Two hares chasing each other, zigzagging from the middle of the field in a vague fashion, as butterflies do, to the boundary fence. Eventually the foremost hare, rather unwillingly, went through into the next field. The other stopped and returned to the centre of the field. It was as if one hare was, in a friendly way, chasing the other out of the field, as if each hare has a field to itself. This chasing was saying "Keep out!"

30th   Ploughing and combining.

September

2nd   Munderfield conker tree changing colour.

5th   Kingfisher seen at Collington Lake by John. Gaffer said he has also seen one on small pond by buildings.

8th   Migraine. Finish combining.

10th   Sue, farm secretary's wedding party at the Oak Hotel, Tenbury Wells. A memorable evening because I met three people from long ago whom I did not recognise. Frank Caldicot, a school mate, had to ask someone else who I was! He, like me, senses a familiar face. Then Elaine Harris, who used to come picking up potatoes with her mother many years ago, was pointed out to me. Mike Perrit recognised me, but I could not put a name to his face, though the eyes were familiar. I used to go swimming with him in Collington's Lake. As I don't socialise much, I was very pleased to meet these people from many years ago. Sue's wedding party seemed to be more of an event than appeared on the surface. So many people she and her husband knew turned out to be people from my past.

15th   Squirrels are eating all the hazelnuts before they have a chance to ripen.

17th   Hawthorn trees exceptionally pretty in their autumn colours. A calm, warm week with light night frosts.

24th   Two herons flew over. Grey wagtail, Park Lake.

28th   Comma butterfly on blackberries, behind Pensons.

October
1st   Baby hare in mustard at Juniper Hill, Grit Hill Farm which now belongs to Netherwood, purchased 1984. It was ploughed up and planted with corn and potatoes. When I ploughed it for the first time I was filled with feelings of nostalgia, for Grit Hill Farm was adjoining The Knowle where I was born and grew up. This was where I had spent a lot of my school days, in its small fields, orchards, tall hedgerows, woodlands and streams. What used to be about 17 fields of different shapes and sizes, is now only four. While travelling backwards and forwards, it seemed I was ploughing 15 acres of memories a day, visualising in my mind's eye, all the different spots where things had happened forty years ago. The apple tree with a hole in, that the nuthatch had made smaller so that my hand was too big to get to its eggs, was still there, and the place where I shot my first rabbit. There was the cider stone we played on and the place where we hid the hedger's tools, where my mate and I compared willies, and where I had a nose bleed, picking up stones, where we cut down wood for firewood and helped bale hay with a stationary baler. I knew the spot where the Worcester apples were, that I used to scrump and the hedgerow bottom that was a mass of blue and white violets. The grave was still there, where I used to go and smell the narcissi and daffodils planted on it, and the field where I did haymaking with a horse. There was the field that I visited each night after school to see if they were cutting it with a binder so as to go rabbiting; where I told a girl how cold her bottom felt to my warm hand and was told, "So would yours be if you'd been sat on the cool ground!" I found the first yellowhammer's nest, in another part where I visualised people, many years ago, cutting this field with scythes or sickles. There are clear pictures in my mind when I travel over where these small fields used to be.

12th   Dab chick, Park Lake.

17th   I have over the years got into the habit of saying "Hello" to the moon each time I see it for the first time at night. When ploughing on my own there is a special pleasure in seeing this comforting light in the sky, especially when turning at the end of the field and swinging round, and faced by it, having just come up over the horizon without my knowing. To-day a full moon suddenly came out from behind the clouds, bathing the valley in its stark light. I seem to have spent much of my life being in two places at the same time, one where my body is, the other where my mind is.

20th   Harvesting today, the gaffer, Lord Darnley, was out on the corn trailer taking the grain from off the combines up to the dryer. We were cutting Far Salleybed field. Roger and I, the combine drivers, had left part of the field down against the brook to dry out a bit more, while we cut the rest of the field. The gaffer had forgotten about this, or did now know it was not cut, being out of sight of the field. He thought we had nearly finished, so left the corn trailer up at the farm and was walking back. As he neared Salleybeds he saw us tearing off down the field and not towards the gate and home and twigged what was happening. His leisurely walk suddenly turned into a mad dash back towards the farm to fetch the tractor and trailer, so that we were able to unload and finish the field. We remembered a time just after he came to Netherwood, and not having had much to do with farming before, he watched Dan and Raymond weigh the pigs, prior to being sent off to Bowketts, Hereford, for slaughter. On the following Monday, there was a call from Bowketts, saying that the pig weights were all wrong. What had probably happened was that the gaffer had been leaning on the scales, so a lot of pigs got sent off before their proper weights had been reached!

22nd While feeling my way back to the farm after ploughing this dark night, along the top of Barnfield, I became aware that I had company. A few yards out, parallel with me, something caused me to stop for a moment and listen, it was like someone breathing with a heavy cold and being half strangled at the same time. It was a most unusual, uncomfortable sound to hear on a dark night and the only thing I could think was that it was a badger. In the last year or two, badgers have set up home near the top of Park Lake, having not been there for the past twenty-five years.

November
7th   Fieldfare back. Many oak trees still have leaves on, the rest are bare.

27th   Cut maize for silage.

December
1st   Trail of jackdaws and crows coming back from the east to roost in Rabbitbury Coppice area as it gets dark.

12th   The berries in the hedgerows that the birds leave, stand out this time of year with all the leaves gone, like dewy, pretty-coloured necklaces. (Black Bryony).

16th   The gaffer cheerfully going up to the woods with saw in hand, came back a little later looking black and disgruntled. Afterwards we found out why. He had some time previously picked out a Christmas tree for himself and on going up to cut it down, found it had gone. Not knowing he had his eye on it, one of us had beaten him to it, and nicked it first. Not a sensible thing for us to have done as this sort of thing can lead to bad gaffer-worker relationships.

1038 Hours Overtime 1986

1987

January
5th   Edvin Loach Church steeple silhouetted in the middle of the red, half-risen sun, looking along possible ley-line, viewed from the Barnfield, adjoining Netherwood Farm buildings. This is past the shortest day but close enough to see the possibilities of some shape near the church that originally was there when ley-lines were the fashion some time or other in the past. It was a most impressive sight. The simplest thing a ley-line could mark, as far as I am concerned, is that it marks the shortest day. Once this is past, there seems to be a lifting of feelings with the knowledge that longer days are on the way. This helps one through the cold weeks that follow, toiling on the farm.

9th   First snow. Grey wagtail, White Meadow.

10th   While waiting to get paid after a day's beating, several of us were hanging about near the archway, shuffling about trying to keep warm. Suddenly, Raymond, one of the beaters, seemed to lose patience. In an unprecedented outburst, he threatened, "I'll get 'im round the neck if the money is not soon forthcoming!" ''Im' being the gaffer, Lord Darnley, we all thought this very funny, as Raymond is about a quarter of the size of the gaffer! We had visions of Raymond trying to leap up to strangle his employer!

23rd   Netherwood is going out of cattle and having more sheep instead. Mink, bottom of Near Salleybed field, staying underwater for a minute at a time in the swollen muddy brook.

27th   Ploughing.

February
1st   Birds giving a bit of twittering song, pair of tree creepers, Park Lake. Spotted woodpecker, The Knowle.

17th   Barn owl seen by Jones, Collington.

28th   A change from a cold frosty east wind to a mild south-west one.

March

2nd   Lots of hazel catkins this year.

7th   Five inches of snow, cleaner and whiter than previous falls this winter.

15th   Coltsfoot in flower. It grew one and a half inches in one day in the lee of a fire, top Calves Hill. Thirty-two blobs frog spawn. Some draining is being done in this spawning ground so these may be the last ones to be seen there.

16th   Primrose out, Knowle drive. Planting spring wheat.

19th   Large flocks of seagulls and one peewit, when planting White Meadow. Hail and snow stopped planting for the day.

21st   Planting spring barley. Snipe seen by Dan on Forty Acres, Pensons.

25th   Frogs spawned in two sessions this year, several weeks apart because of the snow and frost stopping initial spawning.

April

8th   White violets, Park Cottage site.

13th   Yellow wagtail, Big Hopyard. Very pretty yellow.

14th   First fine day's weather this year. Hawthorn buds bursting. Watched grey squirrel eating pussy willow flowers, bottom of Big Hopyard. Planting potatoes.

16th   Toads gathering for spawning, Park Lake. Peacock butterfly.

20th   Wild flowers coming out the same time this spring – primroses, violets, wood anemones, bluebells, cowslips. Saw a snake in Park Lake. Heard cuckoo.

26th   Cuckoo again. Oak before ash. Trees bursting into leaf this last week of hot weather.

May

9th   Swifts.

10th   Flowers and shrubs have come out this year in two short spells of hot weather which normally is spread over a month or so.

12th   The fields of barley look beautiful this year. They come out evenly into ear and the undulating fields are covered in a purple haze as the early morning sun reflects off the dew-laden heads.

19th   Wheatear seen Netherwood drive.

22nd   Green woodpecker seen for the first time this year on Netherwood.

31st   Canoed down River Teme from Little Hereford to Knightwick. The flowers on the river banks remind me of how the roadside hedgerows used to be in my schooldays. Nowadays, the grass verges are covered mostly with cow parsley.

June
8th   Dawn chorus 4.05 am, this cloudy, rainy morning.

July
 6th   Hay making, Coverfield. After several hot, calm days, a breeze came from the north-west, blowing steady for about twenty minutes. Consequently the Coverfield was filled with gently floating white bits of fluff, like thousands of miniature balloonists, going from one side of the field to the other, standing out in sharp contrast against the green of the trees and wood at the top of the field. Poplar tree seeds. Clearing rides in woodland. During this operation I saw more butterflies of one species than I have ever seen before of that or any other sort. This is the Ringlet butterfly. There were hundreds of them, for whenever I went on the farm to clear brambles and grass, there were these butterflies, a dozen or so to each bit of woodland where they were disturbed. These Ringlet butterflies have increased dramatically over the past four or five years since I noticed them first, down by Park Lake, in a patch of blackberry briars in a sheltered sunny position.

13th   Combining winter barley. This has ripened quickly this year, the straw especially turning colour early.

15th   Start of some holiday if weather stops wet and I will catch up on this writing. There seems to have been a lot of different overtime this year. Overtime used only to be done on the farm in connection with tractor work, but it has changed to non-tractor jobs as well, such as building, or work in the woods, or jobs connected with the garden. It seems the farm worker must become even more versatile if he is going to continue in employment, as farming becomes more efficient and its produce ever more in surplus.

   Farmlands seem to be in danger of losing their hold over the people who live and work on them. In these days of easy travel, shorter working hours, the workers no longer need to live on the farm, and this means less personal involvement. Farm work is in danger of becoming like a factory job, where you turn up, do the job, then go home, leaving everything behind. At home, TV transports us to other parts of the globe, creating a desire, in many cases, to go and see these places. There is the temptation to go chasing round the world searching for something that is already here, on one's own doorstep, in the people you have known all your life, the seasons, nature with its wonderful complexity and ability to waste nothing, re-using things in different forms, time and time again. I am not sorry that, for most of the year, I work seven days a week, either at Netherwood or at The Knowle, which is adjoining. Netherwood has kept its hold over me, often taking a lot from me, but also giving a lot back in return. I look forward to seeing the various people that come to Netherwood year after year – the potato pickers, contractors, engineers, salesmen, wood men, lorry drivers, the list goes on and on. For me, there has also been a great joy in finding the remains of past inhabitants of Netherwood from many thousands of years ago, right up to the present day. Handling the pottery and flints I have found, and looking at the world as they did, wondering what their thoughts might have been, is, for me, part of the continuity of Netherwood.

I seem to live two lives now that I commute to Netherwood from Bishops Frome. I wake up in the morning and think about work, but when I come home at night I find that when I reach Summer Pool and round by the Chase Inn, I switch off from my place of work and switch into Bishops Frome, its people and whatever is important at the time. It has taken more than 15 years for me to feel part of this village and what was a large hop-growing community. Moving away from Netherwood, but still working there, has made me more appreciative and aware of things I might so easily have missed, and for all the life around me, I am and shall be forever grateful.

PART THREE

Details of Flints, Tiles and other
Artifacts found on Netherwood
Farms

Netherwood Floor Tiles

Glazed floor tiles occur very rarely. They were used in the richer religious sites during the late Saxon period. The nearest recorded tiles are from Coventry. They then begin to be manufactured in Britain in the late 13thC – the earliest documented tiles are from Westminster Abbey – and continued to be made throughout the 14th and 15th centuries. In the late 15th C–early 16th C there was a major revival of tile quality based on the 'Malvern School' of tiles and it is suggested that tiles of a poorer quality continued to be made into the late 16th and early 17th C, possibly made at pottery kilns in South Herefordshire.

Floor tiles that would be hand manufactured were inevitably expensive so they tend to occur on richer sites only; Abbeys, some churches, palaces and (as excavation increasingly reveals) on richer manor house sites.

Floor tiles in Hereford and Worcester County

There has been little research done on floor tiles in the county generally and even less has been published. From published sources about 100 sites have been identified as producing floor tiles – the majority being churches, several abbeys and cathedrals and castles, and the odd manor site (normally those owned by the church.)

Only two collections of floor tiles have been published for Herefordshire – some of the tiles from Abbey Dore in the late 19th C and a collection of six (78 tiles) from Wigmore Abbey in the 1920s.

With this lack of published sources it is obviously difficult to assess the tiles from Netherwood: but apart from a large collection of floor tiles discovered dumped in a secondary source in Hereford, I think that this may be the largest surviving collection of floor tiles in Herefordshire.

The Netherwood tiles are in generally good condition which implies that they were not left in floors for very long; if they were laid in the 14th C they may well have been removed in the 16th C updating of the house.

The method of production is to make the tile probably by rolling it into a wooden frame – the design would then be stamped onto the tile with a wooden block (or alternatively the design would be stamped, the tile would be given a coating of white slip and the extra wiped off.) The tile would then be glazed with a lead glaze – which gives a brown colour, copper filings added gives the green-black colour range. The tiles would then be stacked in a kiln and fired. The tiles would probably be laid in the room intended into a bed of sand (there is no evidence of them being mortared). They would normally be laid in panels of design and the triangular tiles indicate that the rows, in some panels at least, would be laid diagonally. The tiles with designs — of individual tiles, 4- tile, 9- tile and 16-tile designs would probably be laid inter-mixed with plain tiles to bring out the designs.

The Tile designs The designs (or most of them) have proved relatively easy to identify, as by pure coincidence they occur in two of the three published collections of floor tiles from Worcestershire – Bredon Church and Worcester Cathedral. They fall into two types – coats of arms – de Clare, de Warrenne, Old England, Old France, Audley, Beauchamp, Hereford – and a series of foliage designs. The majority of them occur in Worcester Cathedral with one coat of arms from Bredon Church.

Dating The Worcester Cathedral tiles are dated by documentary sources to 1377. So one has to decide whether the blocks were used at Netherwood before or after that date. The Bredon tiles were dated in about 1940 to c1320, and it has been suggested more recently that they may pre-date this by another 20 years – the reason has never been published, so it may be fallacious. We can say at the moment that the Netherwood tiles are of the fourteenth century, but until research on other tiles in the county has been done, it is impossible to date them much closer.

Place of manufacture Until recently only three suggested tile kiln sites have been identified as Droitwich, Great Malvern and possibly at Lingen. Recent documentary research by Pat Hughes has discovered that one of the roof tile makers at Whitefriars, Worcester had blocks for making floor tiles as well (recorded in his will in the early 16th C). There has always been debate about whether tiles are made in several fixed centres or whether there are migrant tilers who go out to do fixed commissions. Further research probably needs to be done on all the tiles in the county before this can be resolved, but it may be that there was a combination of both – if a local landlord had access to clay, wood for firing, etc and required enough tiles to justify building a new kiln, then the tilers would probably come to his area and save the problems of transporting large quantities of tiles.
If there was a kiln in the Netherwood area we should be looking for seriously over-fired or misshapen tile 'wasters' – there have been none in the collection I have examined.

Importance This is obviously a very important collection of floor tiles – because it comes from a non-religious site; because the tiles are in such good condition, making design identification easier, and because we have designs that are so closely linked with Worcester occurring a substantial distance away.
Publication is obviously to be recommended because of these aspects, but also because so few tiles from the Country have been published and because they remain in a private collection, and would not otherwise come to the attention of future researchers.

Hilary White
Hereford & Worcester
County Museum Archeology Section, May 1989

de Warrenne

Audley

Hereford

Beauchamp

de Clare

Old England

Old France

Flints picked up after ploughing over a 14-year period (1972–1986) on Netherwood Farms, approximately 1250 acres, partly in Thornbury near Bromyard, Herefordshire, and partly in Stoke Bliss near Tenbury Wells, Worcestershire; the largest farm being Netherwood, followed by the Grove Farm, the Hyde Farm, Pensons Farm and part of Grithill Farm. Finds totalling about 23,700 dating from a, just possible, Pre-Palaeolithic "Dawn" tool to the present day, made up of pottery, flint, clay tobacco pipes, tiles, bottles, bones, coins, sharpening stones, quern stones etc.

The finds have been recorded according to the field in which they were found, but in the interests of space have been condensed.

There is no natural flint in the area, and everything found has been brought in by previous generations of different cultures.

Approximate dating in Britain

Lower Palaeolithic	500,000–100,000 years ago
Mid-Palaeolithic	100,000–35/40,000 years ago
Upper Palaeolithic	35/40,000–12,000 B.C.
Mesolithic	12,000–3,000 B.C.
Neolithic	3,000–1,900 B.C.
Bronze Age	1,900–650,600 B.C.
Iron Age	650,600–B.C. onwards

Tile fragments from Flints Field site, Grove Farm

229

Netherwood Manor Farm

Some of the finds from individual fields:

1. Top of Old Roadway, Netherwood Manor Farm; 23 acres

   Upper Palaeolithic, Neolithic, Neo/Bronze:

Flints	150	Roman Pottery	2	Clay Pipes:	
Arrowheads	1	Medieval Pottery	231	1630-40	1
Coins	7	Black Glazed ware	6	1660-80	1
Silver Medal	1	Westerwald ware	0	1670-80	1
Pieces of Lime Burning			37	1680-1720	1

   (Two sites, one Medieval, one Roman, Point to Point Grandstand Field)
   HWCM 4067 and 4061

2. Top of Calves Hill, Netherwood Manor; 15 acres

   Bronze Age:

Flints	31	Roman Pottery	2	Clay pipes	0
Arrowheads	0	Medieval Pottery	1		
Coins	0	Black Glazed Ware	6	Spindle Whorl	1
		Westerwald Ware	0		

   One site, Roman. HWCM 4069

[In the bottom corner of this field was the start of a ditch or canal to carry water about half a mile to keep a pond topped up for milling.]

3. Collingtons, Netherwood Far; 25 acres

   Upper Palaeolithic, Mesolithic, Neolithic, Neo/Bronze:

Flints	194	Roman Pottery	1	Clay pipes	0
Arrowheads	1	Medieval Pottery	2		
Coins	0	Black Glazed Ware	6	Part of Rotary Quern	1
Heavy Scrapers	2	Westerwald Ware	0	Sling Stone	1

   (Only field where heavy scrapers have been found.)

4. Big Hopyard, Netherwood Farm; 25 acres

   Neo-Bronze:

Flints	25	Roman Pottery	2	Clay pipes	2
Arrowheads	0	Medieval Pottery	0		
Coins	3	Black Glazed Ware	11	*Floor Tile	1

[Creosoted ends of hop poles from before 1910 ploughed up from the stiff red clay along top of field. Hops were discontinued about that time.]
* All floor tiles are Medeival unless otherwise specified

5. White Meadow, Netherwood 21 acres

Mesolithic:

Flints	66	Roman Pottery	1	Clay pipes	
Arrowheads	0	Medieval Pottery	0	1670-80	1
Coins	0	Black Glazed Ware	7	1680-1720	1
Floor Tiles	6				

[Ditch running along South-east edge of field from what was a pond on Tythe map fed from canal from higher ground, the ditch ending at a steep drop which would have been suitable for a mill.]

6. Castlefield, Netherwood   18 acres

Mesolithic, Neolithic, Neo/Bronze:

Flints	39	Roman Pottery	0	Clay pipes	
Arrowheads	1	Medieval Pottery	1	1660-80	1
Coins	1	Black Glazed Ware	7		
Floor Tiles	60				

7. Roundcots, Netherwood   31 acres

Neolithic, Neo/Bronze:

Flints	104	Roman Pottery	1	Clay pipes	
Arrowheads	0	Medieval Pottery	2	1650	1
Coins	1	Black Glazed Ware	85	1660-80	1
Floor Tiles	74	Westerwald Ware	2	1740-70	1

[Medieval floor tiles in this and previous field were found mostly near each other over the field boundary.]

8. Far Sallybed, Netherwood   19 acres
Neo/Bronze

Flints	61	Roman Pottery	0	Clay pipes	
Arrowheads	1	Medieval Pottery	3		1
Floor Tiles	1	Westerwald Ware	1	1740-70	1

[This field was covered in what Father called "five bout ridges" – you ploughed round each cop five times, so leaving the land like ridges of corrugated tin.]

9. Near Sallybed, Netherwood   21 acres
Mesolithic:

Flints	18	Roman Pottery	0	Clay pipes	0
Arrowheads	0	Medieval Pottery	0		
Coins	1 Jeton	Black glazed Ware	9		

10. Barnfield, Netherwood;   29 acres

Mesolithic, Neo/Bronze

Flints	111	Roman Pottery	0	Clay pipes:	
Arrowheads	0	Medieval Pottery	5	1650	1
Coins	3	Black Glazed Ware	47	1660-80	1
Floor Tiles	14	Westerwald Ware	5	1670-80	2
		Stone Amulet	1		

[Now ploughed over, stone-walled sheep pens were in the southern part of this field. This is one of the warmest parts of the farm when the wind is from the north.]

11. Big Orchard, Netherwood   34 acres

Lower Palaeolithic, Mesolithic, Neo/Bronze, Iron Age:

Flints	101	Roman Pottery (Site)		Clay pipes:	
Arrowheads	0	Medieval Pottery	28	1650	1
Coins	2	Black Glazed Ware	57	1670-80	2
Floor Tiles	11	Westerwald Ware	1	1670-80	2
Prismatic Core	1				
Part of Polished					
Flint Axe	1				

[Iron Age/Roman/Medieval Site (middle top of field] HWCM 4046

12. Stoneyfield, Netherwood   18 acres

Neolithic:

Flints	15	Roman Pottery	0	Clay pipes:	
Arrowheads	1	Medieval Pottery	1	1650	1
Coins	3	Black Glazed Ware	3	1670-80	2
Floor Tiles	11	Westerwald Ware	1	1670-80	2

13. Behind Cottages, Netherwood   18 acres

Neolithic:

Flints	25	Roman Pottery	2	Clay pipes:	01
Arrowheads	1	Medieval Pottery	5		
Coins	1	Black Glazed Ware	134		
Floor Tiles	29	Westerwald Ware	1		
		Decorated Slip Ware	60		

[Site of a house that once was used as a butcher's many years ago]

14. Peafields, Netherwood 32 acres

Neo/Bronze

Flints	40	Roman Pottery	0	Clay pipes:	
Arrowheads	0	Medieval Pottery	1	1660-80	1
Coins	2	Black Glazed Ware	9	1680-1720	2
Floor Tiles	5	Westerwald Ware	2		

[Local sports were held in this field in the 1920s, then called Roadside Meadows. Whippet racing was one of the events.]

15. 8 Acres, The Top of Drive, Netherwood: 8 acres

Neo/Bronze

Flints	55	Roman Pottery	1	Clay pipes:	
Arrowheads	0	Medieval Pottery	0	1660-80	1
Coins	1	Black Glazed Ware	91	1780-1800	1
Floor Tiles	2	Westerwald Ware	3		

[Long nets were used against the dingleside to catch rabbits in the 1920s. A box of matches was rattled to startle them into the nets.]

16. Stable Meadow, Netherwood   6 acres

Upper Palaeolithic, Neolithic, Neo/Bronze:

Flints	274	Roman Pottery	7	Clay pipes:	
Arrowheads	0	Medieval Pottery	3	1660-80	1
Coins	1	Black Glazed Ware	127	1780-1800	1
Floor Tiles	6	Westerwald Ware	2	Flint knife	1

[Several magnificent beech trees died in the late 1970s/early 1980s after some extra dry hot summers. I still miss those trees and the dignity they gave to Netherwood.]

17. Parks, Netherwood   33 acres

Upper Palaeolithic, Mesolithic, Neolithic, Neo/Bronze

Flints	798	Roman Pottery	(site)	Clay pipes:	1
Arrowheads	2	Medieval Pottery	(site)		
Coins	0	Black Glazed Ware	20	Chert Flakes	121
Floor Tiles	1	Westerwald Ware	2		

Part of polished stone axe, place of manufacture not known

[Site: bottom North East corner of field.] 1600s to 1800s

18. Coverfield, Netherwood 33 acres

Mid Palaeolithic, Upper Palaeolithic, Mesolithic, Neolithic, Neo/Bronze

Flints	281	Roman Pottery	1	Clay pipes:	
Arrowheads	1	Medieval Pottery	1	1800	1
Coins	1	Black Glazed Ware	17	1860-80	1
Floor Tiles	4	Westerwald Ware	3		
Saddle Quern (Neolithic to Roman)			1		

[Grandfather, whilst stacking hay on a horse-drawn waggon, suddenly leaped down to the ground. One of the pitchers had tossed up a couple of snakes in his forkful from a cock of hay!) 1910–1920.

19. The 40 Acres, Pensons Farm

Pre Palaeolithic, Upper Palaeolithic, Mesolithic, Neolithic, Neo/Bronze:

Flints	173	Roman Pottery	5	Clay pipes		
Arrowheads	3	Medieval Pottery	9	1630-40	1	
Coins	1	Black Glazed Ware	84	1650	3	
Floor Tiles	3	Westerwald Ware	4	1660-1680	4	
				1680-1720	1	
				1690-1720	1	

Stamps on base of bowls – ⊕ ✸ 🐦

[Just possible Pre Palaeolithic (half a million years old) Flint Dawn Tool and one other similar. Ball of Flint similar to ones found in poughed fields near High Wycombe. Small Site South East of field (1700s).]

20. Cornerfield, Pensons Farm   6 acres

Upper Palaeolithic:

Flints	2	Roman Pottery	1	Clay pipes	
Arrowheads	0	Medieval Pottery	0		0
Coins	0	Black Glazed Ware	4	Part of Rotary Quern	
Floor Tiles	4	Westerwald Ware	0	(Kyre Brook)	

21. Behind Pensons   25 acres

Neolithic, Neo/Bronze

Flints	61	Roman Pottery	1	Clay pipes	
Arrowheads	1	Medieval Pottery	3	1650	3
Coins	4	Black Glazed Ware	184	1660-80	4
		Westerwald Ware	2	1680-1720	1
				1690-1720	1
				1700	2
				1710-70	1

[Small site house and/or garden, North corner of field.] 1700s
Rest of finds from the whole of Pensons Farm, except Site:

Flint

Flint scrapers	12	18/19 Century Brown/Green/Yellow Glazed Ware	145
Side scrapers	5	Glazed stone ware	3
Disc scrapers	5	Decorated Slip Ware	7
Thumb Nail			
Scrapers	5	Georgian Ware	1
Knives	1	Pottery/Crockery/Glass	48
Utilized Flakes	4	Oyster Shells	10
Microlith (Meso)	4	Sharpening Stone	1
Cores	3	Pieces Lime Burning	1
Flint Nodules	3	Plough Shares	4
		Cider Barrel Tap	1

The Hyde Farm, Stoke Bliss, Worcestershire

22. Brickyards Field, Hyde Farm 12 acres

Neolithic:

Flints	27	Roman Pottery	0	Clay pipes	
Arrowheads	0	Medieval Pottery	0		1
Coins	0	Black Glazed Ware	64	Stamp on base:	
		Westerwald Ware	2		

[Brick kiln site, South corner, near bridge.]

(T3)

23. Bullock Field, Hyde Farm 16 acres

Neo/Bronze:

Flints	24	Roman Pottery	0	Clay pipes	
Arrowheads	0	Medieval Pottery	1	1650	1
Coins	0	Black Glazed Ware	95	1860-80	1
		Westerwald Ware	2		

24. Middle Meadow, Hyde Farm 21 acres: Neo/Bronze

Flints	140	Roman Pottery	0	Clay pipes	
Arrowheads	0	Medieval Pottery	15	1630-40	1
Coins	2	Black Glazed Ware	509	1650	3
Coin, Eliz. 1	1	Westerwald Ware	10	Stamp on Base:	

[Site: West side of field.] HWCM 7049

25. London Field, Hyde Farm 12 acres

Neo/Bronze:

Flints	24	Roman Pottery	0	Clay pipes	
Arrowheads	0	Medieval Pottery	2	1660-80	1
Coins	0	Black Glazed Ware	102	1670-80	1
Lead Pilgrim's					
Badge	1	Westerwald Ware	2	1680-1720	2

(EG)

26. Cow Pasture, Hyde Farm 22 acres

Mesolithic; Neolithic:

Flints	72	Roman Pottery	0	Clay pipes	
Arrowheads	0	Medieval Pottery	2	1670-80	1
Coins	0	Black Glazed Ware	99	1680-1720	1
Lead Pilgrim's		Westerwald Ware	7	1800	1
Badge/Tally	1				

27. Quarry Field, Hyde Farm 15 acres Neo/Bronze

Flints	40	Roman Pottery	0	Clay pipes	
Arrowheads	0	Medieval Pottery	1	Broken stems	
Coins	0	Black Glazed Ware	36	& bowls	3
Flint knife	1	Westerwald Ware	2		

Rest of finds from the whole of Hyde Farm, except sites:

Flint Nodules	15	18/19 C. Yellow/	
Scrapers	6	Brown/Green Glazed Ware	64
Bun Scrapers	2	Glazed Stone Ware	27
Side Scrapers	3	Decorated Slip Ware	179
Notched Scraper	1	Georgian Ware	4
Burin/Scraper	1	Pottery/Crockery/Glass	125
Disc Scraper	3	Oyster Shells	5
End Scraper	2	Pieces Lime Burnings	2
Blades	3		
Microlith(Meso)	1		
Buttons	10		
Lead Shot	1		
Oyster Shells	5		

The Grove Farm, Stoke Bliss, Worcestershire

28. Grove Sling, Grove Farm   18 acres

Palaeolithic, Neo/Bronze:

Flints	20	Roman Pottery	2	Clay pipes:	
Arrowheads	0	Medieval Pottery	0		1
Coins	3	Black Glazed Ware	275	Hammerstone	
		Westerwald Ware	3	possibly	
				Palaeolithic	1

29. Sweet Pleck, Grove Farm   20 acres

Neolithic: Neo/Bronze:

Flints	53	Roman Pottery	0	Clay pipes:	
Arrowheads	0	Medieval Pottery	2	1630-40	1
Coins	1	Black Glazed Ware	275	1650	1
Polished Stone					
Axe	1	Westerwald Ware	3	1660-80	2
(manufactured N. Wales?)				1670-80	1
Roman sharpening					
whetstone	1			1680-1720	2

30. Turnpike, Grove Farm 44 acres

Neolithic, Neo/Bronze:

Flints	115	Roman Pottery	2	Clay pipes:	
Arrowheads	1	Medieval Pottery	2	1650	1
Coins	4	Black Glazed Ware	465	1680-1720	2
Lead Pilgrim's		Westerwald Ware	9	1740-70	2
Badge	1			1780-1800	1

31. Hays (Devil's Dockyard). Grove Farm   9 acres

Upper Palaeolithic, Mesolithic:

Flints	17	Roman Pottery	2	Clay pipes	
Arrowheads	0	Medieval Pottery	7	1650	2
Coins	0	Black Glazed Ware	65	1670-80	1
Microlith	1	Westerwald Ware	2	1800-1950	1

[DUBLIN]

32. Nutwels, Grove Farm 36 acres

Upper Palaeeolithic, Neolithic, Neo/Bronze:

Flints	97	Roman Pottery	3	Clay pipes	
Arrowheads	3	Medieval Pottery	0	1650	1
Coins	3	Black Glazed Ware	93	1660-80	1
End Scrapers	3	Westerwald Ware	2	1800-1950	1

33. Flints Field, Grove Farm   37 acres

Upper Palaeolithic, Mesolithic, Neo/Bronze, Bronze Age:

Flints	84	Roman Pottery	2	Clay pipes	
Arrowheads	1	Medieval Pottery	0	(Site)	
Coins	0	Black Glazed Ware	16		
Burin Point	1	Westerwald Ware	2		
Graver					

(Site: South of middle of field) HWCM 4070

34. Kyre Parks, Grove Farm   32 acres

Upper Palaeolithic, Mesolithic, Neolithic, Neo/Bronze:

Flints	86	Roman Pottery	8	Clay pipes	
Arrowheads	2	Medieval Pottery	2	1630-40	2
Coins	6	Black Glazed Ware	90	1780-1800	1
Flint Knife	1	Westerwald Ware	0	1860-80	1

(Site: West side of field) HWCM 4071

Rest of finds from whole of Grove Farm, except Sites:

Flint Nodules	9	Brown/Yellow/Green/	
Flnt Scrapers	11	Glazed Pottery	120
Bun Scrapers	1	Glazed Stone Ware	47
Side scrapers	7	Decorated slip ware	334
Notched scrapers	2	Georgian ware	16
Disc Scrapers	4	Glass/Pottery/Crockery	226
End scrapers	3	Teeth	40
Thumb Nail		Pieces Lime Burning	1
scrapers	1	Sharpening stone	6
Blades	2	Oyster shells	58
Graver	2		
Cores	1		
Parrots Beak Graver	1		
Knives	2		

Microlith (Meso)	3	Gun striking flint	2
Lead shot	1	Lead Pilgrim's badge	1
Buttons	18		

Grithill Farm, Stoke Bliss, Worcestershire

Flints	16	Roman Pottery	1	Clay pipes	5
Bun Scraper	1	Black Glazed ware	2	Stamp on bases:	
Potboiler	1	Decorated slip ware	5		
Coins	3				
Possibly Butt End					
of Stone Axe	1				

40 Acres
Pensons

Big Orchard
Netherwood

Far Salleybed
Netherwood

Probably natural or
just possibly an
eolith. Pre Palaeo -
lithic "Dawn Tool"

Determination of
these hinges on
finding large
numbers of the

same on site.

Fragment of
belemnite (fossil
cuttlefish) c. 190
million years old.

Prismatic core
from which flakes
have been struck.
Probably Lower

Palaeolithic
c. 500,000 - 100,000
years old.

Cover Field
Netherwood 1977

Bottom Collingtons
Netherwood

Stable Meadow
Netherwood 1980

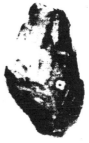

Core from which
primitive flakes
have been struck
? Upper Palaeolithic

Blade trimmed for
use as a scraper
? Upper Palaeolithic

Flake knife
? Mousterian
? Mid Palaeolithic

Top of Old Roadway Netherwood 1977	Bottom Collingtons Netherwood	Top of Old Roadway Netherwood	Nutwells Grove Spring 1980

Graver

? Upper Palaeo-
lithic

Burin (Graver)
Upper Palaeolithic

Blade
Upper Palaeolithic

Knife
? Upper Palaeolithic

40 Acres Pensons

Top of Parks
Netherwood

Hays Grove Farm

Netherwood House
Moat

Small blade
Upper Palaeolithic

Microlithic blade
Late Upper Palaeo-
lithic or Mesolithic

Blunt backed knife
Upper Palaeolithic

Flake from a worked
tool of the
Palaeolithic Age

40 Acres Pensons

Cover Field Neth.

Hays Grove

40 Acres Pensons

Microlith

Mesolithic

Microlithic Blade

Mesolithic

Microlithic Blade

Mesolithic

Microlith

Mesolithic

Flints Grove 1980

Barnfield
Netherwood

Parks Netherwood

40 Acres Pensons

Graver (burin
point)
? Mesolithic

Scalene Triangle

Mesolithic

Microlith

Mesolithic

Microlith

Mesolithic

Stable Meadow
Netherwood

Parks Netherwood

Quarry Field
Hyde

Nutwels Grove

Flint Knife

Neolithic

Knife Blade

Neolithic

Flake Knife
Neolithic. Museum
Comment:- 'lovely'

Side Scraper
Neolithic

Middle Meadow
Hyde Farm

Top of Parks
Netherwood

Hays Grove

Behind Pensons

"Thumb Nail" Scraper

Neolithic

Burin/Scraper

Neolithic

Disc Scraper

Neolithic

Burin/Side Scraper
Neolithic

Top of Parks
Netherwood

Top Old Roadway
Netherwood

Cow Pasture
Hyde Farm

Top Collingtons
Netherwood

Side Scraper

Neolithic

Pot Boiler

Notched Scraper

Neolithic

Heavy Scraper
Neolithic   Museum
Comment:-'lovely'

Stable Meadow
Netherwood

8 Acres Top of Drive
Netherwood

Top Calves Hill
Netherwood

Side Scraper

Neo Bronze

Plano Convex Knife

Neo Bronze

Bronze Age Blade

Sweet Pleck Grove
1977

40 Acres Pensons

Bottom Collingtons
Netherwood

Castle Field
Netherwood

"Parrot's Bill"
Graver

Neo Bronze

Hinge Fracture

Neo Bronze

? Hollow Scraper

Neo Bronze

Notched Scraper

Neo Bronze

Parks Top 75
Netherwood

Turnpike Grove

Stable Meadow
Netherwood

Netherwood Farms
1975

Chert

Gun Striking Flint

Pot Boiler

Neo Bronze

End Scraper

Barn Field
Netherwood

Middle Meadow small
patch Hyde

Barn Field
Netherwood

Bun Scraper

Neo Bronze

Disc Scraper

Neo Bronze

Thumb Nail Scraper

Neo Bronze

Behind Pensons

Tanged and barbed
arrowhead
Late Neolithic

Top of Old Roadway
Top Site.Neth.1978

Tanged and Barbed
arrowhead
Late Neolithic

Bottom Collingtons
Netherwood

Tanged and Barbed
arrowhead
Late Neolithic

40 Acres Pensons

Tanged arrowhead
Neolithic

Top Old Roadway
Netherwood

Tanged and barbed
arrowhead
Late Neolithic

Tea Baun Lake
Netherwood

Leaf shaped arrow
head
Neolithic

Kyre Parks Grove

Single shouldered
tanged arrowhead
Upper Palaeolithic

Cover Field
Netherwood 1985

Bi-facially worked
leaf point
Neolithic
Museum comment:-

"Beautiful"

Turnpike Grove

Tanged arrowhead
Neolithic

Nutwells Grove

Large arrowhead
point probably of
Neolithic date but
representing a
Mesolithic flint
tradition

Parks Netherwood

Projectile Points
(broken)

Meso/Neo

Netherwood Farms

Tanged arrowhead
Neolithic

Castle Field
Netherwood

Large arrowhead
with tang broken
Neolithic

Nutwels Grove

Leaf shaped point
(broken)
Neolithic

Parks Netherwood

Leaf shaped point
(broken)

Neolithic

Parks Netherwood

Tanged arrowhead
(broken)
Neolithic

Kyre Parks Grove

Tanged and barbed
arrowhead (broken)
Late Neolithic

Flints Grove

Tanged and barbed
arrowhead (broken)
Neo Bronze

40 Acres Pensons

Tanged and barbed
arrowhead

Late Neolithic

Stable Meadow
Netherwood

Projectile Point
Neo/Bronze

40 Acres Pensons

Leaf shape arrow
point

Neo Bronze

Far Sallybed
Netherwood

Tanged and barbed
arrowhead
Early Bronze Age

Fealds Grove

Tanged and barbed
arrowhead
Early Bronze Age

Nutwels Grove

Tanged and barbed
arrowhead
Early Bronze Age

Netherwood

Stone Spindle Whorl
from a bow drill
Probably Bronze or
Iron Age date.

Barn Field
Netherwood

Amulet or weight ?

Top Calves Hill
Netherwood

Spindle Whorl

Late Bronze Age

Calves Hill
Netherwood

Polished Stone
native pendant
probably of Bronze
Age date.
Museum Comment:-
"superb"

Bottom Collingtons
Netherwood 1980

Sling Stone

Sweet Pleck Grove

Roman Whetstone

Fealds Grove

Plumb Bob ? Lead

Fealds Site
Grove Farm

Half Spindle Whorl

Roman

Big Orchard Site
Netherwood

Big Orchard Site
Netherwood

Decorated Roof Tile

Roman

Roman wall tile
fragment scored to
form a key for
plasterwork

Netherwood House
Moat

Inscribed Wood

Big Orchard Site
Netherwood

Kyre Park Site
Grove

Iron Age Sherd
c.150 BC – mid 1st
century.

Malvernian tubby
cooking pot
1st – 2nd century AD

Top Calves Hill Site
Netherwood

Top Calves Hill Site
Netherwood

Black burnished ware
type 1
250 – 400 century
Roman

Dorset black
burnished ware
type 1
120 – 400 AD

Top Calves Hill Site
Netherwood

Bottom Site Top Old
Roadway Netherwood

Micaceous imitation
black burnished
ware.

Malvernia
pottery
300-400A.D.
Roman

Top Calves Hill Site
Netherwood

Oxfordshire Ware
(colour coat miss-
ing.)

Big Orchard Site
Netherwood

Buff Ware with
incised decoration

Roman

Top Site Top of Old
Roadway Netherwood

Severn Valley Ware

(Roman)

Big Orchard Site
Netherwood 1983 = 6

Samian Ware
1st/2nd century AD

Kyre Park Site
Grove

Marcette/Hartshill
Roman Mortarium

Top Calves Hill Site
Netherwood

Oxfordshire White
Ware ? Mortarium

Kyre Park Site
Grove

Roman Greyware

Bottom Site Top Old
Netherwood

Roman White Ware
(?) Flag-on handle

Middle Meadow Hyde
1975

Malvern Chase Ware
14th - 17th century

Top Site Top of Old
Roadway Netherwood

Sandy Med. Cooking
Pot

Big Orchard Site
Netherwood

Medieval Pottery
probably Norman

Kyre Parks Site
Grove

Malvernian Med.
Cooking Pot

Top of Old Roadway
Netherwood

Med. Jug Base
13th/14th century

Netherwood
Top Old Roadway

Malvern Glazed Ware
Med. 14th-16th
century

Cow Pasture
Hyde

Bronze Button

Post Medieval

Hays

Pewter Button

17th/18th century

Behind Pensons

Pewter Button
17th/18th century

Netherwood Farms

Victorian Steel

Button

Top of Old Roadway
Netherwood

Jet or Obsidian
Button

Cover Field
Netherwood

Copper Button

Small Pea Fields
Netherwood

Victorian Steel
Button

Grove Sling

Brass Hunting Button

Victorian ?

Fealds Grove

Musketball Lead
Shot

Top of Old Roadway
Netherwood

Lead Shot Ball

Parks Netherwood

Lead Shot Ball

Round Cots
Netherwood

Lead Shot Ball

Stable Meadow
Netherwood

Lead Shot Ball

Stable Meadow
Netherwood

Lead Shot Ball
broken and
distorted.

Top of Old Roadway
Netherwood

.22 Pellet

Top Old Roadway
Netherwood

12 Bore Shot Pellets

Fealds Grove

Silver Penny
possibly Edward VI
London Mint

Middle Meadow Hyde
1975

Elizabeth I (1558–
1603) Silver Six-
pence 1569 third
issue 1561–77

Netherwood House
Moat

Near Salleybed
Netherwood

French 16th
century coins known
Jetons

8 Acres Top of Drive
Netherwood 1979

Shilling
William III

Barn Field
Netherwood

William III (1694–
1702)
Shilling dated 1696

Behind Pensons Farm

George II
Halfpenny

Kyre Parks Grove

George III (1760–
1820) Halfpenny
Irish 1769

Kyre Parks Grove

Sixpence 1816

Top of Old Roadway
Netherwood

Silver Medal
(Civil) made in
B'ham 1915/16

Stable Meadow
Netherwood 1980

Victoria young
head Shilling 1855

Behind Pensons

Lead Wool Tag

London Field Hyde

Lead Disc
Pilgrim's Badge
Medieval

Turnpike Grove

Lead Pilgrim's
Badge

Sweet Pleck Grove

Lead Disc
Pilgrim's Badge
Medieval

Cow Pasture Hyde

Lead Disc
? Pilgrim's Tally
Medieval

├─ 2 cm ─┤

├─ 1 inch ─┤

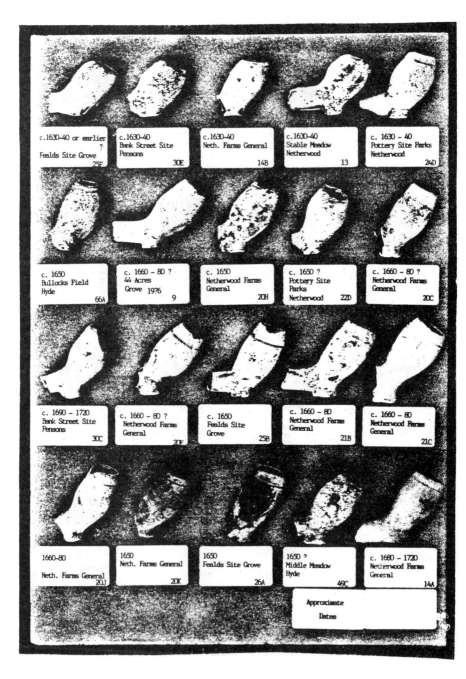

c.1630-40 or earlier
?
Fealds Site Grove
25F

c.1630-40
Bank Street Site
Pensons
30E

c.1630-40
Neth. Farms General
14B

c.1630-40
Stable Meadow
Netherwood
13

c. 1630 - 40
Pottery Site Parks
Netherwood
24D

c. 1650
Bullocks Field
Hyde
66A

c. 1660 - 80 ?
44 Acres
Grove 1976
9

c. 1650
Netherwood Farms
General
20H

c. 1650 ?
Pottery Site
Parks
Netherwood 22D

c. 1660 - 80 ?
Netherwood Farms
General
20C

c. 1690 - 1720
Bank Street Site
Pensons
30C

c. 1660 - 80 ?
Netherwood Farms
General
20F

c. 1650
Fealds Site
Grove
25B

c. 1660 - 80
Netherwood Farms
General
21B

c. 1660 - 80
Netherwood Farms
General
21C

1660-80

Neth. Farms General
20J

1650
Neth. Farms General
20K

1650
Fealds Site Grove
26A

1650 ?
Middle Meadow
Hyde
49C

c. 1680 - 1720
Netherwood Farms
General
14A

Approximate
Dates

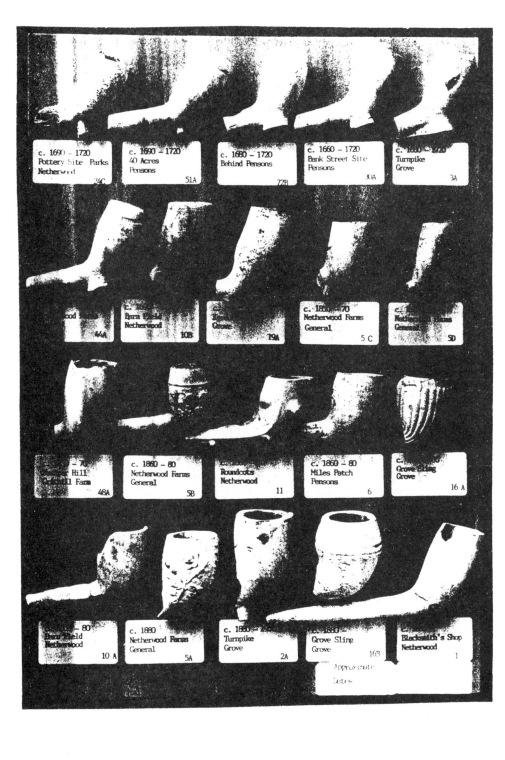

c. 1690 – 1720
Pottery Site Parks
Netherwood
24C

c. 1690 – 1720
40 Acres
Pensons
51A

c. 1680 – 1720
Behind Pensons
72B

c. 1660 – 1720
Bank Street Site
Pensons
30A

c. 1680 – 1720
Turnpike
Grove
3A

ood
44A

c.
Barn Field
Netherwood
10B

c.
Grove
19A

c. 1800 – 70
Netherwood Farms
General
5 C

c.
Netherwood Farms
General
5D

– 70
Hill
Farm
48A

c. 1860 – 80
Netherwood Farms
General
5B

Roundoaks
Netherwood
11

c. 1860 – 80
Miles Patch
Pensons
6

Grove Sling
Grove
16 A

– 80
Barn Field
Netherwood
10 A

c. 1880
Netherwood Farms
General
5A

c. 1860 –
Turnpike
Grove
2A

c. 1880 –
Grove Sling
Grove
16B

Blacksmith's Shop
Netherwood
1

Approximate
Dates

SITES ON NETHERWOOD FARMS

Area of concentrated pottery etc	Field Name	
1 acre (top site	Top of old roadway, Netherwood Farm	HWCM 4067
1/2 acre (bottom site)	Top of old roadway, Netherwood Farm	HWCM 4068
3/4 acre	Top of Calves Hill, Netherwood Farm	HWCM 4069
1 acre	Big Orchard, Netherwood Farm	HWCM 4046
1/2 acre	Parks, Netherwood Farm	
	Netherwood Manor Moat, Netherwood Farm	
1 acre	Middle Meadow, Hyde Farm	HWCM 7049
1/2 acre	Kyre Parks, Grove Farm	HWCM 4071
1 acre	Flints Field, Grove Farm	HWCM 4070

Site HWCM 4067 Netherwood Farm

Flints	4	Roman Severn Valley ware	10
Arrowhead	1	Medieval Pottery	489
Med.sandy cooking pot	4	Roman Black Burnish Ware	1
Med.jug base 13/14 C	8	Med. mostly Malvernian grey Coloured ware	200
Med.Malvernian Pot	8	Med.red orange coloured ware	264
Med.Malvernian cooking pot	2		
Med.Malvernian glazed ware 14/16 C	3		
Glass bead	1		

Near this site a two feet square hole filled with 18 longish (1-1/2 feet approx) irregular stones wedged together – half facing uphill, the other half facing downhill, like giant teeth.
To the south of this site on sloping ground several fire hearts were scattered over approximately 1/2 acre. These were seen when the field was ploughed a bit deeper.

Site HWCM 4068 Netherwood Farm

Roman Severn Valley Ware	345
Roman Samain Ware 2 C AD	2
Roman Burnished Ware type 1	2
Roman White Ware	1
Roman Marcette/Hartshill Morotorium	2
Roman X1 Miaceous Imitation Black Burnished ware	1
Roman Pottery	9
Brick	4
Pieces from field liming	3
	254

Site HWCM 4069 Netherwood Farm

Flints	2
Roman Severn Valley Ware	465
Roman Pottery	123
Roman Black Burnished Ware type 1	11
Roman Oxford Ware (colour coat missing)	2
Roman type Malvernian 1st,2nd C AD	15
Roman Dorset Black Burnished Ware type 1	6
Roman Grey Ware	14
Roman Malvernian Pottery 3rd,4th C	5
Roman White Ware	3
Roman (mixture) Dorset Black, Black Burnished Malvernian, Malvernian	46
Medieval Pottery	1
Medieval Malvernian Chase Bowl 15/16 C	1
Black Slip Ware	2
Teeth	2

Site HWCM 4046 Netherwood Farm

Iron Age Pottery 150 BC -mid 1st C AD	5
Roman Severn Valley Ware	101
Roman Pottery	107
Roman Buff Ware with incised and colour coated decoration	3
Roman Plain Buff Ware	5
Roman Buff Ware bi-colour due to imperfect firing	16
Roman Buff Ware 43 – 400 AD	7
Roman Burnt Samain Ware	1
Roman very worn Samair Ware	1
Roman Amphira	1
Roman Grey Ware	1
Medieval Pottery	6
Medieval - probably Norman	3
Post-Medieval after 1500 AD	6
Posr-Medieval tile	3
Post-Medieval glass	5
Roman fire-place or furnace brick and lining	73
Roman tile/block/tegule	230
Iron working furnace products	16
Roman glass	2
Carbonised wood	26
Roman broken corn grinding stone	1
Possible bolar	1
Oddments	180

Site Parks Field, Netherwood Farm

Flints	11	Clay Tobacco Pipes	
Med. floor tile fragments	8	1630–40	14
Oystershell	2	1650s	13
Westerwold Ware	4	1660–80	4
Georgian Ware	44	1670–80	1
Glazed stone ware	57	1680–1720	2
Decorated slip ware	4	1690–1720	2
17/18/19 Black gl.ware	528	Broken stems and	
Brown/Yellow/Green		bowls	303
Glazed ware	128		
Pieces of glass	65	Stamps on bases:	
Teeth	44		
Bone	13		
Marble	1		
Iron nails	16		
Stone	2		
Sharpening stone pieces	2		
Buttons	2		
Snuff tin	1		
Copper pieces	2		
Ferral for tool handle	1		
Slate fragment	1		
Remains of iron key	1		
Sulphur (for hop drying)	1		
Small fragments/various	430		

Netherwood House and Moat

Flints (one Upper Paleolithic)	2	Pieces of leather shoes possibly	
Roman Pottery	2	18/19 Century	14
Oystershell (Med.or Roman)	14	Copper nail	1
14/15 C Ridge Tile	39	Bones and teeth of horse, sheep,	
Jeton	1	deer, dog not possible to date	26
16 C Incised Bowl sherds	3	Deer antler	1
Inscribed piece of wood	1	19 C Pop bottle marble	1
Medieval Floor tile (plain)	26	Clay tobacco pipe 1660–80	1
-do- (patterned)	24	Broken stems and bowl	3
Medieval Halfs & Triangles	16		
17/18/19 C Black GlazedWare			
(67 body sherds, 30 bases			
30 rims, 9 handles)	136		
18/19 C Brown/Green/			
Yellow Ware	32		
17 C Slip Ware (Toft style)	7		
Similar to above	19		
17 C Slip Ware	2		

17/18 Decorated Slip Ware	42
Cream Coloured Ware	22
Glazed Stone Ware	11
Westerwald	2
White Crockery	8
Willow Pattern Crockery	21
Odd bits of crockery	10
Metal key-hole surround	1
Metal scoop handle	1
Wooden bung	1
Stone Roofing Tile	2
Shaped stones from old Netherwood Chapel	5

Site HWCM 7049, Hyde Farm

Roman Severn Valley Ware	1
Medieval Malvern Chase Ware 14/17C includig 1 Pipkin handle	11
Glazed Medieval	4
Medieval Malvernian 15/16C jar	1
German Stone Ware drinking jug handle, probably 16C	1
Post Medieval 18C plus	2
Oddments	5
Mainly Medieval type pottery	295

Part of cobbled path/yard ploughed up.

Site HWCM 4070, Grove Farm

Flints	54
Arrowhead	1
Flint Scrapers	1
Flint Thumbnail scraper	2
Flint Disc Scraper	1
Flint Side Scraper	1
Flint End Scraper	1
Roman Spindle Whorl	1/2
Roman Malvernian cooking pot 1/2C AD	10
Roman Black Burnished Ware	31
-do- – copy?	3
Roman Saman Ware	2
Roman White Ware	2
Roman Marcette/Hartshill Mortarium	4

Roman Pottery probably incl. some Medieval body sherd	
Malvernian cooking pots	237
Medieval Copper/Bronze pieces	10
Medieval Malvernia cooking pots	88
Medieval Malvernian jug handles	17
Medieval Malvernian rims	11
Medieval Malvernian jug bases	25
Medieval Malvernian pitcher handle	1
Medieval Floor Tile	3
Medieval/Post Medieval pottery undiagnostic body sherds	420
Post Medieval pottery	33
Post Medieval Pottery bases	25
Lead Shot	1

Roman Severn Valley
  Ware   214

16C German Stone Ware   3

17C Pressed Platter Ware   3

17C Wire Bottle neck   1

17C Salt Glazed Stone
  Ware   3

17/18C Glazed Stone ware 5

17/19C   -do-   69

17/19C Salt Glazed and
  Glazed Stone Ware   21

17/18/19C Black Glazed
  Ware   1956

16/18X Mixed Pottery   322

16/18C small pieces   263

18C Glazed Ware   15

18C Stone Ware   17

18C and Victorian   15

Brown Glazed Pottery   786

Brown/Yellow/Green
  Glazed Pottery   265

Georgian pottery   16

Georgian slip ware   2

Decorated Slip ware   20

Victorian Glass   2

Pieces of glass   452

19C Pottery   30

Tile Fragments   7

Pieces of sharpening stone 12

Bottle tops, glass, stones,
  pottery, crockery etc   1547

Coins   2
Burnt bits   25
Incised Stone   2
Marble   1
Oddments   10
Teeth – oxen, pigm dog etc   35
Iron nails   2

Clay Tobacco Pipes
1630-40   6
1650   17
1660-80   12
1680-1720   1
Broken stems and bowls   448

Stamps on bases:

Site HWCM 4071 Grove Farm

Roman Malvernian 'tubby' working pot 1C/2C   2
Roman Burnished Ware type 1 250-400 AD   2
Roman Severn Valley Ware   382
Roman Mortaria   10
Roman Marcette/Hartshill Mortaria   6
Roman Grey Ware   2
Roman White Ware   1
Roman Samair Ware   2
Roman unidentifiable Black/Grey ware   22
Medieval Malvernian cooking pot   1
Black Slip Ware   4
Fragment wet stone   1
Oddments   6

Finds found on Netherwood Farm, Pensons Farm, Hyde Farm, Grove Farm, but not recorded from individual fields.
Palaeolithic, Mesolithic, Neolithic, Neo/Bronze, Roman and Medieval.

Flints total	680
Flint nodules	5
Flint arrowheads	2
Flint potboilers	28
Flint scrapers	40
Flint thumbnail scrapers	8
Flint bun scrapers	6
Flint disc scrapers	3
Flint side scrapers	8
Flint end scrapers	3
Flint cores	15
Flintblades	4
Flint utilized flakes	34
Flint Microlith (Meso)	12
Coins	11
Buttons	16
Oystershell	1
Roman Severn Valley Ware	14
Roman Pottery	2
Medieval Pottery	9
Black Galzed Pottery	820
Brown/Green/Yellow Glazed Pottery	35
Imported German Westerwald Mugs	20
Glazed Stoneware	23
Decorated Slip Ware	62

Pottery/glass/bottle tops etc	202
Teeth	28
Sharpening stones	3
Pieces of lime burning	1

Clay tobacco pipes:

1630-40	2
1650s	2
1660-80	13
1670-80	3
1690-1720	2
1740-70	4
1780-1800	2

Stamps on bases:

Medieval Floor Tiles:

Patterned	11
Plain	17

Horseshoes found on Netherwood Farms 1970s and 1980s Netherwood, Hyde, Grove and Pensons Farm

Horseshoes 350 total.

The labels were unfortunately rendered illegible having become soaked in the oil which was used to preserve the horseshoes, therefore the individual fields in which they were found have been grouped together within the four farms:

Dove shoe 14th C	1
Guildhall shoes 14 & 15C	3
Keyhole shoes 17C	6
Bar toe tip hoes 19 & 20C	2
Donkey shoes	4
Mule shoes	5

The remainder range up to the 1950s when cart horses were last used at Netherwood. From 8 in. diameter cart horse shoes to 3 in diameter pony shoes, plus possibly some Point to Point shoes.

Land Drains, Netherwood Farms

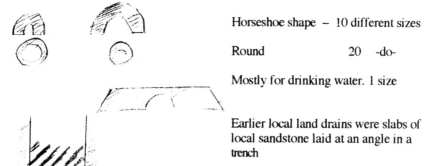

Horseshoe shape – 10 different sizes

Round   20   -do-

Mostly for drinking water. 1 size

Earlier local land drains were slabs of local sandstone laid at an angle in a trench

The horseshoe drains were mostly laid straight onto the trench bottom, a small proportion being laid onto a flat piece of tile:

Lengths ranging from: 11 1/2 in to 13 1/2 in

Diameters from: 1 1/2 in to 10 1/2 in

Bottles, Netherwood Farms

Most of those found were from the Kidderminster area, with not so many being from the Herefordshire part of the country:

Bottles total	180
Fish paste jars	30
Bottle tops	60
Stone ware	20
Ink wells	6